The Social World of the First Christians

# The Social World of the First Christians

John Stambaugh and David Balch

First published in the USA 1986

First published in Great Britain 1986
SPCK
Holy Trinity Church
Marylebone Road
London NW1 4DU



British Library Cataloguing in Publication Data

Stambaugh, John E.
The social world of the first Christians.
1. Christians – Rome 2. Rome – Social life and customs
I. Title II. Balch, David L.
938′ .09 DG78

ISBN 0-281-04263-2

Book design by Gene Harris

Printed in Great Britain by Anchor Press, Tiptree

TO ALISON
AND
TO TOM

# Contents

# Preface

The Christian message, first preached in the villages of Galilee and Judea, then in the temple city of Jerusalem, spread during the period when the books of the New Testament were being composed throughout the Greco-Roman world. In this book we discuss the political, religious, economic, and social features of Palestine and of the cities of the Roman empire and synthesize the results of recent scholarly work, to help the reader understand the relationship between the earliest Christians and the world around them. They lived in that Roman world, and they shared many of its perceptions. They rejected some of its traditions, but it was a conscious rejection of only certain aspects of the world in which they had grown up.

Chapter 1 reviews the background history of the Near East from the third century before the birth of Christ until the reign of Hadrian, when Judaism lost its separate identity in the Holy Land and when the canon of the New Testament was complete. It also surveys the political and legal arrangements of the Roman empire as they affected Palestine and the empire as a whole.

Chapter 2 is concerned with the background of the growth of Christianity throughout the Roman empire, considering the means of communication and how they facilitated the spread, geographically and spiritually, of religious and philosophical sects, of Judaism, and of Christianity. This provides the background for a preliminary survey of the missionary activity of the New Testament church.

Chapter 3 treats the patterns of economic activity in the ancient world, to illustrate the common assumptions in pagan and Christian circles about money and its uses.

Chapter 4 focuses on the Palestinian world of the Jesus movement. Its subject is the urbanization of Galilee, a process that stimulated tension with the rural Jewish peasants. It treats the question of the social context of Jesus' preaching and of his controversies with the Pharisees.

In chapter 5 the focus changes to the Greek and Roman cities of the empire in which the first generations of Christians lived. It offers a survey of the physical environment, the population, and the areas of social interaction: work, play, the family, voluntary groups, and religious cults.

Chapter 6 pulls together the various factors of the social environment of the New Testament, as it compares the organization of the early Christian communities with analogous phenomena in the pagan world. It then surveys the specific urban centers of Christian activity that are important in the New Testament.

Chapters 1, 2, and 3 were written by John Stambaugh; chapter 4 by David Balch. Chapters 5 and 6 contain contributions by both. John Stambaugh is pleased to acknowledge the helpful comments of Paula Carew, Meredith Hoppin, Maureen Dietze, Norman Petersen, and Victor Hill. David Balch wishes to express gratitude to Texas Christian University and Brite Divinity School for research and typing grants which assisted in preparing his chapters. We both owe heartfelt thanks to Wayne Meeks, not only for the initial invitation to collaborate on this book and for generous, sensible, and specific help during writing and editing, but also for awakening our interest in the social world of early Christianity in the first place.

*Epiphany 1985* J. E. S. and D. L. B.

# 1

# Historical Background

When "Jesus was born in Bethlehem of Judea in the days of Herod the king" (Matt. 2:1), he was born into a Jewish kingdom ruled by an Idumaean king with a Greek name, installed and sponsored by the Romans. Jesus grew up in Galilee, near Greek cities where the Greek language was used as commonly as his native Aramaic. And when, after his death in Jerusalem, his disciples told his story to others, they spoke and wrote mainly in Greek to take their message to the whole cosmopolitan world ruled by the Romans. In this first chapter we will consider the reasons for the dominance of Greek culture and Roman institutions in the social environment of the New Testament.

## The Greek World from Alexander to Hadrian

### *Alexander's Conquest of the East*

At the time of Jesus' birth, Greeks had been in uninterrupted contact with the peoples of the Near East for nearly eight centuries, founding full-scale cities on the coast of Asia Minor, establishing trading outposts on the coast of Syria, trading with the Phoenicians and adapting their writing system, and traveling to Egypt for trade, tourism, and service as mercenary soldiers. But it was King Alexander of Macedon who led an army of Greeks and Macedonians on a series of campaigns between 332 and 323 B.C.E. that led to the conquest of the Persian empire, from Asia Minor and Egypt eastward to the borders of India. In terms of the scale and complexity of the lands he brought under his rule, the conquests of Alexander had no precedent in Greek history, and they earned for him the epithet "the Great." He died too soon to work out a satisfactory administrative scheme for his immense kingdom, but two of his policies had a profound effect on the history of the region. The first was the foundation of Greek cities at strategic points, to serve as administrative centers but also to provide a focus and beacon of Greek culture in the alien lands of the Orient. The second policy was openness and tolerance toward the native cultures. The result was that Greek culture exercised a much wider influence on—and also was itself influenced by—the cultures of the East, which until this time it had mostly dismissed with the adjective, as pejorative in classical Greek as in modern English, "barbarian."

### *The Hellenistic Kingdoms*

After Alexander's death in 323 B.C.E., his generals were unable to form a united policy for his empire, and their squabbles and battles resulted in its dismemberment. When the dust of their wars cleared, around 301 B.C.E., Antigonus was in control of the old homeland of Macedonia and exercised a general hegemony over the Greek states on the mainland and the islands of the Aegean. Ptolemy was secure in Egypt, where he founded a dynasty that lasted until the famous Cleopatra VII died in 31 B.C.E. Seleucus emerged as king of Syria and the eastern part of the empire, although its most remote areas in Bactria and Persia soon fell away. During the third century B.C.E. another important kingdom emerged, that of the Attalids, with its capital at Pergamum in western Asia Minor.

In all these kingdoms, a Greek dynasty ruled over a mixed population of Greeks and natives, and all of them encouraged the solidarity of Greek culture by building cities on the old model, just as Alexander had done. The characteristic Greek type of city was the *polis,* a community of relatively small size with temples to the traditional Greek gods and an open-air *agora* for public business. It was administered with some degree of autonomy by magistrates and a council, either recruited from a hereditary oligarchic elite or chosen through democratic election by the citizens who owned property. Sometimes a polis replaced a native center of trade or cult, and sometimes it was a new foundation that coexisted with smaller native villages. Native peoples lived around, outside, and sometimes inside these Greek cities and had some cultural impact on them, but those in them who spoke Greek were more aware of the common heritage they shared with each other and with the old cities of the Greek mainland. In time a common tongue, the *koinē* ("common"), superseded the old Greek regional dialects. This was a slightly simplified form of Attic, the dialect of Athens, which was the home of most of the classics of Greek literature and the most shining example of

Greek culture. This common dialect provided the vehicle for communication throughout the vast world inhabited by Greeks, which they called the *gē oikoumenē* ("inhabited world") or simply *oikoumenē,* which has come into English in the adjective "ecumenical."

### *The Romans in the East*

The Hellenistic world came into direct contact with the Roman empire at the end of the third century B.C.E., when Philip V of the Antigonid dynasty in Macedonia made an alliance with the commercial republic of Carthage, Rome's enemy. This gave the Romans a direct interest in the politics of the Greek mainland, and they soon found themselves using and being used in the political maneuvers of cities and princes throughout the East: Pergamum and Rhodes persuaded the Roman Senate to intervene against Philip V in 201 B.C.E., Pergamum enlisted its help against Antiochus III of Syria in 196 B.C.E., Ptolemy VI had its support in expelling Antiochus IV from Egypt in 168 B.C.E., Ptolemy VI and his brother Ptolemy VII referred to the Senate their rival claims to the throne of Egypt, and the Jewish Hasmonaean king Judas Maccabaeus concluded a treaty with the Romans in 161 B.C.E. as part of his campaign against Demetrius I of Syria. By the middle of the second century the Seleucid monarchy of Syria was in such serious decline that the Romans perceived no threat in it, but the decline invited the various princes on its borders to expand and threaten the stability of the eastern end of Rome's sphere of influence.

The result was even deeper Roman involvement. Wars against King Mithridates of Pontus and King Tigranes of Armenia dragged on from 96 to 63 B.C.E. There was constant trouble from pirates, who harassed shipping and endangered the investments of Roman businessmen. The most successful of the Roman generals was Pompey, who defeated the pirates and preempted the credit for the victories over Mithridates and Tigranes. He then turned to the east and south, where the squabbles of kings and princes did not threaten Rome directly but did upset the general balance of the region. To deal with this unstable situation, Pompey in 64 B.C.E. occupied the Seleucid territory, abolished the monarchy, and established a new province of Syria under a Roman governor. To protect the eastern and southern flank of this province, over the next few years he imposed or negotiated agreements with a series of client kingdoms: to the south, he gave Judea to Antipater, a prince of the Edomites or Idumaeans, an Arab tribe; to the east of the Jordan, he negotiated the adherence of the Nabataean Arabs; and to the northeast of Syria, to guard the frontier toward the Euphrates, he made similar agreements with the client kings of Commagene and Armenia. This changed the political realities of the area: Small principalities no longer followed independent policies aimed at taking advantage of other small principalities. Now they were the eastern outposts of the Roman sphere of influence, assigned a role as buffers against the large kingdom of the Parthians, who had inherited the territory of the Persian empire in Iran and Mesopotamia.

As part of the Roman world, the peoples of the Hellenistic East soon became involved in the big-power struggles of Roman political figures. Several important battles between Pompey and his rival, Julius Caesar, were fought in the east, and Caesar enlisted the loyalty of the Jews by granting them immunity from taxation; when he was assassinated in 44 B.C.E., throngs of Jewish supporters came to honor him at his funeral. In the following years, the avengers of Julius Caesar—led by Octavian, his official heir, and by Mark Antony, the executor of his will—pursued those who favored the old Republican forms that Caesar had challenged. Octavian and Antony then became rivals: Antony claimed the East for his own and attempted to administer it as an oriental monarchy, supported by Cleopatra VII.

When Octavian defeated Antony and Cleopatra in 31 B.C.E., he turned to consolidating his power throughout the empire. He soon eliminated any residual resistance and assumed control of the administration of the Roman world, but he did it with scrupulous regard for the traditional forms of Roman Republican practice. He had received the name Caesar when he was adopted by Julius Caesar; in 27 B.C.E. he received in addition the honorific title Augustus. Modern historians generally refer to him as the first of the Roman emperors, but his own title was the more modest *princeps* ("first man"). With him, Roman history moves from the period of the Republic to that of the Principate, the rule of a succession of such "first men."

In the east, the Parthian threat continued to preoccupy Roman strategic calculations for several centuries. After a series of disastrous defeats, Augustus negotiated a diplomatic settlement in 20 B.C.E. During the first century of the Principate the eastern frontier was, if not completely quiet, at least relatively stable. Indeed, this was true of most of the empire. One of the few real trouble spots was Palestine, which in 6 C.E. had ceased to be a client kingdom and become the Roman province of Judea (chapter 4). Nationalist sentiment broke out into a revolt, which ended only with the destruction of the Temple in Jerusalem in 70 C.E. and the abolition of the Jewish priesthood. In the aftermath the emperor Vespasian reorganized the eastern border of the empire, abolishing the kingdoms of Armenia and Commagene and merging them into the province of Galatia; diplomacy continued to deal successfully with the Parthians, while the Euphrates frontier was secured by new fortifications and a new road through Syria.

The emperor Trajan (98–117 C.E.) undertook extensive military activity in the east. To secure the eastern frontier, in 106 he annexed the kingdom of the Nabataeans as the province of Arabia. Then he took advantage of Parthian weakness to expand the empire all the way to the Persian Gulf, creating the new provinces of Armenia, Assyria, and Mesopotamia. These new conquests turned out to be a strain on the empire's resources, and as soon as he succeeded Trajan in 117, the emperor Hadrian abandoned these three newest provinces and consolidated the frontier closer to the Mediterranean.

For most of the Roman empire, the reign of Hadrian was a time of peaceful security and prosperity, well ruled by an experienced bureaucracy and by a conscientious emperor of culture and sensitivity. Hadrian spent vast sums, particularly in the Greek East, building new buildings and renovating old cities, instilling a sense of pride in traditional Greek civilization. Moved partly by his appreciation for Greek culture, partly by a desire to emphasize the unity and universality of the empire, and partly by security considerations (Jewish inhabitants of Africa, Egypt, and Cyprus had erupted into frantic outbursts against their Gentile neighbors and the authorities between 115 and 117), Hadrian attempted to force the Semitic inhabitants of the East to become assimilated by the dominant culture. He expanded a law prohibiting castration to include the practice of circumcision as a capital crime. This affected Egyptians and Nabataeans as well as Jews, but it was the Palestinian Jews who rose in revolt between 131 and 134; when this revolt was crushed, Roman power in the east remained unchallenged for another century.

## Provincial Organization

### *Administration Under the Roman Republic*

Pompey's settlement in the east added seven new provinces to the Roman empire in the years following 64 B.C.E. When a province was established, it was usually organized on the basis of the cities already there; some of them might already have some treaty with the Romans, and that would often be honored, making them exempt from some of the obligations of provincial status. In provinces that did not have a strong urban tradition, the local administration would often be entrusted to tribal units. The normal and special arrangements were codified in a provincial charter that remained the basic constitutional document for the future.

Each province was permanently occupied by Roman legions under the command of a governor, a *proconsul,* who supervised public order. By the first century B.C.E., the governors were chosen by lot from senators immediately after they had filled the office in Rome of consul or praetor, annual magistrates at the top of the administrative ladder who held *imperium,* the official power to command Roman armies. Naturally such governors were deeply involved in the politics of the city of Rome—the welfare of people who lived in the provinces seldom ranked at the top of their priorities—and were often tempted by easy opportunities of enriching themselves and the politically influential Roman businessmen who flocked to all the provinces.

The governor commanded any legionary troops stationed in the province, with a subordinate *legatus* in command of each additional legion. The governor's staff also included a *quaestor,* responsible for finances and tax collection, and several *praefecti* ("prefects"); a praefectus commanded each non-Roman unit of the auxiliary troops as well as any locally recruited militia.

### *Administration Under the Principate*

In establishing the Principate, Augustus was concerned to improve the quality of provincial administration. Only the most secure provinces, now called "public" or "senatorial," would still be administered in the old way, by a proconsul chosen from members of the Senate who had recently held a major magistracy. The rest of the empire's territory was assigned, along with nearly all the legionary forces of the army, to Augustus himself. The actual administration was divided into individual "imperial" provinces delegated to the emperor's legati, men from the senatorial class specifically chosen by the emperor for their loyalty and administrative skill. Each legatus, as the emperor's representative, was in command of the most important legion in his province. Syria was one of the imperial provinces governed in this way, by a legatus like Quirinius in 6 C.E. (Luke 2:2). A less important province like Judea was administered by a praefectus chosen from the equestrian order, which ranked below the senators in social prestige (see chapter 6). After 44 C.E., the title of these prefects was changed to "procurator," but they remained relatively low-ranking personal emissaries of the emperor.

The governor—whether proconsul, legate, or prefect—wielded the power of Rome in the province. He was bound by the provincial charter to honor specific arrangements for tax exemption and other prerogatives, and the provincials could complain about his administration to the Senate or emperor, but otherwise his exercise of imperium was very nearly absolute. He dealt with the local authorities in the cities or tribes. He exercised police powers through his command of the legions, if any were stationed in the province, or else a smaller military unit made up of auxiliary troops composed of non-Roman citizens. He heard law cases and pronounced capital sentences by virtue of his imperium, and he moved through the province regularly, holding hearings in various important assize cities. Tax collection was normally delegated to the cities.

Local administration was performed by the cities, subject to the supervision of the governor. Throughout the empire there were three main types of communities.

During most of the Principate, the most prestigious type was the Roman colony. Its original settlers were Roman citizens sent out from Italy or from Roman legions, and non-Romans who lived in or around them were often granted Roman citizenship as well. Colonies, because of their Roman citizenship, were exempt from tribute and most forms of taxation, and their government was based on a Roman model. As the author of Acts tells us (16:12), Philippi was such a colony. So was Corinth, where Roman colonists lived together with non-citizen Jews and Greeks (Acts 18:4–8).

Other cities were known as *municipia.* This title originally referred to free cities that enjoyed specific treaty privileges guaranteeing at least some degree of autonomy; during the Principate it came to denote communities that had received a wholesale grant of Roman citizenship.

Still other cities simply continued their old constitutions, especially in the Greek East where a democratic form of government survived. These had a citizen assembly, a smaller council, and a board of magistrates who often retained the titles they had had in the old days of Greek freedom and who were often elected by the assembly. We see the meeting of such a vigorous popular assembly at Ephesus (Acts 19:24–40), although the secretary of the assembly worried that immoderate behavior would cause the Roman authorities to limit its power. And certainly Roman influence made itself felt; many cities added a new magistrate to serve as priest of the imperial cult, and Roman policy generally favored an oligarchical style of government. Even when democratic institutions were retained, they were rearranged so that the real power of policy-making resided in the council, which increasingly was made up of those wealthy enough to hold office as magistrates and conservative enough to be reliable partisans of Rome. These upper-class members of the local aristocracy were satisfied with and proud of their membership in the Roman empire. Throughout the Principate the local aristocracies remained steadfast in their loyalty to Rome. Judea, as we shall see, was an exception, but it was virtually the only one, and even there the ruling Sadducees seemed content to collaborate with the Roman authorities.

## Palestine

### *Under the Ptolemies and Seleucids, 320–142 B.C.E.*

Because of its geographical position, Palestine was constantly involved in the big-power politics of the ancient Near East. In the Bronze Age, it saw infiltrations and invasions of Canaanites, Amorites, and Israelites from the Arabian desert, of Akkadians from Mesopotamia, of Egyptians from Egypt, of Hittites from Asia Minor, of Hyksos and Philistines from unknown parts. A big-power vacuum around 1000 B.C.E. permitted David and Solomon to establish an independent kingdom in Palestine, with its capital in Jerusalem. When it fragmented during the following century, its parts eventually fell to sustained attacks from Assyrians and Babylonians. In 587 B.C.E. Jerusalem was captured, Solomon's Temple destroyed, and the population of Jerusalem taken captive to Babylonia. Jews returned only when the Persian king Darius conquered Babylon in 519 B.C.E. and allowed the exiled peoples to return to their homelands. A sacral state was formed in Judea that owed a vassal's allegiance to the Persian throne, and in Jerusalem a second temple was begun.

This Jewish state came under the control of Alexander the Great in 332 B.C.E., and after his death it was gradually taken over by Ptolemy, once he had established his rule in Egypt. During the third century B.C.E. the Ptolemaic kings of Egypt regarded Palestine as a buffer against the rival dynasty of the Seleucids to the north in Syria. They established several colonies as outposts of Ptolemaic culture in Palestine—at Gaza, Ptolemais, and Philadelphia—all important centers of communication. They did not interfere with the internal administration of the various districts and regarded the little state around Jerusalem as temple land, which in Egyptian terms meant that it enjoyed considerable autonomy as long as it paid its assessed tax to the king each year.

The Seleucid dynasty in Syria was in several ways more aggressive than that of the Ptolemies. At certain times under Antiochus III (223–187 B.C.E.), their kingdom included Armenia and Parthia and even part of India. In 200 B.C.E. their rivalry with the Ptolemies culminated in a battle at Paneas in northern Palestine, which brought the region under Seleucid domination. At first this meant little change for the Jewish state at Jerusalem. Antiochus went on, however, to various intrigues in Asia Minor, in the course of which he ran afoul of the Romans. They were in a position to require him to pay enormous reparations, and in attempting to meet these debts, Antiochus' son Seleucus IV planned to confiscate the temple treasury at Jerusalem. He died before he could do this, and his successor, Antiochus IV, devoted himself to a policy of appeasement and reconciliation with the Romans.

The seductiveness of Hellenistic culture was apparent to the Jews of Palestine. Some of them, chiefly the upper-class nobility in Jerusalem, were tempted to assimilate, to adopt Greek ways and accept the social and economic benefits of Greek society. Others, members of the old priestly families (led by the Oniads) followed by the peasants of the countryside, resisted this attempt and, in reaction, increased their emphasis on the traditional defining markers of Judaism embodied in the books of the Torah. Antiochus' need for money and his general inclination to rule a culturally unified kingdom provided the Jewish Hellenizers with the political opportunity to seize power. Between 175 and 163 B.C.E., the Hellenizers, whose interests were impeded by the detailed regulations of the Torah, chipped away at the traditionalist institutions. They established, with the encouragement of Antiochus, a Greek-style polis in Jerusalem, complete with a gymnasium and a council dominated by the nonpriestly nobles of the Tobiad family. The attempt reached a climax in 167 when Antiochus tore down the city walls of Jerusalem and built a new fortress (the Acra) for a Syrian garrison. In the Temple itself, a cult addressed to the Greek god Zeus was established, and Antiochus issued a decree prohibiting the practice of the Jewish religion in Judea.[1]

The traditionalists responded with armed revolt. Under the leadership of a family of wealthy rural priests who are usually called the Maccabees, the war against the Seleucids continued for twenty years. In 164 B.C.E., Judas Maccabaeus overturned the cult of Zeus, which came to be known as the "abomination of desolation," and reestablished the traditional cult of the Jews, an event still celebrated in the holiday of Hannukah. The Romans, who were interested in keeping the Seleucids weak, supported the Maccabees, and an accommodation was reached in 152 B.C.E., when Jonathan was named high priest. He became, in effect, the governor of a Syrian province, paying tribute to one of several pretenders to the Seleucid throne.

### *The Hasmonaean Dynasty, 142–63 B.C.E.*

Jonathan was succeeded in 143 B.C.E. by his brother Simon as leader of the people and high priest. By exploiting the rivalry of several Seleucid princes, he managed in 142 B.C.E. to achieve for Judea exemption from taxes and tribute. This was a major turning point, for it made Judea an independent state. Simon was proclaimed high priest for life, general and *ethnarch* ("leader of the nation") for eternity. A new dynasty, called the Hasmonaean, after their legendary ancestor Hasmon, was thus founded.

In their foreign policy, the early Hasmonaeans frequently enlisted the power of Rome against their Syrian neighbors. Encouraged by the Roman alliance, by Syrian weakness, and by their own nationalistic zeal, the Hasmonaeans expanded their territory constantly. Starting from their power base in Judea, they first conquered the Samaritans, destroying their temple on Mount Gerizim in 128 B.C.E. and their capital city Samaria in 109 B.C.E. To the south, the Hasmonaeans annexed the territory of the Arab tribe of the Idumaeans and forcibly converted them to Judaism. They also captured most of the Greek cities along the seacoast and those in the Decapolis ("the land of ten cities") on the east bank of the Jordan. They attacked the basic social structure of the Greek cities, abolishing such typical institutions as the gymnasium and the pagan temples, which were abhorrent to the Hasmonaean rulers. They forced the populations to accept Judaism or to leave. Many accepted, although the acceptance was undoubtedly perfunctory in the more hellenized territory. In Galilee (which Aristobulus conquered in 104 B.C.E.), however, it seems that the Greeks and the local hellenized aristocracy tended to leave, while the rest of the local population, which spoke the Aramaic of its ancestors, accepted the Jewish religion and remained faithful to it.

By the time of Jannaeus, who ruled with the title of king from 103 to 76 B.C.E., this Jewish state was virtually as large as David's, nine hundred years earlier. When Jannaeus died, a dispute arose over the succession. This precipitated a civil war, and the resultant instability tempted the Romans to intervene.

### *Roman Domination, 63 B.C.E.–66 C.E.*

The intervention came in the wake of the Roman conquest of Syria and the abolition of the Seleucid monarchy. We have seen how Pompey protected the southern and eastern borders of the empire with client kingdoms. His policy was to keep these small, and the Hasmonaean kingdom was reduced in size and power. The Greek cities along the Mediterranean coast and in the Decapolis, where the Hasmonaeans had imposed Judaism, were given autonomy, and the Greek population returned to them. The cities of Strato's Tower, Sepphoris, and Scythopolis also recovered their autonomy, to form an effective barrier between the Jewish territories—Galilee in the north and Judea and Idumaea in the south. From the Roman point of view this simply returned the area to its former inhabitants, who could be expected to be loyal to their Roman patrons, and contained the Jewish territory within secure limits. To Jewish nationalists, it was an unjust encroachment on the legitimate holdings of the Hasmonaean kingdom. Furthermore, many Jews expelled from these cities in Galilee, the Decapolis, and the coast lost their trade and property as they crowded into the restricted territory of Judea.

But the Hasmonaean princes were more concerned with their war with each other, and as a client state of the Romans Judea became a pawn in the machinations of the big politicians in Rome. In 55 B.C.E. a new ruler was appointed by the Romans, to rule Judea with the title "procurator." This was Antipater, a prince of the Idumaean tribe (which had been forcibly converted to Judaism by the Hasmonaeans) who was regarded as an outsider by traditionalists.

Antipater's son Herod learned to play the Romans' game even better than his father, and he succeeded in being recognized in 43 B.C.E. as "king" of a Judea that included Galilee, Peraea, and Samaria. The high priesthood was separated from the temporal rule, and there was considerable religious resistance to Herod's kingship; it took several years for Herod to capture Jerusalem, for instance, and when he finally took it, in 37 B.C.E., he needed a Roman garrison to enforce his rule. In 27 B.C.E. he received from the emperor Augustus the rule over a number of old Greek cities on the coast and in the interior, and later he received a large territory east and northeast of Galilee including Gaulanitis, the modern Golan Heights. This territory was sparsely inhabited, so Herod took the opportunity of founding new cities there, to relieve overpopulation in the Judean homeland. The Jews who settled in these cities were more loyal to him than those of Judea, who always regarded him as an alien, more partial to Hellenism than Judaism. And in many ways he played the part of a pagan Hellenistic monarch. On the site of Samaria he founded a new city of Sebaste, and at Strato's Tower on the coast he founded the new city of Caesarea. Significantly, both were named for and included temples of members of the imperial family. A Greek theater and a hippodrome were built in Jerusalem. Greek was the official language of administration. Greek tutors taught in the royal household. On the other hand, to mollify Jewish sentiment Herod invested in an elaborate rebuilding of the Temple in Jerusalem. Tremendous walls, one of which survives as the Western Wall, or Wailing Wall, supported a great terrace on which the new temple was built, on an unprecedented scale of size and decoration. Work began in 23 B.C.E. and was not completed until 64 C.E.

In the memory of the next generation or two, Herod was an outsider who treated the Jews contemptuously, tortured the faithful Pharisees who resisted his hellenizing activity, and even murdered three of his own sons. At his death, resentment turned to active resistance throughout his kingdom. In Jerusalem, in the Judean countryside, in Peraea, and in Galilee, bands of guerrillas organized themselves around charismatic figures who to their followers seemed to embody the features of the long-expected Messiah; today, depending on our point of view, we would call them freedom fighters or terrorists. The disturbances required the Roman governor of Syria, Quinctilius Varus, to intervene militarily on two separate occasions in 4 B.C.E. His campaigns ended in Jerusalem with the crucifixion of two thousand Jewish prisoners, thus augmenting the general legacy of resentment and resistance that Herod's successors inherited.

According to the Gospels, Jesus was born shortly before Herod's death in 4 B.C.E.

In his will Herod left his kingdom to his three surviving adult sons, and after long discussions in Rome (for which nearly all the members of Herod's family managed to be present and make their case) the emperor Augustus ratified this arrangement. (The event may be reflected in the story of the king who went on a great journey in the parable of the pounds, Luke 19:12–27.) The southern part, Judea and Samaria, was to be ruled by Archelaus, who was granted the title ethnarch. Galilee and Peraea were assigned to Archelaus' brother, Herod Antipas, who is often referred to in the Gospels simply as Herod. Archelaus' half brother, Philip, was given the northeastern part of the kingdom, the new regions Herod had received between 23 and 20 B.C.E. Both Antipas and Philip received the title *tetrarch* ("leader of a fourth").

Philip's tetrarchy, which he ruled until his death in 34 C.E., included many Greek cities, and even the Jews here were relatively content with the Herodian family. As a result, Philip's rule was tranquil. He rebuilt the fishing village of Bethsaida at the northeastern corner of the Sea of Galilee (Mark 6:45; Luke 9:10) as a Hellenistic city named Julias in honor of Augustus' daughter, and farther north he replaced Paneas with the new Hellenistic city called Caesarea Philippi (Matt. 16:13 and parallels).

Herod Antipas ruled Galilee as tetrarch until the emperor Gaius deposed him in 39 C.E., his subjects including both Jesus of Nazareth and John the Baptist. Antipas comes most vividly to our attention in the Gospels because of his execution of John, who had made a public issue over Antipas' marriage to Herodias, a marriage that violated two Jewish laws (Matt. 14:1–11; Luke 3:19–20). Mark's version (6:17–27) gives us a glimpse of life in Antipas' court, peopled by courtiers, military officers, leading men, a conniving queen, and even a royal dancing lady (Salome, Herodias' daughter and wife of the tetrarch Philip). The casual way in which Antipas observed Jewish proprieties is also shown in the new capital city that he built on the Sea of Galilee. Although named Tiberias, in honor of the emperor who reigned from 14 to 37 C.E., it was intended to be more a Jewish city than a Gentile one. During the construction, however, an old cemetery was discovered within the city limits, which made it unfit for habitation in the eyes of the orthodox. Herod went on with the construction but was only able to persuade a small number of Jews to go there to live.

The least happy of Herod's successors was Archelaus (Matt. 2:22), who encountered political opposition from the beginning of his reign. We are not well informed about the details, but by 6 C.E., Samaritans and Jews alike united in an embassy to Rome that succeeded in persuading Augustus to depose Archelaus and exile him to Gaul.

Archelaus' territory was annexed to the Roman empire as an imperial province under the control of a prefect of equestrian rank. The governor of the much more important province of Syria exercised supervisory oversight and on occasion intervened in Judean affairs. For instance, when the province of Judea was being organized, Quirinius, the governor of Syria, conducted a general census of the new province, which is probably that referred to in Luke's story of the nativity of Jesus (2:2).[2] It resulted in the imposition of a per capita tax on the population, which Matthew (22:15–22) and Mark (12:14–17) refer to with the Latin word *census;* Luke (20: 21–26) uses the Greek word for tribute. The administrative center of the province of Judea was on the Mediterranean coast in Herod's Hellenistic city of Caesarea, from which the governor commanded a small number of troops. In Jerusalem, the Sanhedrin functioned as the provincial senate, its members drawn from leading families in the usual provincial pattern. The presiding officer was the high priest, who at the beginning (from 6 to 15 C.E.) was Annas; even after the office was transferred to others, the high priest continued to be the most important political person in Judea after the governor (Matt. 26:3; Luke 3:2; John 18:24; Acts 4:5–6).

The official policy of the Romans was scrupulous in maintaining Jewish autonomy in religious matters and in permitting Jews all over the world to pay the annual tax of half a shekel for the maintenance of the Temple. Jews were exempt from the normal requirement to participate in the imperial cult. Instead, sacrifices (two lambs and a bull) were offered every day in the Temple on behalf of the emperor.

In many ways, Roman rule was mild, but certain incidents grated on the sensibilities of Jewish traditionalists who remembered the great independent power of the Hasmonaeans and who had seen so many shufflings of administrative arrangements. For instance, the vestments worn by the high priest for solemn festivals were not in his custody but were kept in the Antonia fortress, guarded by Roman soldiers. The census of Quirinius was itself the cause of great resentment, which crystallized around a charismatic figure from Galilee named Judas (Acts 5:37), whose followers came to be known in subsequent years as Zealots.

None of the Roman governors of Judea between 6 and 66 C.E. seem to have been conspicuous for their tact. We know most about Pontius Pilate, governor from 26 to 36; given the nature of our sources, what we know are his collisions with the opponents of Roman rule. Early in his term, for instance, he installed a new unit on garrison duty in the Antonia fortress in Jerusalem. The new unit, unlike any of its predecessors, was identified by standards that bore medallion busts of the emperor. This seemed a deliberate affront to the Jewish prohibition of graven images. Later, to finance a new aqueduct in Jerusalem, Pilate appropriated money from the temple treasury, a violation of Roman as well as Jewish law. In another episode, he installed shields inscribed with his own name and that of the emperor Tiberius on the walls of Herod's palace, his own residence in Jerusalem. In all these incidents, Pilate was forced to back down, usually by the threat or reality of Jewish violence. Diplomatic maneuvering also played a role. Sejanus, chief adviser to the emperor Tiberius (14–37 C.E.), seems to have encouraged anti-Jewish behavior throughout the empire; after Sejanus was condemned for treason in 31 C.E., Tiberius seems to have been more sympathetic to the wishes of the local Jewish authorities in the Sanhedrin. In defense of his position, therefore, Pilate seems to have had to proceed rather gingerly in dealing with the high priest and his associates. This may explain his conduct at the trial of Jesus. It may also explain the role of Barabbas, who may well have been one of the Zealots; if so, his terrorist activities would have led to his arrest (Mark 15:7).

Pilate was replaced as prefect in 36 C.E., and the governor of Syria, Vitellius, attempted to mollify the Jews by a series of conciliatory acts that included the return of the solemn vestments to the high priest's keeping.

The reign of the emperor Gaius (37–41 C.E.), nicknamed Caligula, was marked by his attempt to abolish the Jewish cult at Jerusalem and in its place install a statue of himself for worship on the Temple Mount. This was in revenge for an episode at Jamnia, where the Jews had attacked and desecrated a new altar that the Greeks living in the town had erected in honor of the imperial cult. The emperor was assassinated before he could push the project to completion. One of those whose arguments and pleas delayed the plan was Agrippa I, grandson of Herod the Great. He had grown up in Rome and become a good friend of Gaius and also of Claudius, who succeeded Gaius as emperor and reigned from 41 until 54 C.E.

In order to calm the tensions rising in Judea, Claudius appointed Agrippa king: from 41 C.E. until his death in 44, he ruled Galilee, Peraea, and Judea. There existed once more an independent kingdom under the Herodian royal house that could claim at least some legitimacy in Jewish eyes. Within his kingdom Agrippa, whose grandmother was a member of the Hasmonaean dynasty, presented himself as a devoted and pious Jew. He observed the festivals, offered daily sacrifices, and asserted the dominance of Pharisaic Judaism over dissident sects by executing and imprisoning leaders of the Christian community in Jerusalem (Acts 12:1–19). On the other hand, his upbringing in Rome had given him decidedly pro-Roman sympathies and Hellenistic taste. He preferred to live in the Greek city of Caesarea rather than Jerusalem, his coins were stamped with his image, and he was celebrating a festival of the imperial cult when he was stricken with appendicitis and died in great pain—the victim, the pious said, of divine retribution for permitting the crowd to greet him in terms appropriate to the ruler cult of Hellenistic kings.

When Agrippa I died, the emperor once more made Judea a Roman province, thus making Roman control more solid but also frustrating Jewish nationalist hopes. This was the third time in recent memory that a Jewish kingdom had been supplanted by Roman administration—in 63 B.C.E., in 6 C.E., and now in 44. Incidents of Roman insensitivity compounded the sense of disappointment: The first Roman governor, now called a procurator, attempted to regain custody of the high priestly vestments; under Cumanus, procurator from 48 to 52, a soldier on guard duty indecently exposed himself to the crowd at Passover; and when a group of Jewish pilgrims from Galilee were waylaid by Samaritan bandits, the authorities did not respond. The Zealot movement increased the number and effectiveness of its terrorist attacks, threatening with death any Jew who collaborated with the Roman authorities. One raid came out of the desert and nearly captured Jerusalem; it was led by a Zealot called "the Egyptian," who was still a concern to the authorities at the time of Paul's arrest (Acts 21:38). The religious and political authorities of the Sanhedrin exploited the unrest for their own ends, undercutting their opponents at every opportunity and persecuting dissidents like the Christians. Charismatic leaders appeared in many parts of the province, and hopes of a speedy deliverance from Roman domination were fueled by prophetic sermons and apocalyptic literature predicting that the Jews would overcome under a Messiah who would arrive soon. The Romans reacted with countermeasures, executing the terrorists and arresting the crowds who flocked to the preaching of the "prophets" and "Messiahs." Two of the procurators of this period appear in the New Testament narrative: Felix (52–60 C.E.) married to Drusilla, the daughter of Agrippa I (Acts 24:24), under whom Paul's trial dragged on and on for two years (Acts 24:27), and Porcius Festus (60–62 C.E.), who heard Paul's case with dispatch and, after consulting Agrippa II, Drusilla's brother and the ruler of a small client kingdom based on Philip's old tetrarchy, acceded to Paul's request to be sent to Rome for trial (Acts 24:27 to 26:32).

### *The Jewish Wars and Their Aftermath*

The progressive breakdown of law and order in the province of Judea led to a full-scale revolt against Roman authority in 66 C.E. A dispute between Greeks and Jews in Caesarea led to an unsympathetic show of force by Gessius Florus, the procurator. The Zealots responded by seizing the fortress Herod had built at Masada and massacring its Roman garrison. The priestly establishment in Jerusalem joined the revolt by discontinuing the sacrifices on behalf of the emperor, which amounted to a declaration of war against the Roman empire. The Roman empire responded by sending Vespasian and his son Titus against the rebel province. By the middle of 68 C.E., their armies had regained control of the whole territory except eastern Judea. The death of the emperor Nero interrupted the Roman campaign, and a Roman civil war dragged on for a year. The victor was Vespasian himself, the new emperor.

Titus continued the war. He besieged Jerusalem for a full year and finally stormed onto the Temple Mount in the middle of 70. He entered the Holy of Holies, carried off the sacred implements to adorn his triumph in Rome, and then set fire to the Temple itself. Another month was needed to root out the last resistance within the city, and then Titus ordered the destruction of the city walls and the enclosure of the Temple. Mopping-up operations continued against the fortresses occupied by the Zealots. The last to fall, in 73 C.E., was Masada.

The Romans took strenuous measures to guarantee the tranquillity of Judea in the years after 70 C.E. The post of governor was upgraded to the rank of imperial legate and given to well-qualified individuals with experience in provincial administration. The military garrison was also strengthened, and a full legion of professional soldiers was stationed in Jerusalem, the most likely location of future trouble. A careful eye was kept to intercept any potential Messiahs before they gained a following, and the descendants of the house of David were subject to special scrutiny and persecution.[3]

The destruction of the Temple and the obliteration of the priesthood and the Sanhedrin represented a catastrophic turning point in Jewish history. The sacrifices mandated in the books of the Torah could no longer be performed but could only be maintained in the memory of the Jewish people. The old custom, tolerated by the Romans, of paying a half-shekel tax per person per year for the maintenance of the temple cult in Jerusalem was now rendered pointless, but the Romans required all Jews throughout the empire to pay the equivalent amount, two drachmas, to the empire, ostensibly for the maintenance of the cult of Jupiter, who had defeated Yahweh and his people. To cope with what had happened, some Jews, like the Pharisees, strove to maintain the memory of the old traditions and adapt them to the new circumstances. Others, like the Zealots, took comfort in the expectation of a Messiah who would restore the Jews to power. Both looked and hoped for the restitution of the full priestly cult in Jerusalem.

Between 115 and 117 C.E., both Roman and Jewish sources tell us about widespread Jewish unrest in Cyrene, Egypt, and Cyprus. Responding to the promises of self-proclaimed Messiahs, these Jews rose up violently against their Gentile neighbors and against the authorities. There may have been some similar uprising at this time in Palestine as well, but we do not have any direct evidence concerning it.[4] Instead, we hear of the revolt that broke out in 132 C.E. led by Shimon bar-Kosiba, a messianic figure who was called Bar Kokhba ("Son of the Star") by his followers and later, by bitter rabbis, Bar-Kozeba ("Son of the Lie"). The outbreak may well have been triggered by the emperor Hadrian's ban on circumcision, which amounted to a ban on the practice of the Jewish religion, even if that was not Hadrian's intention. Palestinian Christians would have resisted Bar Kokhba's claim to be the Messiah and probably did not join the revolt. New documents recently discovered in the caves used as hiding places by the rebels seem to show, however, that some Gentiles joined Jews in the resistance and that Bar Kokhba was proclaimed the "*nasi* ('prince') of Israel."[5] The Romans sent some of their best commanders with eight legions, and by 135 C.E. the revolt had been crushed, the rebels starved into submission in caves in the Judean hills and their survivors crucified by the hundreds. The expectation that the Messiah would come soon was shattered. The city of Jerusalem was rebuilt as a Hellenistic city named Aelia Capitolina in honor of the emperor's family. A temple of Zeus crowned the Temple Mount, and Jews were forbidden even to enter the city.

## Roman Law and Local Law

### *Citizenship*

As the empire grew and Roman authority became more widespread throughout the Mediterranean world, one of the means by which the Romans rewarded and co-opted the loyalty of the people they dominated was through grants of Roman citizenship. Roman citizenship involved the responsibility of service in the legions of the army, but it also involved the privileges of a vote in the Roman popular assemblies, the full protection of Roman law, and exemption from paying most taxes.

Roman citizenship could be acquired in several ways. The simplest was to be born as the child of a Roman father. Another was to be the citizen of a foreign city that had been granted, wholesale, the Roman franchise. Sometimes citizenship was granted to the aristocratic governing class of a certain provincial city, or individuals might receive it—from the emperor, the Senate, or a general in the field—as a reward for faithful service. Such citizen status would, of course, be inherited by children. The regular legions of the army were reserved for citizens; noncitizen soldiers served as "auxiliaries"; when they were honorably discharged, usually after about twenty-five years' service, they received Roman citizenship, which could also be passed on to their children. Finally, slaves who were set free by citizen masters also received limited rights of citizenship; their children born after manumission were considered full citizens.

Although as late as the first century B.C.E. legal thinkers like Cicero had worried that it was not possible to be both a Roman citizen and the citizen of another municipality, these scruples had been overcome by the time of the Principate. Paul, for example, could claim to be a citizen both of Tarsus, "no mean city" (Acts 21:39), and of Rome (Acts 22:25–28).

Within the Roman empire, everybody came under the general jurisdiction of the Roman authorities. The only exceptions were cities with special treaties specifying autonomy of jurisdiction. Depending on the treaty, Roman citizens in such autonomous cities might or might not be subject to the local authorities; usually they were not. Natives who had acquired Roman citizenship enjoyed the same status as any other Roman citizens, although according to a decree of Augustus they had to continue to make contributions to the welfare and maintenance of their hometown even after they received Roman citizenship. Both Roman citizens and citizens of free cities were able to choose whether to be tried by local courts or Roman courts, those either of the governor or of the emperor. Inhabitants of the Greek East who were not Roman citizens were normally subject to local laws wherever they were.

In Rome, Romans were subject to the old Republican laws and the courts and penalties provided in them. Cases involving Romans and foreigners were heard before a special magistrate. Roman citizens always had the right to appeal a capital sentence: In the Republic, they could appeal over the head of any magistrate to the sovereign assembly of the citizens; in the Principate, they could appeal to the emperor. We do not know that these appeals were always tolerated by provincial governors, although our best documented example is that of Paul before Festus, who makes his appeal to

Caesar *before* the case is heard. Festus grants the appeal, but it is not certain that he was compelled to do so; he may just have wanted to get rid of a troublesome case.[6]

### Legislation and Jurisdiction

According to the usages of the Roman Republic, which at least in legal theory continued to be valid through the first century or two of the Principate, a law properly so-called (*lex*) could only be made by the popular assembly of citizens in Rome. At the beginning of the Principate, new legislation continued to take this form; whether initiated by emperor or Senate, it was passed formally by one of the citizen assemblies in Rome. But during the first century C.E. the citizen assemblies fell into neglect, and decrees of the Senate (always in concert with the emperor's wishes) took on the force of law. So also, by the second century, did direct pronouncements from the emperor.

The laws regulating criminal acts had established separate jury courts to hear trials under specific categories: adultery, forgery, murder, bribery, and treason. These tended to be the crimes of the rich and powerful. There were other types of behavior that also required regulation, even though they did not come under one of the "ordinary" categories of the criminal law. To deal with them, the appropriate magistrate had the power to determine what was legal behavior, what was illegal, and what an appropriate punishment was, in accordance with the advice of a council. In the city of Rome, the appropriate magistrate was the prefect of the city, who at the beginning of his appointment issued an edict listing the principles by which he and his council would decide such "extraordinary" cases—the proceeding was known as a *cognitio extraordinaria.* The emperor himself, attended by his own council, also heard such cases as a court of last resort or, in serious cases such as treason, of first resort.

In the provinces, the appropriate magistrate was the governor. Since there was no formal law defining the charges heard in such a trial and specifying the penalty, a magistrate hearing such a cognitio extraordinaria had a great deal of freedom in dealing with the case. First he had to decide whether or not to accept the charge, to determine whether he considered the alleged conduct to be a crime or not. We see this happen at Corinth when Paul was hauled before Annius Gallio, the proconsul of the province of Achaia (Acts 18: 12–17). The Jewish leaders accused Paul of "persuading men to worship God contrary to the law." The proconsul decided that it was an internal dispute within the Jewish community and refused to hear the case. This also presented a problem to Pliny the Younger, when he was governor of Bithynia at the beginning of the second century. In his correspondence with the emperor Trajan (*Letters* 10.96) he expresses a great deal of confusion as to what constitutes the crime: simply confessing the name of Christ, or the attendant subversive actions of refusing to offer incense to the emperor's image, or the various immoral actions that were being alleged against the Christians in his province of Bithynia. This shows that there was no specific legislation forbidding Christianity, but that judges all over the empire dealt with Christians on a largely individual basis. It also helps explain why the persecution of Christians was not continuous but happened only sporadically, at specific times and places. Trajan, followed by Hadrian, laid down confusing guidelines: Christians were not to be accused anonymously or hunted out, but if they were accused and convicted of being Christians they were to be punished.[7]

Within a province, the governor tended to be involved only in more serious cases involving public order. Smaller legal matters were left in the hands of local officials, who continued to observe the old systems of the individual cities or kingdoms. In Judea, then, the Sanhedrin and the high priest continued to observe and enforce the laws of Moses recorded in the Torah and could expect the Roman authorities to recognize their right to do so. In the Greek cities, the local authority of one city's laws was limited to its own territory, a fact which Paul and Barnabas and their hosts exploit by keeping on the move; when they are brought before the magistrates in one town like Thessalonica, they pay a security deposit and move on to another town like Beroea, where their accusers have to start all over again with a new set of magistrates and laws (Acts 17:5–10).

On some occasions, matters of jurisdiction are not clear to us and may not have been very clear to the people involved. For example, scholars have not come to any agreement about whether or not the Jewish authorities in Jerusalem had the power to execute condemned criminals. They do it in the case of James and the case of Stephen, and this has led P. Winter, E. Mary Smallwood, and others to argue that the Sanhedrin could pronounce and carry out the death sentence.[8] In this view, the Gospels are wrong when they say that the Jews were really responsible for Jesus' death; the fact that Pilate executed Jesus would mean that the trial was a Roman proceeding, based on the charge of sedition. On the other hand, A. N. Sherwin-White argues that all the evidence from elsewhere in the empire indicates that local courts did not have the jurisdiction to execute criminals, a duty the Romans reserved to themselves.[9] In his view, the Jewish authorities may well have said, "It is not lawful for us to put any person to death" (John 18:31), and the executions of Stephen and James are more in the nature of lynchings than legitimate death sentences. This may also be the case with the woman taken in adultery (John 8:1–11).

All the New Testament trials illustrate a common principle of procedure in Greek and Roman law, the lack of a public prosecutor. Just as in civil cases the offended party had to take the initiative against the defendant, so in criminal proceedings some individual had to bring the action against the accused. Public police forces did not normally do detective work.

### *Police*

In the individual cities of the empire, the authorities generally exercised police power through a board of locally recruited watchmen. They were never terribly effective, except at Antioch and Philippi, both Roman colonies. By the second century, the governor appointed local boards of "peace wardens" to deal with serious crime and to police the countryside. In Jerusalem the high priest had his own police force, the Temple Guard, under the command of the captain of the Temple. This was the unit that came to arrest Jesus (John 18:3, 12) and the apostles (Acts 5:24–26) and was posted to guard the tomb of Jesus (Matt. 27:65).

The Roman governor also enforced public order through the troops under his command. In the "imperial" provinces, these included one or more legions with 5,000 men each. In Judea up until 66 C.E., the governor had to do his work with only six cohorts (including, apparently, the "Italian cohort" of Acts 10:1). Each cohort contained 500 to 600 men; a tribune recruited from the prestigious equestrian order was in command (John 18:12; Acts 21:31–40; 25:23). Centurions were the noncommissioned officers, in charge of 100 soldiers (Mark 15:39; Luke 23:47; Acts 10:1). They usually rose up from the ranks, and some of them attained special status which admitted them, on discharge, to the status of equestrian. The soldiers' duties included crowd control and carrying out executions (John 19:1–37). Special assignments were sometimes entrusted, in the early Principate, to a military police corps of *speculatores,* one of whom performs the execution of John the Baptist (Mark 6:27). Police duties like the escort of prisoners were also assigned to soldiers: thus Julius, a centurion of the "Augustan cohort" (Acts 27:1) commands a small group of prisoners. Many soldiers surely supplemented their salaries through less official activities, including clear-cut extortion; there is no reason to suspect that the soldiers were well liked by the populace, especially in a restive province like Judea.

### *Punishments*

In old Roman civil law, a convicted defendant was liable to monetary payments or retaliatory punishments that could even include death. Fines and death were also the most common punishments decreed by the criminal laws, although by the end of the Republic enforcement was routinely lax enough that there was time for a convicted person to go into voluntary exile outside Italy and escape execution.

Under the Principate, as we have seen, judicial magistrates had a great deal of discretion in deciding on punishments, and a wide and not especially consistent variety of punishments were used. Even before the trial, suspects were imprisoned and beaten with whips or cudgels as part of the preliminary examination of the evidence, the *coercitio.* The penalties imposed after conviction varied with the mood or judgment of the magistrate and his council, with the nature of the crime, and with any extenuating or aggravating circumstances. A relatively lenient penalty was a fine. Imprisonment was not a punishment in itself but simply detention, before the trial or the carrying out of the sentence. The equivalent of long incarceration was exile, in which the convicted person, usually belonging to the upper classes, was relegated to an island or remote city for an indefinite period, often life. In more serious cases, or if the convicted person was of lower status, he might be deprived of his liberty, sold as a slave or condemned to lifelong toil in the mines or the gladiatorial arena. Before being sent off, such a convicted prisoner was beaten severely with a *flagellum,* a vicious flail tipped with pieces of bone or metal. Such a beating also preceded most forms of capital punishment. Some death penalties were specific to certain crimes: In Rome, for example, a parricide was sewn into a sack and thrown into the river, a vestal virgin who violated her oath of chastity was buried alive, and those convicted of certain other crimes were thrown off the Tarpeian rock. Distinguished Romans and prisoners of war were efficiently strangled in prison or simply ordered to commit suicide by the emperor. Or the condemned prisoner was tied to a stake naked and whipped with rods, then blindfolded, made to kneel, and beheaded with an ax (during the Republic) or a sword (during the Principate). More brutal and sadistic executions were also used. Crucifixion was usually reserved for slaves and particularly vicious prisoners of war, although it was inflicted on citizens from time to time. Death on the cross was slow, as the condemned person's weight hung on his arms; muscle spasms, cramps, and insects added to the pain, and death usually came through gradual suffocation. Breaking the legs increased the weight and brought death more quickly. Burning at the stake was originally an old Roman retaliatory punishment for arsonists. There was thus a grisly appropriateness to Nero's burning the Christians whom he had accused of setting fire to Rome in 64 C.E. It was such an unusual punishment that there was widespread revulsion in the city. There was less revulsion when prisoners were condemned "to the beasts" at the gladiatorial shows. The condemned were tied to stakes, and lions or other wild animals were released into the arena to kill them as slowly or as quickly as luck would have it.

Jewish law was very specific about the imposition of punishments. The Law of Moses specified flogging for certain sexual crimes and allowed judges to impose it for other offenses as well, up to a maximum of forty blows (Deut. 25:2–4). To avoid any possibility of violating that injunction, "forty lashes save one" became a normal punishment handed out by Jewish courts (2 Cor. 11:24). The traditional form of capital punishment was stoning, prescribed for idolatry, sorcery, and adultery. As we have seen, it is unclear whether the Romans permitted the Jewish authorities to exercise the death penalty, although in one case a kind of legalized lynching was sanctioned: An inscription on the Temple clearly warned that any Gentile—including a Roman citizen—who violated the sacred area was liable to immediate death by stoning.

# 2

# Mobility and Mission

Throughout the New Testament, people are on the move. In Luke's Gospel, for example, Mary makes three trips between Galilee and Judea within a single, albeit eventful, year (Luke 1:39–56; 2:1–5, 22–39). In the Gospel of John, Jesus and his disciples walk from Galilee to Jerusalem several times (e.g., John 2:13; 5:1; 7:1–10). In the days after the resurrection, we read about Philip's trips to Samaria, Gaza, and Caesarea (Acts 8:5, 26, 40) and about Peter's visits to Samaria, Lydda, Joppa, Caesarea, Antioch, and possibly even Corinth (Acts 8:14; 9:35–39; 10:1–24; Gal. 2:11; 1 Cor. 1:12). Paul's travels are known best: to Antioch, Cyprus, Pamphylia, Pisidia (Acts 13 to 14); to Troas, Macedonia, Achaia, Ephesus (Acts 15:41 to 21:17); to Rome (Acts 27:1 to 28:16); to Arabia (Gal. 1:17); to Crete (Titus 1:5); and repeatedly to Jerusalem (Acts 9:26; 11:29–30; 15: 1–29; 21:17).

## Communications

### *Highways*

A high degree of mobility was typical of the Roman empire in the first century, a time when, over a wide expanse of territory, travel was easier than it had ever been before. Roads connected all the provinces and cities of the empire. Army patrols reduced the dangers from highwaymen. Roman power kept the sea free from pirates. A standard coinage was universally accepted, and the Hellenistic-Roman cultural unity allowed a traveler who knew both Greek and Latin to be understood everywhere.

Roman roads were paved, to withstand the wear of hobnail boots and heavy loaded wagons. In valleys, the roads tended to hug the side of the hill. They climbed to mountain passes in a series of steep switchbacks and crossed rivers by means of fords, ferries, or bridges of wood or stone. Most people walked, but those who could afford it might ride a donkey, a horse, or even a camel. The well-to-do, like the Ethiopian eunuch (Acts 8:26–31) traveled in chariots or carriages pulled by mules or horses.

For a long trip, you took along a sack with a change of clothes or two and carried money in a purse tied to your belt or worn on a cord around your neck. Once on the road, you might encounter farmers who would come up to the roadside to sell produce or handmade trinkets, but the main landmarks between cities were the inns and way stations constructed for the messengers of the imperial bureaucracy. *Mansiones* ("inns") were located at intervals of a good day's journey, twenty-five to thirty-five miles apart, depending on the terrain. These usually had a number of sleeping and eating rooms available, and fairly elaborate facilities for stabling and tending animals. At more frequent intervals, perhaps every ten miles or so, were *mutationes,* smaller stations where official couriers could change horses and where ordinary travelers could find something to eat and a bed. Towns along the road offered more complete hospitality—a variety of places to eat, heated bathing establishments, and lodgings of many different types, ranging from luxurious villas converted for use as comfortable hotels to very cheap dives, the walls covered with graffiti and the beds infested with bugs.

Such travel involved discomforts and dangers. Paul, who knew them from personal experience, lists floods, robbers, shipwreck, sleeplessness, hunger, thirst, and cold (2 Cor. 11:25–27). In the first century, the main roads were relatively free of highwaymen, but on smaller roads in politically unsettled provinces it was perfectly possible for a traveler to be set upon by thieves, as the parable of the good Samaritan shows (Luke 10:29–37).

The most secure way to travel was to rely on the hospitality of friends or some other personal contact. A very old tradition emphasized the importance of hospitality, of the shared obligations of providing food and shelter to visitors, in the assurance that they would extend the same hospitality to you when you traveled near their home. The upper classes stayed at the villas of relatives or associates or even maintained hostels along routes they traveled frequently. More humble folk, too, would exploit friendships and acquaintances when they traveled. Paul for instance stayed whenever possible in private houses (Acts 16:12–15; 17:5; 21:16; 28:7, 14; cf. Philemon 22).

### *Seafaring*

Because it was faster and often more comfortable than a land journey, many preferred to travel by ship. During the first and second centuries the best service was available between Alexandria and Rome, the route of the great ships that transported grain from Egypt. When the favorable northerly winds were blowing, the trip from the port of Rome to Alexandria could take as little as ten days, although the return could require up to two months. When Paul sailed from Palestine to Rome, he changed ships at Myra on the southern coast of Asia Minor. The ship he took had sailed due north from Alexandria on a route to Rome that would avoid open seas. It was apparently the off season, but the large grain ship took on 276 passengers (Acts 27:1–8).

Since all the ships were designed primarily for cargo, passengers provided their own mattresses, blankets, clothes, materials for washing, food, and cookware. The exact moment of departure depended on many factors, not least on the presence of good omens, for ancient sailors were superstitious. Because of the very real dangers of the enterprise, a sea journey could often be an emotionally draining, tense experience. Piracy—with its attendant robbery, rape, kidnapping, and murder—had been a significant danger during the classical and Hellenistic period, but Pompey eliminated that danger in 67 B.C.E., and the imperial fleet continued to offer assurance against pirate raids in the first and second centuries. The great unavoidable risk was shipwreck, whether from dangerous shallow waters or from storm. The safest time to sail was between May and October, but even then rough weather could put a ship in serious peril. When that happened, feverish prayers were offered to the gods of the sea, and all those aboard, crew and passengers, were put to work (Acts 27:19–38).

### *Letter Writing*

An easier way to communicate across distances, whether great or small, was by means of the letter. A standard format was developed, which was followed in official communications from kings, edicts of city councils, memos between business associates, open letters of advice from oracles or counselors, and private communications between friends, lovers, or relatives. Rhetoricians even wrote handbooks laying down the rules for specific types of letters. Letters served as means of introduction and recommendation (2 Cor. 3: 1–3; 3 John), conveyed news (2 Cor. 8:1–7), requested favors (Rom.

16:1–2; Philemon), expressed thanks (Phil. 1:3–7; 4:10–14), and offered encouragement (1 Thessalonians) or advice (Galatians; 1 Corinthians 7; 2 Corinthians 8).[1]

The upper classes dictated letters to secretaries—slaves or freedmen. Ordinary people could find scribes available in public squares, who for a small fee would prepare a letter in the proper format. The writers of the epistles in the New Testament used secretaries (Rom. 16:22; 1 Peter 5:12), although Paul normally added a note at the end in his own hand (1 Cor. 16:21; Gal. 6:11; Col. 4:18; 2 Thess. 3:17).

Roman officials used the *cursus publicus,* horsemen stationed along the road system, to dispatch official communications. Wealthy private individuals sent their own slaves, as we see in the voluminous correspondence of Cicero. Others used friends (Rom. 16:1–2) or entrusted the letter to a stranger who happened to be going in the right direction.

### *The Traveling Public*

Those with first claim to the facilities of the Roman road system and the galleys of the navy were those on government service: individual messengers bearing official dispatches, ambassadors from cities or client kingdoms delivering petitions, provincial governors going out to their provinces or moving about in them to administer justice, soldiers marching from one post to another. Occasionally, the emperor himself, surrounded by an immense retinue, would tour the world or lead the army into battle.

Another important group of travelers were businessmen: the shippers, entrepreneurs, and their agents who traveled about making contracts and supervising the shipment of goods. On a smaller scale, itinerant merchants shuttled back and forth, buying goods in one spot and selling them in cities and towns across the seas.

Some slaves were trusted to carry messages for their masters or to supervise some business enterprise on their behalf. Presumably it was a common sight to see a strange slave traveling, by himself or with a few others, on his master's business. Thus a runaway like Onesimus (Philemon 10–18) would not necessarily be very conspicuous.

Other travelers included the touring companies of actors known as Dionysiac artists; athletes or religious pilgrims headed to a major festival at Delphi or Olympia or Jerusalem, or to a shrine of Asclepius for healing, or to a local fair; wandering philosophers, Cynics, teachers, and wonder-workers; or tourists simply out to see the sights.

### *Migration*

Not all traveling was temporary. Some people went to stay. One pattern of permanent migration was the colony, in which a group of residents of one city went out to found a new one, to form the core of a new citizen elite and engage in all the agricultural, commercial, and (usually) political activities of an independent city.

Another pattern included the men and women who left one city to go and live, usually as noncitizen aliens, in some established city. Such migrants were often traders and craftspeople, exemplified in the tentmakers Priscilla and Aquila, whose movements can be traced in the New Testament record. Aquila, the husband, was a Jew from Pontus, in northern Asia Minor, but he and Priscilla had already moved to Rome by the reign of Claudius, since they were among the Jews he expelled from the city. They moved to Corinth, where Paul, a fellow tentmaker, went to stay with them. When Paul left Corinth for Syria, Priscilla and Aquila went with him as far as Ephesus, where they soon became leaders of the Christian community and probably continued to practice their trade (Acts 18:1–3, 18–28; Rom. 16:3; 1 Cor. 16:19). When, later, Paul wrote to the community in Rome, they were there again and hosts of another house church, as they had been in Ephesus (Rom. 16:5).

Normally, such artisans and traders lived under the laws and customs of the host city, with specific liabilities and privileges according to the individual situation. They organized themselves and met regularly for business and to celebrate their common heritage. In some cases it was convenient for the political authorities to recognize such a community of foreigners as an autonomous entity, known in Greek as a *politeuma* (cf. Phil. 3:20). As such, the group could enjoy a certain amount of social independence, although always subject of course to the general political control of the state.[2]

## The Movement of Religions

### *The Reception of New Cults*

Sometime near the end of the third century B.C.E., on Apollo's sacred island of Delos in the middle of the Aegean Sea, a man named Apollonius, the grandson of an Egyptian immigrant, bought a plot of ground in an exclusive residential area, cleaned out the refuse that had been dumped there over the years, and began to build a temple to Sarapis, an Egyptian god who was popular among the Greeks in Alexandria. The god's statue had been brought to

Delos two generations earlier by Apollonius' grandfather, who in Egypt had belonged to a minor priestly family. In that first generation, the statue was installed in a small private shrine in the priest's rented quarters, and when he died his son took over the priestly duties, adding a statue of himself to the religious decor of the little household shrine. After he died, Apollonius saw a dream vision of the god, who ordered him to obtain a suitable lot and build a proper temple.

Apollonius' efforts were resisted by some members of Delian society, perhaps on the grounds that he should not introduce public foreign cults on Apollo's sacred island, perhaps on the grounds that he was not entitled to buy property, or that the temple he was building in some way violated the terms of his purchase agreement. In any event, a hearing was held, the accusers were struck dumb, the god and his priest were vindicated, and the temple was built. Apollonius erected a column on which he inscribed a prose account of what had happened, along with a poem, commissioned for the occasion, singing the praises of Sarapis in appropriately solemn verse. Within a generation of the building of this temple, two more cult associations were organized in honor of the Egyptian gods. By 180 B.C.E., this worship was recognized by the state as an official Delian cult.

The cult of Sarapis at Delos is particularly well documented, since all three temples have been excavated, along with a large number of inscriptions. It is an individual case, and yet many of its features are typical of the way in which pagan cults spread in the ancient world. When merchants or other migrants from the Orient arrived in the cities of the old Greek world, they brought with them their native gods and ceremonies. They then worshiped them as individuals or in company with fellow countrymen who lived in the same place. Other cults were spread by colonists or soldiers, who erected shrines to official gods of the state or foreign ones encountered on the way.[3]

Professional holy men also appear in classical literature, wandering from place to place and introducing new cults. The sources usually portray them as charlatans, hucksters of religion, working on the susceptibilities of their audiences to bilk them of money and food. One very unflattering picture of this sort is preserved for us in an essay by Lucian of the second century C.E. Here we meet Alexander of Abunoteichus, who traveled widely throughout western Asia Minor, preaching the blessings of Asclepius and supporting his claims as a wonder-worker by setting up a mobile oracle that specialized in faked miracles; he claimed, for example, that the god "made predictions, discovered fugitive slaves, detected thieves and robbers, caused treasures to be dug up, healed the sick, and in some cases actually raised the dead" (Lucian, *Alexander the False Prophet* 24).

Healing miracles were typical of the cult of Asclepius and were characteristic of certain types of holy men, including the emperor Vespasian, who healed a blind man when he visited Alexandria. The news of such miracles was spread by personal contact and also by written and oral recitations—called aretalogies—of the god's blessings. The deeds of new and old gods were also publicized through such colorful ceremonies as processions and sacrifices, which would attract attention in the city streets.

The core members of most imported cults were immigrants or descendants of immigrants, who reached out to new members through various means of religious propaganda. The propaganda was seldom very aggressive, however. Potential adherents could come and read the testimonia or watch the processions, but the initiative for joining the cult lay with them as individuals. Once they joined, they would normally participate in rites and ceremonies and make some financial contribution, but wholehearted conversion, in the sense of exclusive devotion to the god of the cult, was not normally expected. The gods of paganism were not jealous gods.

### *Meeting Places*

In the case of Sarapis at Delos, the statue of the god was installed in a private house and was tended almost as an individual or family cult. Similarly, when several merchants from Cyprus found themselves together in the harbor town of Athens, or shippers from Berytus got together to further their common interests in the Italian port of Puteoli, they erected a shrine to their ancestral god or gods in rented or purchased quarters.[4]

These shrines were often designed to remind the worshipers of home; traditional rituals were continued, a priest might be brought from the country of origin, architectural features and statues echoed particular cultural traditions. There does not seem to have been any strict standardization, however, and each cult society had a great deal of autonomy. Hierarchical titles were sometimes those of the cult and paralleled cults of the same god in other places, but often the titles were those of the local community. Within a generation or two, there was a tendency for these shrines to take on more and more the normal features of Greek or Roman temples in the cities where they were located. As with any group in a Greco-Roman city, there was an important role for the patron, a wealthy member of the group, perhaps the founder or one of his descendants.

Allegiance to such a cult could offer a special focus for an individual's life, an opportunity to donate time, attention, and money. Since most members met at regular intervals to celebrate their god with sacrifices and a common meal, they offered some sense of belonging and specialness within a large and impersonal world. Some of these cults offered their adherents specialized, even secret, knowledge, along with the promise of salvation from certain evils of the world, and thus erected barriers between themselves and the larger society outside. Such barriers were not absolute, however, for these pagan cults held values and systems of belief in common with the pagan society of the cities and the empire.

### *Syncretism*

The quickened pace of contact between peoples and cultures produced the mutual influence and intermingling that historians call "syncretism." Syncretism can be perceived as a general cultural phenomenon, the adoption of certain of one social group's customs and ways of thought by another, or it can be a specifically religious phenomenon.

People tended to think of the gods of other nations as similar or identical to those they already knew at home. Thus Greeks considered the Egyptian god Osiris to be identical to their own Dionysus. In the Roman empire, native individuals in northern Africa made dedications to their traditional god Baal but used the Roman name Saturn, because that was a generally accepted equivalent and seemed more appropriate in an inscription written in Latin. (The trend also appeared in Jerusalem itself, during the hellenizing movement under Antiochus IV, when Yahweh was identified with Zeus.) In a related sense, syncretism was the tendency for one god to accumulate the attributes of other gods, so that Isis came to be seen as incorporating in herself the divine qualities of Aphrodite, Demeter, Athena, and many others, taking on the appearance of a single all-inclusive divinity. In Egypt, for instance, theologians for millennia had tended to interpret different individual gods as manifestations of a single godhead; Greco-Roman theologians, relying on oriental sources, also identified various gods in a single godhead, expressed in popular exclamations such as "Zeus Hades Helius Dionysus is one," or "Zeus Sarapis is one."[5]

The forms of this pagan syncretism help us appreciate the extent to which those who participated in these cults were incorporated into the society of the Greco-Roman city. They shared with the larger culture a sense that the whole world was controlled by divine powers, which manifested themselves in a variety of ways but shared common attributes and personalities.

### *Attitudes of the Authorities*

Normally, these kinds of cults did not pose any threat to the established order of a Greek city or kingdom or to the Roman empire. Consequently, the established order accommodated and even encouraged their practice. It was in general a good thing to keep all the gods well tended and favorably disposed toward the state.

This included even strange and exotic gods. The Great Mother of Phrygia, for example, was served by priests who had castrated themselves, and therefore the Roman Republic did not allow its citizens to be initiated; on the other hand, it welcomed the goddess into Rome in 204 B.C.E., gave her a temple at a prominent central location, and celebrated her festival as an official holiday. When Roman authorities did ban or restrict the practice of certain foreign cults (such as the cult of Dionysus in the second century B.C.E., or that of the Druids), it was on the grounds that they posed some threat to public order.

### *Philosophical Sects*

If we define "conversion" in some way that includes a change in life and attitudes and an allegiance to some system of belief that is significantly different from a society's prevailing ones, we find only a few examples in Greek paganism. As early as the sixth century B.C.E., Orphic preachers had gone about in Greece citing a sacred literature, offering purifications, and exemplifying an ascetic way of living. At about the same time communities of Pythagoreans were organized, bound together by a secret knowledge of the nature of the universe and by a peculiar disciplined life. Pythagorean doctrines, taught in small groups, seem to have enjoyed a surge in popularity in the first century B.C.E. and the first century C.E.[6]

Philosophical teachings, for their part, did often advocate some major reorientation of moral and spiritual life. The doctrines of Cynics, Stoics, and Epicureans were well known, at least in outline, throughout the Greco-Roman world. Cynics gave their characteristic harangues on street corners and in marketplaces. They engaged in earnest attempts to convince others of the superiority of their way of life, shedding old conventions and living simply in accordance with the demands of nature. Their example of poverty inspired many wandering Stoic teachers, who also (like the followers of Plato in the Academy and those of Aristotle in the Lyceum) taught in lecture halls and public gymnasia. These Stoics preached a unity of all mankind that overcame any local or ethnic allegiances, and a way of life in which reason tamed the passions into obedience to an orderly, beneficent nature. The Epicureans' doctrine emphasized the need to gain happiness through quiet contentment and withdrawal from the world, so their recruitment policies were less direct. They held up the personal example of Epicurus himself, memorialized in statues, and composed essays that were published or inscribed in public places. They emphasized friendship and strong cohesion within the group.[7]

Philosophy attracted converts in a way that pagan religions did not. Normally, adherents of these philosophical sects were expected to experience a significant change in attitude and life-style. They did sometimes challenge traditional ways of thinking, and occasionally they experienced persecution. Tradition, or history, tells how the natural philosophers Anaxagoras, Protagoras, and Diagoras were prosecuted for impiety in Athens in the fifth century B.C.E., and atheism was one of the charges on which Socrates was convicted and executed in 399 B.C.E. In Rome, foreigners who professed one sect or another of philosophy were expelled from the city in 173 and 161 B.C.E. Under the Principate, too, specific philosophers were sometimes sent into exile, and several Stoic teachers were convicted of treasonable plots against the emperor.[8] For the most part, however, philosophers remained within the larger society, and they never seem to have refused to participate in the official cults of the state. As a result, attacks by the established authorities were rare.

## The Jewish Diaspora

### *The Jews in the Gentile World*

At Sardis, in western Asia Minor, Jewish immigrants may have arrived as early as the sixth century B.C.E., when Jerusalem was destroyed by Nebuchadnezzar. There was certainly a permanent Jewish community by the late third century. In the first century B.C.E., according to the Jewish historian Josephus, the Roman governor of Asia Minor issued a decree confirming the right of the Jews of Sardis to lead a communal life, celebrate their festivals, settle lawsuits among themselves, and build a synagogue for their common use (Josephus, *Antiquities* 14.235, 259–261). A later synagogue (from the fourth century C.E.) has been excavated at Sardis and shows that the Jewish community there continued to be important and powerful. The large building with columns and colorful mosaics stands at a major crossroads, its courtyard open to the view of crowds passing along the street or entering the public gymnasium next door.[9]

In some places, and Sardis was one of them, Jewish residents were active in city life, enjoying privileges and prominence. In other places, the Jews were few, one obscure minority among others, distinguished only by their peculiar customs. But they were virtually everywhere, in what is known as the Diaspora ("Dispersion").

By the beginning of the Christian era, Jews were found throughout the Roman empire and beyond its eastern borders, in town and in the country. They represented nearly every social class. Jewish soldiers served in the armies of the Hellenistic kings, and some of them rose to the highest ranks. Jews served as government officials, especially in Egypt; the papyri tell us of policemen, magistrates, clerks, tax collectors, and granary clerks. There were Jewish landowners and peasants and agricultural workers, both free and slave, and craftsmen, merchants, shippers, and moneylenders. One estimate holds that fully one fifth of the population of the eastern Mediterranean was Jewish; this may well be too high, but certainly Jews were a common phenomenon in the towns and cities of the Greco-Roman world, and their customs were widely known, if not always very well understood.[10]

Attracted by the monotheistic rigor, high moral standards, and sincerity of the Jews, and by their well-defined notion of who they were, sympathetic individuals manifested various degrees of allegiance to Judaism. Josephus (*Antiquities* 20.17–48) gives one example in his account of Jewish sympathizers among the royalty of small eastern kingdoms during the first century B.C.E. Jewish traveling merchants were the missionary agents, and we get the impression that they were all over the world. In this story alone, one such merchant converts the queen mother at home in Adiabene on the upper Tigris. Another, in a small principality at the southern tip of Mesopotamia, persuades the royal ladies there to adopt Jewish ways of worship, and through them he also converts Izates, a visiting prince of Adiabene. Izates, accompanied by his Jewish mentor, soon is recalled to Adiabene to become king, where his mother and his mentor agree that he should not be circumcised because it would offend his subjects for him to declare such complete allegiance to a foreign god. Soon thereafter still another Jewish traveler, a strict practitioner from Galilee, arrives in Adiabene and persuades Izates to be circumcised in obedience to the Mosaic Law. Such high-level conversions were hardly very common, and yet the story does demonstrate the active role of traveling Jewish merchants in gaining converts, and a certain difference of opinion concerning the necessity of circumcision.[11]

A Gentile who entered the community as a full member was called a "proselyte." He or she had to adhere faithfully to the dietary laws and the commands of the Torah. New proselytes often received a formal baptismal cleansing when they were received, and normally males were circumcised.[12] Given the severity of these requirements, the number of proselytes was relatively small (Matt. 23:15; Acts 6:5). In the Diaspora more women than men were converted, and more people from the lower social classes than the upper. We do hear occasionally, however, about the conversion of upper-class ladies, like Fulvia in the reign of Tiberius (Josephus, *Antiquities* 18.81–84).

Other men and women accepted certain Jewish ways of doing things and made what contributions they could to the life of the synagogues without becoming full members. These included individuals at the very top levels of Roman society, like Flavia Domitilla, niece of the emperor Domitian (Dio Cassius, 67. 14.1–3). It was possible to sympathize in this way with Jewish ways without renouncing polytheism and such public duties as sacrificing to the official gods. Prosperous Judaizers often expressed their devotion by contributing money or facilities to the synagogue. They were honored as patrons of the Jewish community, with some such title as "Father" or "Mother" of the synagogue. If we can believe the hostile testimony of Juvenal (*Satires* 14.99), the children of such Judaizers often became full converts and were circumcised.

### Synagogues

The Greek term *synagōgē* ("assemblage") generally referred to a group of people, a community, or a congregation. Meetings were often held in private houses while the group was small, but normally we can assume that, like the adherents of pagan cults, the local Jews would eventually acquire a house or other site for their communal activities. This was called a synagogue or a *proseuchē* ("place of prayer"), and its architecture depended on the size and resources of the community. A small synagogue on the island of Delos, in use from the first century B.C.E. to the second century C.E., consisted of a simple room with benches; it was entered from a courtyard through three doors facing eastward toward Jerusalem. On the other hand, the Jews of Sardis were able to construct a much more impressive synagogue.

We can form some idea of the organization of these synagogue communities from the inscriptions and other remaining records. The *archisynagōgos* was spiritual leader and chief teacher (Acts 13:15; 18:17). An executive committee attended to the secular affairs of the community; its members were called "elders" or, like the chief magistrates of a Greek city, "archons." The inscriptions also refer to a secretary, who would keep records and handle correspondence. An attendant (*hypēretēs* in Greek, Luke 4:20; cf. John 7:32) took care of the building, kept order during the service, made announcements, led the prayers if necessary, and administered corporal punishment in accordance with the Law.

In larger cities there were several synagogues (Rome, for example, had at least eleven—see chapter 6). They seem to have enjoyed considerable autonomy, although there is evidence that in some cities an umbrella organization coordinated their activities, such as maintaining common burial grounds.[13]

The synagogue was a place of prayer, where the congregation gathered on the Sabbath and on holy days. It was also a school, where the Torah was studied; some of the excavated synagogues included separate rooms for instruction. And it was a community center, where members could gather for specific reasons like baking unleavened bread or for more general purposes of conviviality.

An important social function of the synagogue was to provide a sense of belonging and to facilitate contacts. A vignette from the Mishnah describes the great central synagogue in Alexandria in Egypt during the third century C.E. Among its rows of columns were specific locations where the goldsmiths, silversmiths, blacksmiths, carpetmakers, and weavers sat together. "Thus when a poor man entered, he could recognize the members of his own craft and apply to them, and in this way gain a livelihood for himself and his family."[14] This would have been very important to traveling merchants and craftsmen and provided one very tangible reason for a Jew to maintain contacts with other Jews upon reaching a new city. In this way, the tentmaker Paul goes to the synagogue when he arrives in a new town and is able to make contact with other tentmakers.

In several ways, then, the synagogue strengthened the Jews' sense of themselves as special and separate. The community offered a place where the rules of the Torah—circumcision, the Sabbath, the festivals, the dietary laws—were respected and enforced. The commitment of the individual to the group was strengthened by the sense of special separateness in a place that was cut off from the world outside but was open to its influence.

### *Hellenization*

Inevitably, the pagan culture of the Greco-Roman world had an impact on the Jews living within it. Language made the most marked impact. In the Greek world, Jews spoke Greek like everybody else. By the second century B.C.E. a significant number of them must have spoken only Greek and no Hebrew, because it was necessary for the Jewish community of Alexandria to commission a translation of the traditional Hebrew scriptures into Greek, which we know as the Septuagint. Papyri found in Egypt and Jewish inscriptions found throughout the empire also make it clear that the Diaspora Jews used Greek for nearly all communications, personal and official.

Greek ways of doing things tended to become normal for Diaspora Jews in many areas of their life. Synagogue assemblies passed decrees that echoed the format and phrasing of official decrees of the Greek cities, just as the titles of their officers imitated those of Greek magistrates. Even in the regulation of their private life, Jewish families seem to have followed the prevailing custom of their neighbors; at least, this seems to be the implication of records found in papyri from Ptolemaic and Roman Egypt, in which Jewish women are regulated by Greek rather than Jewish laws of guardianship.[15]

Greek education also exerted its claim, for many Jews in the Diaspora attended the gymnasium and participated in its athletic and rhetorical training.

Such Jews learned Greek modes of thought, and we can detect a syncretism of Greek forms and Jewish content. The "Letter of Aristeas," for instance, written in Alexandria in the second century B.C.E., describes Judaism in terms usually reserved for Greek philosophy. It even equates Zeus, head of the Greek pantheon, with the God of Israel. And there is some evidence, not accepted by all scholars, that proselytizing Jews in Rome in the second century B.C.E. adopted the name Juppiter Sabazios for their God.[16] This tendency is most fully developed in the works of Philo, who wrote in the first century C.E., also in Alexandria. Many of his essays are in effect a translation of Jewish belief and practice into terms that will be understandable to a pagan educated in the principles of Greek philosophy.

In general, the Jews in the Diaspora made certain accommodations to the pagan world in which they lived. They were not immune to its attractions and amenities, and some of them deserted Jewish ways altogether to enter pagan society without restraint. There are even a few rare cases in which people with unmistakably Jewish names made dedications to pagan gods or made dedications to some unnamed god that was erected in a pagan temple.[17] But the institution of the synagogue and the peculiar customs of the Jewish Law, along with their continuing contact with Jerusalem, functioned to remind the Jews of their special position, in many ways at odds with the world around them.

### *Attitudes of the Authorities Toward the Jews*

The societies of the Greco-Roman world expected certain behavior from their members. Whether free or slave, male or female, citizen or noncitizen, all people were expected to respect the sovereign (whether king, emperor, or law), to contribute services according to their means (which could involve military or corvee duty, or financial contributions to pay for some public work), and to participate in the society's common cults.

In regard to many of these expectations, however, Jews who lived by the Torah could not behave in the normal way. They could respect the sovereign and pray on his behalf, but they could not offer incense to his image or participate in any of the sacrifices of the state cults. Nor was it easy for them to serve in the armies, because that would interfere with their observance of the Sabbath and because soldiers were expected to take part in sacrifices. (Occasionally, special Jewish companies seem to have been formed, although the evidence is not absolutely clear.) And at public ceremonial occasions they could not join everybody else in consuming meat sacrificed to pagan gods, a practice that violated Jewish scruples on several counts.

Religious Jews, therefore, had to hold back from much commonly accepted and expected behavior. In order to avoid trouble, they often petitioned the authorities for specific exemptions, arguing that although their Law forbade certain specific observances, they were loyal members of society and prayed for the sovereign in accordance with the ways of their fathers. With the respect for other gods and for local traditions that was usual in ancient society, and perhaps in recognition of proven loyalty, the exemptions were often granted—by the Persian king in the sixth century B.C.E., by individual cities, by the Hellenistic Ptolemies and Seleucids, and by Roman governors and emperors. Among the specific privileges granted were the right to observe the Sabbath and send each year a half-shekel tax to Jerusalem for the maintenance of the Temple, exemption from participating in civic cults and from making the usual contributions to their celebration, and autonomy to exercise legal jurisdiction within their own community, which formed a politeuma, as we have seen.

Jews claimed a kind of equal citizenship in the cities where they lived. This came to be resented: The Jews seemed to enjoy the city's prosperity and amenities but were excused from most of the annoying duties. During the later first century B.C.E. and the first century C.E., several Greek cities moved to curtail such special Jewish privileges. Ever since the days of the Maccabees, the Jews had been allied with the Romans against one Hellenistic kingdom or other, and in the cities of the Diaspora, the hostility of the Greeks both reflected the Jews' past loyalty to Rome and assured that the Jewish-Roman bond would continue.

The attitude of the Roman emperors varied with the individual but tended to be favorable toward the Jews. When hostility against the Jews in Alexandria broke out into a terrible pogrom in 38 C.E., for instance, the emperor Gaius showed little sympathy, and in 41 Claudius handed down stern warnings to both Greeks and Jews, but he reaffirmed the Jews' rights both in Alexandria and in all the towns of the empire. This protection continued even after the conquest of Judea by Titus in 70 C.E.[18]

On the other hand, in the wake of the destruction of the Temple and the requirement that Jews pay the old half-shekel tax to the Roman state rather than to the priestly establishment in Jerusalem, resentment of Rome spread among some Jews in several Diaspora centers. The Jewish guerrilla fighters known as *sicarii* fled from Roman-occupied Judea and urged Diaspora Jews in Egypt and Cyrene to resist the Romans. Much Jewish writing took on a violently anti-Roman tone. The apocalyptic vision that the Messiah would come became more widespread—and more narrowly focused on Rome as the enemy of Israel.[19]

## Social Characteristics of Christian Missions

### *Social Transitions*

Conversion to Christianity made a decisive impact, both in terms of the individual's self-perception and in the social context of a new fellowship. That Christian fellowship itself experienced certain transitions in the generation following Jesus' death and resurrection, most significantly from a Jewish movement to a Gentile one and from a rural to an urban environment.

The transition from a Jewish to a Gentile movement is presented in its most linear, schematic form by the author of Acts, writing a generation or two after the events. Acts portrays an early opposition between hellenizing Jews and more traditional ones (6:1); the speech of Stephen, who represents the "Hellenists," implies that they minimized the importance of strict adherence to the Law (7: 44–53).[20] When a few Gentiles are converted, controversy arises as to whether they need to become Jewish proselytes and be circumcised; the story of Cornelius the centurion, based in the Roman capital at Caesarea (Acts 10), exemplifies the issue, which becomes more pressing as Jewish Christians preach to non-Jews at Antioch (11:19–26) and elsewhere (13:44 to 14:7). Eventually, a conference of Christian leaders at Jerusalem produces a compromise between the Judaistic and Hellenistic factions (15:1–29; 21:25). Many Jews, however, still refuse to accept the gospel. Preachers are rejected by Jewish audiences in the Temple and in synagogues, leading to Paul's decision finally to go only to the Gentiles (Acts 13; 18; 28).

On the other hand, Paul himself indicates that he addressed his mission to Gentiles from the beginning and that tension between Judaizers and Hellenists continued for a long time (Galatians 2; cf. Romans 15). He never mentions preaching to Jews in their synagogues, and he alludes to persistent disagreements about table fellowship. He criticizes Peter, who recognized the validity of the Gentile mission but then refused to eat with non-Jewish Christians in Antioch (Gal. 2:11–13). Regardless of the details, however, it is clear that the transition from a Jewish to a Gentile movement was principally owing to the admission of Gentiles into the church without requiring them to become Jews first.

Parallel to this transition from Jewish to Gentile moved another, from the countryside to the city. The dominant imagery of the Gospels is rural, and the occupations of the Twelve tend to be those of the countryside. Towns often seem somewhat threatening, with Jerusalem the most threatening of all. Those who "came out to hear" Jesus, however, usually came from towns. The Diaspora Jews who were present at Pentecost took back the message to the cities of the Greco-Roman world (Acts 2). The rural imagery of the Gospels is replaced in Acts by scenes set in urban synagogues and city streets, harbor waterfronts and government courtrooms and jails. The countryside was not completely abandoned as a mission field; —chased out of Iconium in southern Asia Minor, Paul and Barnabas went into the surrounding countryside of Lycaonia to preach (Acts 14:5–7), and at the end of the first century a hostile Roman source tells us that many rural residents of Bithynia, in northwestern Asia

Minor, had become Christians (Pliny, *Letters* 10.96). Still, in general the gospel made its most notable progress in the cities, a fact that involves a great shift in the cultural horizon of Christianity—from a reform impulse within Palestinian Judaism to a Greek-speaking movement based in the cosmopolitan cities of the Greco-Roman world.

In its first generation, of course, the leaders of the Christian movement were Jewish. The book of Acts (18:17) suggests that some synagogue leaders were receptive to the Christian message, as were well-to-do women and men like Priscilla and Aquila. The most influential members, especially the missionaries and principal patrons, came from the upper social levels of Hellenistic Judaism.[21]

Early Christians came as well from all levels of Gentile society except the very highest. Upper-class women outnumbered upper-class men, because they were less in the public eye and enjoyed within the group a higher status than they could in Greco-Roman society. Prosperous men and women served as patrons, and whole households sometimes followed their masters and mistresses into the Christian way (Acts 11:14; 16:15; 18:8). Freed men and women, whose position in society was ambiguous (their formal status was low, but they were often wealthy and influential), also joined the community. Slaves were attracted by the promise of spiritual, if not legal, emancipation and were converted as members of households or, sometimes, as individuals. The poor were attracted by the Christians' promise of salvation hereafter and by their practice of taking care of those in need during this life.

### *The Christian Community*

The Christian message was brought to the cities of the Roman empire by ordinary Jews of the sort who were present at Pentecost and by "apostles," who included the original disciples of Jesus as well as Paul and other men and probably women and who moved about preaching and establishing Christian cells, invoking direct charismatic authority from God (Rom. 16:7; 1 Cor. 15:5–9; Gal. 1:1, 17, 19).

According to the account in Acts, when an apostle arrives in a new city, he makes his first contacts at the synagogue (as at Thessalonica, Acts 17:1–2) or in the Jewish residential quarter, or among the craftsmen whose trade he knows (as with Priscilla and Aquila at Corinth, Acts 18:2–4). Paul, to judge from his own words (Rom. 1:5, 13–15; 11:13–14; 15:15–21; Gal. 1:16; 2:7–9), addressed his mission primarily to Gentiles. He refers to his first converts as the "firstfruits." They often seem to be wealthy Gentiles attached to the Jewish community (Acts 13:43), excluded from full membership in the synagogue but valued for their support. The loss of their allegiance may well have accounted for some of the bitterness of the synagogue leaders' opposition.[22]

The apostle would often lodge with these initial converts and make further contacts among their circle of acquaintances at home or at work. In the book of Acts, Paul rents a place to stay and evangelize in Ephesus (19:9) and Rome (28:16, 30), speaks in public at Athens (17:17–34) and elsewhere (14:8–18; 16:16–39; 19:11–20), and also uses trials and hearings before government officials as an opportunity to deliver the Christian message (13:7–12; 16:25–34; 21:37 to 22:24; 22:30 to 23:10; ch. 24; 25:6 to 26:29).

For the most part, however, converts at first heard the Christian message on the more intimate scale of personal contact, through friends and acquaintances who then took them to one of the group's weekly meetings.

A typical Christian cell was normally small, limited by the physical capacity of the house in which it met. The owner of the house functioned as host or patron; his or her name often was used as identification (Acts 18:7–8; Rom. 16:23; 1 Cor. 1:16; Col. 4:15). The group was organized on determinedly egalitarian lines. The early Christians in Jerusalem practiced community ownership of property (Acts 2:44–47). Women played as prominent a role as men. Slaves and freed men and women shared equally with the freeborn. Within the group, at least in the early decades, there was a conscious rejection of the status-conscious norms of society, a rejection summarized in the admonition that within the community of the baptized there was "neither Jew nor Greek . . . slave nor free . . . male nor female" (Gal. 3:28; cf. James 2:2–12).[23]

Other passages of the New Testament, on the other hand, especially the admonitions to orderly family life known as the "Haustafeln" (Col. 3:18 to 4:4; Eph. 5:21–33; 1 Tim. 2:9–15; 1 Peter 3:1–7), seem to show an attempt in the next generation of Christian leaders to impose a more patriarchal order, patterned more closely on the traditional Greco-Roman (and Jewish) family. This reflected the formation of Christian cells conceived as households (see chapter 6).[24]

The Christian leaders emphasized the worldwide nature of their mission. Stoic philosophy was emphasizing the cosmopolitan nature of mankind, which transcended the old ethnic boundaries of cities and kingdoms, and the Roman consolidation of Alexander's empire presented a physical incorporation of that idea. Frequent visits and written communications bound the various cells together. The New

Testament is full of references to this intercommunication and is itself a product of this interdependence and mutual hospitality. The Letter to the Hebrews (chs. 12 to 13), for instance, recommends openhearted generosity in receiving itinerant Christian teachers (cf. 1 Peter 4:9). Problems soon arose, however, in deciding which teachers were of the proper doctrinal purity, and followers of different groups refused hospitality to some who felt they had a claim to it (2 John 4–10; 3 John 5–10; cf. Mark 6:10–11; Luke 10:4–11; in the second century, *Didache* 11–12; Lucian, *Passing of Peregrinus* 11).[25]

Perhaps the most conspicuous quality of Christians was their charity, their generosity toward the poor. Matthew's Gospel is especially emphatic on the necessity of clothing the naked and visiting the sick (5:42 to 6:4; 19:16–22 and parallels; 25:31–46), and in Acts we see individual acts of charity (3:1–10; 9:36; 10:2–4) as well as more institutionalized provision for the poor—the distributions to the widows at Jerusalem (6:1) and the collection for victims of famine (11:27–30; 24:17). There are many exhortations to charity (Acts 20:33–35; Rom. 12:13; Eph. 4:28; 1 Tim. 5:3; Heb. 13:1–3; James 2:14–17; 1 John 3:17–23), which in the following generations was recognized by outsiders as one of the characteristic qualities of the Christian community (Lucian, *Passing of Peregrinus* 12–13; Julian, *Misopogon* 363a–b; *Letters* 430d, ed. Spanheim).[26]

### *Proclaiming the Message: Preaching and Ritual*

The Christian message exercised a powerful attraction on converts and held their enthusiasm in spite of hostility, rejection, and persecution. The Christians' joy and strength of conviction are clear in the New Testament and in the accounts of the witness of Christian martyrs facing execution (Justin Martyr, *Dialogue with Trypho* 110; *Second Apology* 12).

Their message preached one God. In this they were sharply distinct from the mass of their contemporaries, and in this they resembled the Jews from whom they derived the belief. But they also believed and preached that the Messiah had truly come, that he had died on a tree and had come back to life again, that his continuing Spirit allowed individual believers to be saved from the hazards of their old life and to experience a new life, and that he would return to earth again. To express this new teaching—new life and new community—the Christians abolished, within a generation of Jesus' death, the ceremonial requirements of the Jewish Law and developed new ones to replace them.

The early Christians spread their message through personal involvement, witness, and example, through sermons addressed to small or large groups, through letters of introduction and exhortation. These same techniques were also used within the Christian groups to reinforce commitment and strengthen faith. In the internal dynamics of the Christian groups, they were expressed in more or less formal rituals.

The theme of the oneness of the living and true God was used to emphasize the distinctiveness of the Christian community. It was what separated Christians from the polytheistic pagans from whom the Gentile converts had come (1 Cor. 8:4–6; 12:2–3; 1 Thess. 1:9). Paul and his followers also used it to emphasize the internal coherence of the Christian community: The oneness of God demanded that the body of the church also be one, that there be no internal boundaries between members (1 Corinthians 12; Gal. 3:28; Eph. 4:1–16; Colossians 2).[27]

The oneness of God and the abolition of the Jewish Law were also connected, in Pauline teaching, with the doctrine of the crucified Messiah who reconciled both Jews and Gentiles to God "in one body through the cross" (Eph. 2:16). The notion that the Messiah had been executed as a common criminal and then came back to life was radically opposed to normal Jewish expectations (Deut. 21:23; 1 Cor. 1:18–25; Gal. 3:13). Once it was accepted as truth, however, it became a central image in justifying the abolition of traditional Jewish observances and in substituting a new set of symbols that distinguished a Christian from a non-Christian. The image of the crucified and risen Messiah helped Christian teachers and preachers encourage Christians who confronted persecution that they could expect to rise to new life just as their Lord had (1 Thess. 3:2–4; 4:13–18; 1 Peter 1:3–21).

As the body of Christ, the worldwide organism of individual cells incorporated the continuing presence of God. That presence is articulated in intimate terms drawn from the vocabulary of the family: God is the father, the Christians are children and heirs (Romans 8; Gal. 3:26 to 4:7). He acts directly and personally, participating in the intimate life of the local household assembly.

These new communities were distinct in their sense of newness, of change. Their new order required a unique new life-style, and much early Christian teaching in the New Testament exhorts the believers to live in an appropriate manner. They are urged to keep sexually pure, in terms that emphasize carnal impurity as a characteristic of the outside world (1 Cor. 6:9–11; Gal. 5:19–24; Eph. 4:22 to 5:20; Col. 3:5–14; 1 Peter 4:3–5; Rev. 22:14–15). They are urged to conduct their affairs in peace and tranquillity, in order to reflect their unity in Christ and to present a good impression to the outside world (Eph. 5:22 to 6:9; Col. 3:18 to 4:1; 1 Peter 2:16 to 3:9). This would have helped the believers define themselves in terms of the Christian community and reinforce their allegiance to its God.

A final theme, made most explicit in Revelation but frequently used in Pauline literature and the Gospels, is apocalyptic, the expectation that Jesus will return in ultimate triumph, amid destruction and judgment. In that coming wrath, which was expected urgently and imminently, Jesus would save the believers and deliver them (1 Thess. 4:13 to 5:11). The final world order, which would make sense of the anomalous social status of the Christians and place them among the elect, was still to come.

When the communities of Christians "came together" (1 Cor. 11:17–34) in their house churches, they were reminded of their distinctness. They met in private houses, discreetly closed off from the street, and what went on in those meetings reinforced their sense that their true allegiance lay here rather than in the world outside. They met regularly, apparently on Sunday (Acts 20:7; 1 Cor. 16:2). They chanted psalms and sang hymns intended both to glorify God and to edify the congregation (Eph. 5:18–20; Col. 3: 16–17), and the New Testament seems to preserve quotations or paraphrases from some of the hymns (1 Corinthians 13; Phil. 2: 6–11; Col. 1:15–20; Rev. 4:11; 11:17–18). Free prayer and witness also had its part; Paul's picture of the coming together of the Corinthian Christians (1 Corinthians 14) describes, if not a free-for-all, at least a dynamic, exciting ritual that permitted each individual to contribute "a psalm, a teaching, a revelation, a tongue, an interpretation." Speaking in tongues was a charismatic manifestation of the Spirit that Paul acknowledged but tried to channel into more rational, edifying directions. Reading from the Jewish scriptures probably had a place in the ritual, since the authors of the New Testament assume that even Gentile converts will know something of the content of the Old Testament. In addition to the testimonies and instruction offered by individuals, it seems likely that there may have been opportunity for a sermon by a local leader or a visiting apostle, or for a reading from one of the letters in circulation.[28] Prayers were offered standing, with hands extended (1 Tim. 2:8), both "with the spirit" and "with the mind" (1 Cor. 14:15), which probably means both spontaneously and more formally. The petition known as the "Lord's Prayer" (Matt. 6:9–15; Luke 11:2–4) is an example. Other prayers were adapted from Jewish worship patterns (1 Cor. 15:57; 2 Cor. 1:3–4; Eph. 3:21), concluding with a congregational "Amen" (1 Cor. 14:16; 2 Cor. 1:20; Rev. 5:14).

The Lord's Supper, in which bread was broken and shared with a cup of wine in commemoration of Christ's death and resurrection, formed a regular part of these meetings (Acts 2:42; 1 Cor. 10:14–22; 11:17–34). Many groups in Greco-Roman society met regularly for ritual banquets, but the Lord's Supper of the Christians was different. Strict monotheism separated Christians from the pagan world, and that separation was emphasized and reinforced in its exclusiveness: "You cannot drink the cup of the Lord and the cup of demons" (1 Cor. 10:21). This insistence on purity in table fellowship was typical of Jewish groups, especially the Pharisees and Essenes, but as Christian practice developed, the boundaries of that table fellowship changed, and ceremonial rigor was relaxed so that the whole Christian community, Jew and Gentile, slave and free, male and female, shared equally in the table of the Lord (Gal. 2:12–14). That unity of the Christian body was represented in the sharing of a single loaf at the Eucharist (1 Cor. 10:17).

The Eucharist also expressed for the participants the reality of the death and resurrection of the Messiah. The breaking of bread and drinking of wine was a memorial, a representation of Christ's death (1 Cor. 11:23–26). Eating and drinking in memory of a deceased relative or comrade was normal practice among both Jews and pagans, but in the Lord's Supper the Christians remembered their Lord's death week by week. It was a memorial, according to Paul, but it was also more. It was communion or participation in the body and blood of Christ (1 Cor. 10:16), a celebration of the continuing presence of Christ and his Spirit among them.

The eucharistic ritual also crystallized the new life in Christ and the apocalyptic expectation of his return. When some Christians tried to turn their Lord's Supper into a dinner party in the style of the status-conscious pagan society of Corinth, Paul rebuked them for their failure to meet the egalitarian social requirements of their new way of life (1 Cor. 11:18–22; cf. Jude 12–13). And he insisted that those who receive the bread and cup should do so in a way appropriate to their new life in Christ. In the same passage, Paul connected the Eucharist with the apocalyptic theme of Christ's return: The celebration proclaims Christ's death "until he comes," and judgment at that last coming awaits those who eat and drink unworthily (1 Cor. 11:26–32).

Baptism was the other important ritual, which initiated the new convert into the Christian fellowship. At first, baptism could apparently follow immediately upon exposure to the Christian message (Acts 8:26–39); later, preliminary instruction became more extensive. The rite was conducted in the living water of a river, if possible, or perhaps in a synagogue or public bath or in the private bath of a house church. The converts removed their clothing and were immersed, or else they stood in water while some of it was poured over their head. There is evidence that the ceremony ended with the newly baptized person proclaiming that "Jesus is Lord" (Acts 22:16; Rom. 10:9) and taking a seat on a throne (Eph. 2:6). Ritual washing was common in both pagan and Jewish practice, as part of some other ceremony requiring physical or spiritual cleanliness. Christian baptism was distinctive because it was *the* central initiation rite, performed just once for each individual, rather than a repeated act. The fact that baptism was a single "once-for-all" act meant that the barrier between those who were clean and those who were not was permanent, not temporary as in the ritual cleansings of pagans and Pharisees.

The rich symbolism of the baptismal ritual allowed early Christian thinkers to relate it to the distinctive themes of Christian social life. The single act of baptism was related to the singleness of God (Eph. 4:4–6) and the unity and solidarity of believing Christians, in which the old status categories of Jew, Greek, slave, free, male, and female ceased to exist (Col. 3:10–11). The death and resurrection were symbolized for the individual being baptized in the physical act of submersion, "being buried with Christ," and rising up out of the water (Rom. 6:3–4; Eph. 2:1–5; Col. 2:12–13). Baptism symbolized the participation of the believer in the Spirit—the continuing presence of God in his or her heart (Acts 10:44–48). In the ritual itself, the death-and-life theme was symbolized. The death of the old life was reflected in the submersion, and the shedding of old habits in the removal of clothes (Col. 3:9–10). Writers and preachers constantly reminded the believers of the change in their lives that came with baptism, when they "died to the elemental spirits of the universe" (Col. 2:20), and encouraged them to live in harmony with that momentous event. This was especially important, according to a passage in Hebrews (10:21–31), for those who, once having been cleansed by the Son of God in baptism, risk severe punishment at the apocalyptic Judgment Day if they have sinned deliberately in the meantime.

### *Attitudes of the Authorities Toward the Christians*

The tumult caused by the preaching of Stephen and his subsequent death (Acts 6:8 to 8:3) was the first open hostility of the Jewish authorities to the followers of Jesus, who responded by leaving Jerusalem. When they made new converts in Gaza, Samaria, Damascus, Antioch, Caesarea, and Cyprus (Acts 8:14 to 11:30), they added Gentiles to their fellowship. This prompted Herod Agrippa in 41 C.E., anxious to appear as a defender of the Jewish Law, to institute a somewhat more sustained persecution (Acts 12:1–19). In the years that followed, the belief that Jesus was the Messiah and the dispute over the place of the Law in Christian practice put the Christians in conflict with the established Jewish authorities. As they moved farther and farther out into the Roman empire, that dispute was repeated in town after town, as the missionaries first went to the synagogues, making some impact, but eventually turned to a wider audience of Gentiles; this at any rate is the pattern repeated in Acts (14:19; 17:5–7).

Not infrequently, the leaders of the synagogue hauled Paul before the Roman authorities, but these officials usually viewed the matter as an internal disturbance among Jews and refused to hear the case. In its first three decades, the Christian movement appeared to the pagans as just another variant of Judaism, so it was the beneficiary, rather than the victim, of Roman justice. Roman officials first separated Christians out as a target of prosecution in 64 C.E., when they blamed them for a disastrous fire at Rome under the emperor Nero. They were therefore punished as incendiaries by being burned alive. (Apocalyptic talk of the imminent fiery end of the world would have given credibility to the charges.) There is no evidence that the religion was banned at this time, and yet there is no doubt that Christians were subject to arrest, trial, and execution. Like the Jews, they refused to offer sacrifice to the gods of the state and claimed an allegiance to a higher power. Unlike the Jews, they could not claim to be an ancient ethnic religion, and their insistence on converting non-Jews to their new religion threatened to divert attention and sacrifice away from the gods who protected the state.

We have already seen how vague the Roman charges against the Christians were. If all was quiet, and the local authorities were not anxious about Christians, life could go on in relative tranquillity. But there was always the awareness of danger, and when opposition broke out, it was vicious and supported by the state: at Rome in 64, 137, and 165; in Asia Minor from 164 to 168 and from 176 to 178; at Lyons in 177. The danger is palpable in many passages of the New Testament.

One response, traceable especially in the later Pauline writings, was to encourage loyalty to the state, to acknowledge its authority as the chief bulwark against the anarchy that the Antichrist would try to impose (Rom. 13:1–7; 2 Thess. 2:3; 1 Tim. 2:2; Titus 3:1; also 1 Peter 2:13–14, 17). Apologetic writings attempted to show that the Christians fit into society and posed no political or social threat.[29] The admonitions to domestic tranquillity (1 Tim. 2:1–3) show a desire not to offend conventional morality; the internal organization of the Christian communities took on a more conventionally patriarchal order; the wild-eyed tone of apocalyptic rhetoric was softened. In Luke and Acts there is no enmity between Christ and Caesar: Joseph dutifully registers for the census (Luke 2:1–5); tax collectors appear in a favorable light (Luke 18:10–13; 19:1–10); Pilate finds Jesus innocent of political agitation (Luke 23:1–4); the Roman authorities treat Paul fairly (Acts 13:7–12; 16:35–39; 18: 12–17; 21:37–40; 23:16–31; 25:1–12). In Matthew (22:15–22), Jesus himself acknowledges the authority of the constituted government.

A more militant approach justified the dangers of the present day by holding out the promise of an eventual day of judgment in which the devilish adversary—clearly the Roman empire—would be punished (2 Thess. 2:6–12; 1 Peter 5:8–11; Revelation 18). The sufferings of Jesus were the model for Christians to follow, and the Gospels contained predictions of the troubles waiting for his followers, along with the assurance of eventual victory (e.g., Matt. 16:24–28; Luke 21:12–28; John 15:20; Hebrews 12).

# 3

# The Ancient Economy

The cultures of the classical world were based in a tradition that was older than money. Greeks, Romans, and Hebrews all looked back to a time when wealth and status were measured in terms of land or flocks and power was measured in terms of family allegiances. By the time of the New Testament, money and movable wealth had become much more important. Still, the basic social fabric of these civilizations was woven of the familiar fiber of personal contacts: of favors done, returns expected, allegiance owed.

## The Economy of Social Relations

In the society of early Greece, aristocrats helped each other in a mutually rewarding way. They extended hospitality to friends visiting from other areas, exchanged gifts, and formed alliances with other important families in the same area. They looked to their poorer relations and neighbors for political support and for help with harvests and in feuds with rival aristocrats, and these poorer relations and neighbors in turn looked to them for physical protection and for loans or gifts in time of need.

In the Roman tradition, too, aristocrats developed reciprocal ties of friendship. Friends of similar social station could be counted on to provide hospitality when you were traveling or loans when you needed them or political support when you were running for office. The relationship between social superiors and their inferiors was formalized in the institution of the *clientela,* in which the influential "patron" provided protection and support to dependent "clients." The clients in turn provided votes at election time and, by swelling the numbers of their patron's entourage, helped demonstrate to the world how important he was. The phenomenon operated on many different levels, and a given individual—say, a moderately important member of the aristocratic council in a provincial city—might well have a large body of personal clients and also himself be the client of, in ascending rank, one or more important provincial aristocrats or Roman equestrians or senators. By the time of the late Republic, powerful politicians had through their successes in overseas wars become the patrons of whole cities and client kingdoms. Herod the Great, for example, was the client first of Mark Antony and then of Augustus.

The Gospels imply that some similar institution governed the relationships between classes in Palestine. The parable of the husbandmen (Matt. 21:33–41; Mark 12:1–9; Luke 20:9–16) illustrates the subordinate position of the tenants to the wealthy property owner. Luke contains several stories (12:35–38; 14:12–24; 17:7–10) about the relationship of the rich and the poor at meals. He also reports the story of the importunate woman who prevails on her patron for help (18:2–5).

The most important element in the equations governing these personal and social relationships was reciprocity. The favors of patrons to clients were extended in expectation of a return. Social superiors gave food or money to their inferiors; municipal patrons gave buildings and endowments to cities; princes donated aqueducts and temples to client kingdoms. But they all did so in the expectation of loyalty, of honor, of military support, not of monetary return.

An important parallel phenomenon is that "charity" in the modern sense was virtually unknown, at least in the Greco-Roman part of the ancient world. If a politican provided handouts of grain or oil or money, as was often done, he did it in the expectation that the recipients would express their gratitude in ways the world could measure and from which he would himself benefit—in terms of honorific decrees passed, commemorative statues erected, political support mustered, or military help provided. Charity for the poor and destitute, who could not offer anything in exchange, was virtually unknown. Even when we do hear of donations of food or money, the largest portions always go to the more prosperous members of the recipient population, those who can make the most impressive return. If the most needy do receive something, it seems to be coincidental to the main purpose of the donation.[1]

Among the Hebrews, there did exist a tradition of extending help and mercy to the poor. Even so, this is often phrased in a way that parallels the Greco-Roman concern for reciprocity. Giving to the poor brings redemption to the giver, and the heavenly reward can be seen as real if long-term gratification.[2]

## Private Finances

### *The Wealthy*

The material wealth of the Greco-Roman world was distributed very unevenly. A tiny fraction of the population owned a vast proportion of the land and resources, and the mass of men and women had to make do with moderate means or scrape by on very little. Not everybody who was rich had a correspondingly high social status, but all members of the social elite had plenty of money. The aristocrats spent ostentatiously in election campaigns and then spent ostentatiously during their term in office. Conspicuous consumption was a required life-style of the upper classes; wealth functioned as a proof of social and political status, and spending money in a flashy way typically seemed more important than saving and investing it.

Such a life of conspicuous consumption, of course, required goods to consume, money to spend, and resources to exploit. Since land produced food, which was the one indispensable commodity in antiquity, it was always a rewarding investment, especially for one who was rich enough to ride out a few lean years. Hence the wealth of the elite was based on land, whether inherited or acquired from insolvent neighbors or debtors or as the spoils of war. So too in the Galilean world of the Gospels, every rich man whose source of income is identified owes his wealth (with two exceptions) to agriculture (Matt. 13:3–4; 21:28; 25:14–30; Luke 19:11–27). One exception is the merchant who finds the pearl of great value (Matt. 13: 45–46); the other is Zacchaeus, the customs collector, who pays for his untraditional source of wealth by accepting a low social status (Luke 19:1–10).

The steady income from agricultural investments was not always sufficient for the needs of the elite. Campaigning for elected office and contributing to public games or buildings were expensive, and the costs of government service at the higher levels far outweighed any income from it. Senior Roman magistrates, however, could look forward to several subsequent years of service as a provincial governor, and that involved the opportunity for regaining much more—in perquisites, business contacts, and extortion—than the costs of running for and holding office. And there were other sources of supplementary income. Gifts from the emperor went occasionally to favorite individuals. Military booty provided a rich reward for army commanders. Urban real estate could be as lucrative as agricultural land: One of Cicero's letters of the first century B.C.E., for example, shows this leading member of the senatorial class worrying about the cheapest way to restore some slum property to a minimally acceptable state (*Letters to Atticus* 14.9.1). The upper classes also found ways to invest in commercial enterprises. Normally they did it by using clients and freedmen as agents to take part in large cooperative corporations that invested in a variety of enterprises. Such an indirect approach was desirable both because it was less risky and because the official moral rhetoric of the upper classes looked on commercial transactions with a great deal of disdain.[3]

Pliny the Younger, whom we have already met as the governor of Bithynia at the end of the first century C.E., provides a good example of a Roman senator at the top of the financial pyramid. He inherited immense tracts of farmland in northern and central Italy, which he considered his main financial resource; just one of these farms, in Tuscany, brought in 400,000 *sestertii* a year, equivalent to 100,000 *denarii,* a sum large enough by itself to make a person a member of the economic elite of the empire. In addition, he received generous bequests in the wills of friends and associates. Some of his liquid reserves were lent out at interest. His other assets included several townhouses and country villas and hundreds of slaves. Pliny was generous with his wealth, perhaps untypically so. He gave liberally to his hometown of Comum, endowing a library, a school, a bath, a fund for the maintenance of children, and another for an annual banquet for the ordinary citizens. He also gave a temple to a town near his Tuscan estate and made gifts and interest-free loans to a large number of friends.[4]

The actual work of maintaining and increasing private fortunes was usually left to talented accountants: to freed and slave bailiffs and supervisors. But we have enough glimpses into the private affairs of important men like Cicero and Pliny to know that they took a personal interest in their financial affairs and in the details of their investments. The rich man whom Jesus describes (Luke 12:16–21) as obsessed with the desire to improve his holdings had his counterparts at the highest levels of Greco-Roman society.

In that society, wealth was indispensable for a "virtuous" life—which is to say, a life of aristocratic leisure. The poor man who had to work with his hands and hire himself out at the behest of another was regarded with disgust rather than pity, as passages from the whole range of classical literature make plain. The notion that the poor were in some way "blessed" (Matt. 5:3; Luke 6:20) would have struck as preposterous anybody raised in the aristocratic circles of Greco-Roman society. Such an idea is paralleled, however, in writings from the ancient Near East and in the Jewish conceptual world of the psalms and prophets.[5]

Still, in the Greek and Roman cities, there were those people who had not inherited great fortunes of land and could not afford such lofty attitudes toward the more down-to-earth details of making a living. Some of them were able to become very wealthy. Such newly rich people appear with some frequency in classical literature, which from its generally upper-class bias tends to treat them with undisguised condescension. The sarcasm becomes all the more bitter when the parvenu in question is, as is often the case, a former slave. The most famous example is the freedman Trimalchio, whose personality and career are sketched in a long detailed episode in Petronius (*Satyricon* 76). Trimalchio is a fictitious character loaded with pretentious gaucheries, but he would make effective satire only if he reflected, in however exaggerated a form, a type familiar to the author's aristocratic audience during the first century in Nero's Rome. In describing his career, Petronius has Trimalchio say that he originally came from Asia as a slave and then worked as his master's financial agent. When the master died, he was set free and inherited a vast fortune, much of which he invested in shipping and soon lost. But he scraped together enough to outfit another ship and with the profits was able to buy up his former master's property. This sort of investment in land was, as we have seen, the one really secure and respectable investment, but Trimalchio continued to invest in commercial enterprises—first trading slaves and cattle, then lending money to other upwardly mobile freedmen.[6]

Both Trimalchio and the aristocrats initially acquired their wealth through inheritance, but we also know of specific individuals who were able to become fabulously rich through extraordinary talent or luck or diligence. We hear of sculptors and painters who were paid extraordinary fees for single works, or doctors who earned tremendous salaries tending the highest circles of society, or teachers who collected the income from generous endowments, or prostitutes who profited from the generosity of a devoted patron, or shippers who like Trimalchio made big profits in a hurry. In the smaller Roman cities of North Africa, tomb inscriptions tell us of men who started from humble beginnings and made money in agriculture. One detailed example is a farmer in Mactaris who started as a member of a band of migrant harvesters. He became the foreman of the troop, eventually was able to acquire his own farm, and became so prosperous that he entered the local aristocracy. He even served as censor, one of the most distinguished magistracies in the city.[7]

### *Agriculture*

The importance of landed wealth reflected the fact that ancient society, like any society, was dependent on food. When all was said and done, you had to earn your daily bread by the sweat of your own or your servants' brow. The great majority of the Roman empire's work force was engaged in farming and herding, and the pages of the New Testament show more awareness than most Greco-Roman literature of the realities, often harsh, of subsistence economics. The Synoptic Gospels devote much attention to the processes of planting seed, harvesting fruit, grinding grain, eating bread. Sometimes there is a surplus to gather into barns. Sometimes it is a matter of bare subsistence: When the disciples do not catch any fish, they expect to go hungry (Luke 5:1–11; John 21:3–5).

Agricultural land was exploited in different ways. Some small private farms were tended by their owners, with help from their families and perhaps a couple of slaves. Vegetables and cereals could be efficiently grown on such small, individually owned farms, in an era before farm machinery existed, and a few flocks or herds would supply milk, wool, and meat. At some places, the holdings of a wealthy landowner would be divided into small individual plots to be let out to tenant farmers on some kind of lease arrangement (Matt. 21:33–41; Mark 12:1–9; Luke 20:9–16; cf. Varro, *On Agriculture* 1.17.2–3; Columella, *On Agriculture* 1.7; Pliny the Younger, *Letters* 3.19; 9.37). At others, large tracts were farmed directly by gangs of slaves, under the supervision of one or more stewards; these stewards were themselves often slaves who had demonstrated loyalty and skill at organization. Such large enterprises may have been more efficient for the cultivation of cash crops, like olives and grapes, and for the tending of large flocks of sheep, goats, and pigs.

At busy seasons, peasants would help each other with chores or hire extra workers by the day. Help was available from individuals like those we glimpse lounging about in the marketplace waiting to be hired (Matt. 20:1–16) or in gangs like those we read of on the tombstone of the harvester of Mactaris. A Roman source tells us of an entrepreneur in the first century B.C.E. who assembled gangs of agricultural workers, presumably but not necessarily slaves, to work the hill farms of central Italy (Suetonius, *Life of Vespasian* 1.4; cf. James 5:4).

Man does not live by grain and vegetables alone. Bees provided honey. Birds provided meat and eggs. Sheep, goats, and cattle provided milk, wool, meat, and skins. The figure of the herdsman recurs in the Gospels (Matt. 12:11–12; 18:12–13; Luke 14:5; 15:4–6; John

21:15–16), in the images of the Good Shepherd (John 10), the shepherds on the hillsides at the Nativity (Luke 2:8–20), and the swineherds from Gadara, over in the Gentile territory of the Decapolis (Matt. 8:28–34; Mark 5:11–17; Luke 8:32–36).

Fishing could presumably be done on an individual basis, but the cost of basic equipment was high and maintenance required many man-hours. The Gospels imply that fishermen on the Sea of Galilee like Simon and the sons of Zebedee formed small cooperatives (Luke 5:1–11), which were able to hire additional help (Mark 1:20). A tombstone from Jaffa indicates a similar arrangement on the coast of Palestine; it identifies two members of a fishing cooperative organized, apparently, by a certain Lysas.[8]

The surplus from small farms was usually brought to market by the farmers themselves. Some of them will have owned their own mules, donkeys, and carts. At markets held in the squares of towns and cities and outside the city gates, locally produced grain, fruit, wine, oil, and wool were sold. Butchers acquired the meat left over from sacrifices and sold it to the public. (Pliny the Younger, *Letters* 10.96.9–10, shows that, in the late first century C.E., conversions to Christianity had seriously depressed the market for this kind of meat in some quarters.)

Bakeries ground the grain and provided finished bread in Roman cities, but in the rural economy of the Gospels, breadmaking seems to be confined to the individual household (Matt. 13:33; 24:41). The sale and transport of grain was normally a matter of private enterprise, but the cities usually took on the responsibility of making sure that a reasonable supply was available for the urban population. A couple of consecutive years of drought or other natural disaster could cause a desperate shortage of grain, and the ancient sources list many serious famines in all parts of the Roman world at various times. It was unusual to transport food very far, but really big cities like Athens and Alexandria did need to make arrangements for receiving grain shipments from overseas. Otherwise, the only provisions that were regularly shipped long distances were specialty wines, exotic dried fruits, and luxury spices.

### *Crafts and Commerce*

Individuals with resources to invest and an instinct for taking risks could make great fortunes in commerce. Shipping involved many hazards from shipwreck and piracy, but it could pay off handsomely, in real life as well as in the fictional situation of a Trimalchio. Some made money as government contractors for public works: constructing roads, aqueducts, and major buildings; manufacturing military supplies; baking bread for the public dole.

Much more commonly, people engaged in manufacturing, distribution, and service occupations on a small scale to meet local needs. Such trade was mostly a phenomenon of towns and cities, where there was a market for a variety of goods (James 4:13). Potters made dishes and vases for everyday use, fullers and weavers produced cloth, workers in leather sewed shoes and awnings, blacksmiths made farm implements and artisans' tools, carpenters made furniture and wagons, sculptors made statues and decorative reliefs. They ordinarily used raw materials that were produced near at hand and sold their finished wares in their own workshops, either on a free market or to fill some specific contract. Often, slaves and freed slaves operated this sort of small enterprise on behalf of their masters and patrons. But whether free, freed, or slave, the men and women who operated these businesses generally did most of the work themselves, helped by spouse and children and by a few slaves or hired hands. Hired workers were sometimes skilled artisans employed on the basis of a verbal or written contract, sometimes unskilled laborers hired more informally by the day, sometimes slaves with or without specialized skills, rented from their owner.

This is the pattern we see in a variety of documents from the ancient world. In the fourth century B.C.E., it is attested in the records for the building of the temple at Tegea in southern Greece, where individual contractors provided gangs of between five and ten workmen. In the third century B.C.E., it appears in the papyrus accounts of an Egyptian businessman who hired free workers by the day to dig clay for bricks on the east bank of the Jordan; the workers do not appear to be highly skilled but might on other occasions make contracts directly with a city or temple to produce bricks on their own. In the early Principate we can discern the way in which the pottery industry was organized at Arretium in central Italy, a major source of high-quality tableware. Detailed studies show that the pottery was produced in nearly a hundred small factories. A small number of skilled slave artisans (fewer than ten at most of them; about sixty in the three largest firms) produced the bowls, assisted by a larger but unknown number of others who dug and cleaned the clay, applied slip, and tended the kilns. As the market for these wares spread, new factories were established, at first apparently by the freed agents of individual Arretine families in other parts of the empire. Small workshops like these provided the economic context for the work of the goldsmiths we encounter in the "War Rule" of the Dead Sea Scrolls (1QM 5.6, 9–11), or the silversmiths whose livelihood at Ephesus was dependent on the tourists who came to visit the temple of Artemis (Acts 19:24–27), or more basic craftsmen like the carpenter Joseph (Matt. 13:55; Mark 6:3) or the tentmakers Prisca, Aquila, and Paul (Acts 18:2–3).[9]

The economy of ordinary life was too basic, too close to a subsistence level, to encourage the sale of luxury goods, except to the upper classes in the larger cities. To meet the limited demand in more remote areas, itinerant merchants with small luxury items made the rounds of annual fairs held at festivals of the gods throughout the empire. In this way fine silks imported from the Orient, or the linens for which Tarsus was known in the second century C.E., were brought to their customers. Fine dyes were also transported over large distances and could provide a comfortable income. We meet Lydia, a merchant of such dyes, in Acts (16:14, 40). This "seller of purple" came from Thyatira in Asia Minor and was a prosperous resident of Philippi, with social ties to the synagogue there. Her name implies that she may have been a freedwoman. Traders in luxury purple dye at Rome were often freed, and often women; several of those whose names are known from grave inscriptions seem to have been former slaves of the same family, which may have given them their start.

A variety of other occupations provided essential services for a complex society. Lawyers and physicians offered their varying degrees of expertise. Innkeepers and barbers were independent businessmen or servants of a rich patron; for the ordinary folk of the lower classes, the neighborhood barber dispensed the most accessible and affordable medical care. The poor who had no special skills had to sell their labor on the open market, at low pay, on farms and vineyards, or in construction, or as porters at the docks, sailors on ships, or attendants at the baths. Otherwise, they could sometimes find support on the public dole, if they lived in a city that had one and if they satisfied requirements of citizenship, age, sex, and the like. If that failed, some of the destitute turned to robbery (Luke 10:30).

Dealers and brokers could make money from the trade in slaves, especially when wars produced a good supply of captives. (In general, the slave trade was less active in the peaceful years of the Principate, and the majority of new slaves were born and raised in captivity.) Slaves were used, depending on their talents and their masters' needs, for skilled work as teachers, cooks, physicians, and managers; for routine household service; and for brute physical work in mills, baths, mines, and fields. In some ways they were more efficient than free hired labor, because they were always available to their owners, either for personal use or to be hired out to contractors. In other ways they were more troublesome, because they had to be housed and fed even when there was no need for their work. Slaves thus represented competition to the free labor market, but they did not replace the hired hand. At various times and places and under various circumstances, both slave or bonded laborers and free hired workers were used. Some scholars, like G.E.M. de Ste. Croix, emphasize the evidence for slavery to argue, using Marxist categories, that the ancient economy depended on the exploitation by the propertied classes of the productive capacity of an unfree, oppressed population of workers. Others, like Moses Finley, emphasize the evidence for hired workers to argue that slavery was less important than the operation of a more or less free labor force.[10] The evidence is ambiguous and does not allow us to take a census to determine whether in fact at any given time free or slave labor predominated; thus, by stressing certain specific items, both sides are able to argue with conviction. Clearly, however, slavery was an important element in the ancient economy.

### *Moneylending and Tax Collecting*

Banking operations were often a function of social relations. Among the upper classes, as occasions arose when an individual needed money, he borrowed it from friends; on other occasions, he lent to friends who needed it. Members of the upper classes were also often asked for loans by their dependents and clients, as part of the reciprocal relationship between them. Those of great political influence, such as the great Roman generals of the first century B.C.E., included among their clients whole cities and kingdoms, and we know that they made loans on a vast scale to such cities and kingdoms. In one scandalous episode, Brutus ("the noblest Roman of them all") lent a tremendous amount to the city of Salamis on Cyprus, at the equally tremendous interest rate of 48 percent; we know about it from Cicero (*Letters to Atticus* 5.21.10–13; 6.1.3–7), who shook his head in disapproval. Cicero himself, on other occasions, borrowed large sums from professional moneylenders (*Letters to His Friends* 5.6.2) and from friends and allies (*Letters to Atticus* 5.4.3; 7.3.11; 7.8.5) in order to finance his personal and political affairs. Another technique of the rich for raising cash in a hurry was to demand payment of outstanding loans from their debtors (Pliny the Younger, *Letters* 3.19).[11]

Those who lent money, either formally or informally, were well protected from default. Under Greek, Roman, and oriental law, creditors were apparently able to bind into permanent slavery or temporary debt bondage those debtors who did not or could not pay. The parable of the unmerciful servant (Matt. 18:23–35) illustrates the options. When the king demands payment, perhaps like Pliny to cover some new expenses of his own, and the servant cannot pay, he threatens to sell him into permanent slavery. When this servant in turn is confronted with a defaulting debtor, he threatens to place him under temporary debt bondage. He does this on his own authority. Elsewhere (Matt. 5:25–26; Luke 12:58–59) we understand that the law courts would also cooperate in enforcing this type of temporary debt bondage. Apparently some Christians later used such a procedure, in effect selling themselves into bondage to ransom others or into outright slavery in order to raise money for the congregations in Rome.[12]

Moneylending was a profession in which equestrians and smaller businessmen became involved. We hear about them in Roman literary and legal documents and in the Gospels (Matt. 21:12; Mark 11:15–17), as money changers, who performed the essential service of converting small bronze coins into larger silver or gold denominations or exchanging the coins of one city for equivalent coins of another city. They also functioned as banks, receiving money at fixed rates of interest and lending it out to other borrowers (Matt. 25:27; Luke 19:23). Individuals also lent out money and invested in business enterprises in the expectation of profit (Matt. 25:14–30; Luke 19:12–27).

On the other hand, such deposits and investments did not inspire as much general confidence as modern savings accounts in federally insured banks. To protect their savings, some people deposited them in temples in the hope that the gods would protect them (Juvenal, *Satires* 14.261–262). Others entrusted precious objects and cash reserves to strongboxes in the safest room in their house, with a nagging fear that moth and rust might well consume and that thieves might break in and steal (Matt. 6:19; 12:29; 13:52; 24:43; Mark 3:27; Luke 11:21–22; 12:39; James 5:1–6). Modest fortunes worth 1,000 or 2,000 denarii, for instance, were found in strongboxes at some of the largest houses in Pompeii, while bankers' records from the same place show deposits up to ten times that amount; this implies that many of the rich kept a small portion of their liquid cash at home but deposited most of it at interest with the moneylenders.[13] A few may have buried their treasures in fields, risking the danger of becoming a source of sudden wealth to someone else (Matt. 13:44).

## Municipal Finances

### *Expenses*

The basis of the ancient economy was agricultural, but the basis of Greek and Roman civilization was urban. Society was organized around the cities, and they provided the amenities of culture and market facilities. Farmers and herdsmen from the surrounding hinterland came into the towns and cities to sell their products and buy manufactured items and specialty goods, at daily markets, weekly fairs, or annual holiday bazaars.

The city also provided a physical environment in the public buildings that it constructed and maintained. It supplied temples, altars, animals, and incense for sacrifice. It administered law and order and provided meetinghouses and archives for administration, oil and fuel for the gymnasia and public baths, prizes and (in the Roman period) wild animals for games, an adequate supply of grain, and aqueducts to bring good water to public fountains. In addition, there were publicly supported professors and doctors in many of the larger cities, and even smaller Greek cities in the East paid for teachers and trainers in the gymnasia. Magistrates were assisted by a staff of attendants and public slaves supported by the municipal treasury. Watchmen were paid to provide police and fire service, and public slaves attended the baths and helped maintain the public buildings, aqueducts, and roads.

### *Sources of Income*

The most important source of revenue for most cities of the Roman empire was real estate. Public land, even belonging to temples, was rented out for farming. The land was often within the political territory controlled by the city, but not necessarily. It was also usual for the cities to build public marketplaces and to charge merchants for the stalls they occupied. Residential properties might also be owned by cities and rented out to tenants, and the cities' cash revenues could be lent out in short-term loans to earn interest.

The cities sometimes collected direct taxes, but they did so as agents for the imperial government and passed the money on to the Roman authorities. Tolls and custom duties, on the other hand, came into the municipal treasuries. These were usually relatively low, around 2 or 2½ percent on imports and exports, but big commercial cities that were major centers of trade depended heavily on them.

In the case of most cities, rents on public lands and tolls on imports and exports fell far short of expenditures. There is no real evidence that anybody drew up a proper annual budget for an ancient city, and we do know that when certain cities in Asia Minor overextended themselves in the first and second centuries C.E., they turned to the provincial governor for help, which did not always materialize (Pliny the Younger, *Letters* 10.39–40, 77–78, 98–99, 108–109).

### *Municipal Benefactors*

To balance their accounts and provide the more comfortable amenities of urban life, the Greek and Roman cities exploited the economics of social relationships. The members of the ruling classes, who had the financial resources and the honor of municipal office, were expected to contribute from their own wealth for the benefit of the entire community. In Greek cities, wealthy men were assessed certain *leitourgiai* ("liturgies," literally "people works"). These included the responsibilities of paying the expenses of a festival, or a dramatic performance, or the maintenance or construction of a public building, or the annual upkeep of a ship, or the oil supply for the gymnasium. In some Roman communities, laws required those who had received the honor of a magistracy and a place in the local council to pay certain fees into the city treasury and to make specific contributions to the expenses of games. In addition, men and women of the ruling class, motivated by public spirit or political ambition, often made lavish additional contributions, boasting of the beautiful buildings they had donated, the elaborate games they had sponsored, or the endowments that established a school or university or provided oil for the gymnasia, fuel for the baths, or cemetery plots for all citizens. Emperors and senators also played the benefactor to cities, paying for new temples or establishing endowments. The communities showed their gratitude by erecting statues or by granting honorary citizenship, golden crowns, seats of honor at the theater, free meals in the town hall, and immunity from taxation or by issuing decrees of thanks in praise of the benefactor's good character, enthusiasm, zeal, and generosity. The relationship between the municipal benefactor, his or her gifts, and the beneficiaries was so embedded in Greco-Roman society that its vocabulary frequently appears in the New Testament, particularly Luke–Acts and the letters of Paul. Thus Jesus refers (Luke 22:25) to the way in which "those in authority" expected the honor that belonged to the title *euergetēs* ("benefactor"). Words referring to liturgies are used for the duties in faith of Christians (Phil. 2:17, 25–30). Others referring to the provision of choruses at dramatic festivals are used for the way in which God supplies spiritual benefits to believers (Gal. 3:5; Phil. 1:19; 1 Peter 4:11) and bodily needs to the poor (2 Cor. 9:9–10).[14]

## Imperial Finances

### *Patterns of Economic Activity*

On the global scale of the empire, the major routes of activity were all those proverbial roads that led to Rome, whether physical highways or (more often, given the high cost of land transport) sea lanes. Food and building materials were the main items of long-distance trade, and this sort of commerce was in the hands of private entrepreneurs, although the imperial government was normally the only large-scale customer. The present consensus among students of the ancient economy is that business deals were very specific and long-range systematic thought about economic patterns was unknown. In this way Finley explains the dearth of economic theory in classical literature and the absence of large-scale corporations which set about "making money" in any way parallel to modern capitalism.[15] It also helps explain why no regime in the Roman empire ever drew up a detailed long-range budget, and why famines could strike with such devastating force, because no contingency plans had been made in advance. This does not mean, of course, that people in the ancient world did not know how to invest to make money; the parable of the talents (Matt. 25:14–30; Luke 19:12–27) shows clearly that they did. But such investments were limited to a relatively small scale.

Similarly, most commercial activity in the Roman empire was local. Farms within easy distance of towns supplied their food and most raw materials. Manufacturing was done in small workshops for local consumption. We know of occasional long-distance trade in exotic foodstuffs or luxury textiles, but it also seems to have been in the hands of individual traders or groups of traders working with very specific cargoes.

### *Public Expenditures*

The public *aerarium,* the treasury of the old Roman Republic, continued under the Principate to pay for the public services of the city of Rome and the administrative expenses of those provinces under the nominal control of the Senate. The much larger expenses of administering the "imperial" provinces were borne by the *fiscus,* the funds at the disposition of the emperor, who thus functioned, through his personal largess, as patron to the entire empire.

The emperor provided the purse that financed the offices of his prefects in the provinces. He employed an immense household of slaves and freedmen. He paid the salaries of soldiers throughout the empire, as well as bonuses to reward troops for victories or induce them to stay loyal. A special fund provided separation pay when a soldier was honorably discharged from the army.

Most of the construction and maintenance of public buildings in the provinces was paid for by the cities, as we have seen, but the imperial treasury paid for special projects like harbor works, roads, and military camps. Frequently the emperors exhibited their beneficence in the form of elaborate games and spectacles, or special handouts to all the citizens (larger ones to the rich than to the poor), or some special construction. At the end of the first century C.E., Trajan established a special fund to ensure specified amounts of grain to all the citizen children in Italy.

### *Sources of Income*

In keeping with the rest of the ancient economy, land provided most of the revenue. The proceeds from public land flowed into the aerarium, and revenues from the increasing number of estates owned by the emperor flowed into the fiscus.

Taxes, of course, were an important source of income. In the Republic, direct taxes were not levied on Roman citizens, but they were collected from the conquered territories in the provinces. The machinery of administration in the provinces was, however, not elaborate enough to collect taxes efficiently. The Senate therefore contracted with Roman businessmen, who paid the taxes due and then were relatively free to use any appropriate means to collect money to reimburse themselves—at a profit. Since these men were engaged on public business, they were known as *publicani.* In the individual towns and villages the work of tax collecting was performed by agents of the great businessmen, and they were themselves known to the local population as "publicans." At the end of the Republic the great corporations of publicani were abolished, and the local cities took over the job of collecting taxes. They continued to use the same kind of local tax collectors—small, sometimes quite prosperous, businessmen whose low social status is well illustrated by their appearances in the Gospels (Matt. 9:9–13; Mark 2:14–17; Luke 3:12–13; 19:1–10).

Under the Principate there were two main types of taxes or tribute: *tributum soli* and *tributum capitis.* The former was a property tax assessed within a province at a fixed rate on land, houses, slaves, and ships. The rate in the province of Syria, we know, was 1 percent annually. The other form of tribute was a head tax, levied at a flat rate on adults between the ages of twelve or fourteen and sixty-five —apparently one denarius per person per year (Matt. 22:15–22; Mark 12:14–17; Luke 20:21–26); in some provinces it applied only to males, but in Syria, among other places, it applied to everybody. Since these taxes were assessed at a flat rate, it was always easier for a rich person to pay than a poor one, and this tended to accentuate even further the gap between rich and poor. A census was necessary to count the heads and enforce the tax, and during the reign of Augustus surveys were held in all the provinces: Luke uses such a census as the occasion for Mary and Joseph's trip to Bethlehem. In spite of Luke's words, it is unlikely that this was a universal census: a census was held within each province to determine liability for the head tax, and we know that one was held in Judea in 6 C.E. (see chapter 1).

Customs duties provided an important source of revenue (Matt. 9:9; Mark 2:14; Luke 5:29). Jericho, where Jesus met the customs official Zacchaeus (Luke 19:1–10), was a frontier post between the Roman province of Judea and Peraea, part of the tetrarchy of Herod Antipas. Other sources of revenue included a tax on manumissions of slaves and several new taxes introduced by Augustus: a 1 percent sales tax, a 4 percent special tax on the sale of slaves, and a 5 percent tax on all inheritances over 100,000 sestertii, except those from very near relatives. After Titus' destruction of the Temple in Jerusalem in 70 C.E., all Jews in the empire were required to pay a special extra head tax of 2 denarii each year; it was the equivalent (half a shekel) of the tax they had paid earlier for the maintenance of the Temple, the *didrachma* (Matt. 17:24–27).

Residents of the provinces were liable as well for nonmonetary payments. The well-to-do were expected to play host to Roman dignitaries passing through, and anyone could be required to provide animals, wagons, and supplies for official messengers or military troops. Many documents, especially from the second century, complain about the way soldiers in particular abused their right to make such demands.

### *Coinage*

Casual allusions in the Gospels and classical literature, and the abundance of coins found in every archaeological excavation of the Roman period, show that the society of the empire depended thoroughly on the use of coinage. The imperial government used coins to pay its troops and its bills to suppliers and contractors, and then they circulated through all strata of society.

Large denominations of silver and gold were minted by the Roman imperial mints; they bore the image of the emperor on one side and some other variable device on the other. The standard silver denomination was the denarius, known in the East by its equivalent in Greek, *drachma.* The parable of the vineyard (Matt. 20:1–16) implies that a denarius was a generous day's wage for agricultural workers, just as in the fifth century B.C.E. a drachma had been the standard wage for skilled workers on the buildings of the Acropolis in Athens. Such day workers, of course, suffered a great deal of uncertainty about employment, and it is unlikely that they were able to earn at anything like that rate through the whole year. Soldiers in the Roman legions, on the other hand, received an annual salary: In the first century their annual pay was 225 denarii; in the second, 300. Out of this they were expected to buy their own food, clothing, and weapons. Auxiliary troops received much less: 200 denarii for elite troops, 150 for cavalry, only 100 for infantry.

For day-to-day transactions, smaller denominations of bronze were in circulation—in the western part of the empire, these were produced at central mints, but in the eastern part, individual cities and territories provided the small change. The standard denomination was the *as,* often known in Greek as *assarion.* At the official rate of exchange, a denarius was worth 16 asses, although documents of the Principate show that especially in the East it took 18, 20, or even 24 asses to buy a denarius. The best guess of scholars is that the money changers took the extra asses as their fee.[16] Money changers were necessary on several levels: If you had bronze coins from your hometown and were in another city, they would have to be changed into the local bronze currency or into denarii, which were accepted everywhere; if you had been paid in silver denarii you might well need smaller coins to buy groceries and other everyday necessities; if you were a small businessman, you usually took in bronze coins and would need to change them into larger silver or gold denominations to pay your bills.

The Gospels give an idea of price levels. Two asses will buy four or five small sparrows (Matt. 10:29; Luke 12:6). Bread to feed the Five Thousand is estimated at 200 denarii (Mark 6:37), which implies that a denarius would buy enough bread for twenty-five lunches; one portion would cost less than one as. The good Samaritan assumes that two denarii will cover most, but possibly not all, of the costs for several days' food and lodging at a country inn (Luke 10:35). These prices compare in order of magnitude to those we know from Italy, where in the first century enough good-quality flour to make a pound of bread cost two asses and a measure of wine varied according to its quality from one to four asses. An itemized bill for a night at an inn in central Italy lists wine at ⅙ as, bread at 1 as, and main dinner course at 2 asses; a girl for the night cost 8 asses, and hay for the customer's mule cost 2 asses. An inscription from Pompeii lists expenses for nine days for (apparently) a group of three persons, with an average expense of 1½ denarii a day.[17]

For the needs of everyday life, a greater variety of coin denominations was in circulation. The as was broken down into a half piece (the *semis*) and a quarter piece (the *quadrans*). Local currencies might well circulate even smaller denominations, like the *lepton:* The widow's mite (Mark 12:42; Luke 21:2) consists of two lepta, which Mark explains is equivalent to one quadrans. The gap between the as and the denarius was filled by a series of brass coins: *dupondii,* worth two asses, and *sestertii,* worth four asses, or one quarter of a denarius. The Romans usually referred to prices in terms of sestertii rather than denarii.

Old Greek terms for large amounts were still in use in New Testament times as well. The *mina* (Luke 19:12–27) was worth 100 drachmas; the *talent* (Matt. 18:24) was an immense amount, worth 6,000 drachmas.

Everybody knows how foolish it is to try to convert ancient prices into modern equivalents. But if we assume, just for the sake of illustration, $15 to $20 as a minimum daily wage, we could take an as to be roughly equivalent to a dollar. A sparrow then costs 50 cents or so, a loaf of bread about $2, a liter of wine about $1 or $2, the widow's mite about a quarter. The mina that the nobleman apportions to each of ten servants (Luke 19:12–20) was worth 60 drachmas, something in excess of $1,000 on these arbitrary calculations. And when Judas suggests selling the woman's ointment and giving it to the poor, he imagines that it would bring 300 denarii (Mark 14:5), around $5,000. To the modern American reader, remembering that $20 a day represents a minimum wage, the prices, especially of luxury goods, will seem disproportionately high. It is certainly safe to suppose that the average wage earner had much less left over for luxuries than his modern American counterpart.

# 4

# Society in Palestine

Fundamental questions about Palestinian society in these centuries remain unanswered. Had Jews continuously resided in Galilee, relatively isolated from the processes of urbanization and Hellenization? When and where did the Jews begin to build synagogues and study the Torah in them? What role did the rural peasants play in the social unrest of this period? Did the common people speak primarily Aramaic, or did many of them converse daily in Greek, which would also mean that they accepted some Greek values? Who were the Pharisees? In what social context did Jesus preach, and how are the controversies between him and the Pharisees to be understood? This chapter addresses these questions.

## Demography

The boundary system at the time of Jesus has been described in chapter 1: we will review some historical events in the light of our present concern with the ethnic and religious composition of the population. The Maccabee Simon partially evacuated Jews from western Galilee (1 Macc. 5:15, 23). His successor, John Hyrcanus, conquered Samaritans to the north and Idumaeans to the south. From the beginning it was Maccabaean policy to tolerate no Gentiles in their land, so those who were conquered either converted or left; the Idumaeans accepted circumcision, remaining loyal even during the later war against the Romans. Aristobulus reigned only one year (104–103 B.C.E.), but he added Galilee to Jewish dominions, forcing Ituraeans to evacuate it (Josephus, *Antiquities* 13.318), so Sepphoris became a Jewish town.

The Roman general Pompey reversed much of this Jewish expansion in 63 B.C.E. by freeing all the Greek cities along the Mediterranean coast, as well as some inland cities, including Samaria, Scythopolis, and the cities east of the Jordan. Still, Judea remained significantly larger than it had been in pre-Maccabaean times. Parts of Idumaea, Samaria, and Peraea east of the Jordan were still Jewish, and Galilee was separate but culturally attached to Judea. Further, Julius Caesar reversed some of Pompey's actions by restoring Joppa and the Jezreel valley in 47 B.C.E. (Josephus, *Antiquities* 14.205, 207).

The geography of Palestine at the time of Jesus is easier to determine than are population figures and the extent of ethnic and religious groups. The population of Jews in Judea was compact and included the coastal areas of Joppa and Jamnia, although the latter city included Gentiles among its residents. Herod the Great introduced some Gentiles into Jerusalem, as did Herod Antipas into Tiberias. The population of Capernaum was also mixed.

The Bar Kokhba war (132–135 C.E.) brought decisive changes in the demography of Judea. Hadrian expelled all the "circumcised" (including Jewish Christians) from the region of Jerusalem. After this second war against Rome, Galilee remained the main stronghold of Palestinian Judaism.

Estimating the size of the population in Palestine at this time is very difficult; ancient sources give exaggerated figures and modern guesses vary widely. Michael Avi-Yonah gives a total of two and a half million for all of Palestine; more recent figures give at least three million.[1]

## The Pattern of Life

The vast majority of Jews in Jesus' lifetime in Galilee, Transjordan, and Judea lived in small towns, not in the large cities such as Tiberias and Jerusalem.[2] Franciscan excavations have uncovered housing in Capernaum from Jesus' time. There are several blocks of houses whose walls were unevenly constructed of basalt blocks, not strong enough to support a second story. Staircases led to the roof, which was usually flat. The rooms below were very small with inadequate ventilation and tiny windows; rooftops gave privacy and provided cooler temperatures. Larger rooms in Capernaum were about 18 feet wide; it would have been difficult to find wooden beams any longer for the roof. Floors were made of large, uneven pieces of basalt, not closely fitted together, where it would be easy to lose a coin (Luke 15:8). The blocks of houses were surrounded by streets or alleys. One block contained four family apartments, all of which faced onto a common courtyard. If each family had about eight persons, the thirty-two people living in such a small space would never be alone.

### *Daily Life: The Family*

In small towns, some families lived in one room, but most had several; the "family" often means the patriarchal one, including the wives and children of married sons. Some extended families slept in one bedroom, but usually each couple and their children had their own. The bed was the most essential item, although chairs and benches were common. Ovens were vital; bread was baked weekly by the whole family.

It was rare for persons to remain unmarried. Until the tenth century C.E., oral law allowed a man to have more than one wife, but only a few cases of bigamy are known. The Essenes read Genesis 1:27 as prescribing monogamy (Cairo Damascus Document 4.20–21; cf. Matt. 19:4). Greco-Roman practices of abortion and of exposing babies were alien to the Jewish way (cf. *Didache* 2.2).

At birth, children's limbs were straightened and swaddled (Luke 2:7) so that they would grow properly. Sons were named at circumcision (Luke 1:59–60; 2:21); only Gentiles, not Jews, celebrated birthdays. Firstborn sons were to be redeemed (Ex. 34:20); that is, the priests were given dues. There were differences about whether the dues could be given to a local priest or whether this had to be done in Jerusalem; Luke indicates (2:22) that Jesus' parents went to Jerusalem. Although Bar Mitzvah originated later, a boy led in prayer in the synagogue only after he became thirteen.

The dead were buried the same day (Acts 5:6–10) to the sounds of pipers and hired mourners (Matt. 9:23). The corpse was buried in a shroud of linen (John 11:44; 19:39–40) in a wooden coffin, less often in a stone sarcophagus. The grave was not filled with dirt; it was blocked with a stone door or large rock (Matt. 28:2). It was customary to visit the grave, roll back the stone, and make sure that the person was really dead (Matt. 28:1). After the flesh decomposed, the bones were collected and placed in a chest, which was set in a niche. Many such ossuaries have been found by archaeologists.

The rabbis made many efforts to encourage widows to remarry, but in some circles it was praiseworthy for them to remain unmarried (Judith 8:4; 1 Cor. 7:39–40). For the husband, divorce was a simple announcement that the wife was free to marry any other man. Apparently, the wife could also demand that the court compel a husband to divorce her (M. Ketuboth 5:6).[3]

### *The Synagogue*

The villagers assembled for religious services in the synagogue, which also served as a town hall for community affairs. The people took turns reciting prayers and reading scripture. The earliest synagogue found by archaeologists, if it is correctly identified as a synagogue, is on the Greek island of Delos and dates from the first century B.C.E.,[4] although there are synagogue inscriptions from as early as the third century B.C.E.[5] In Palestine, buildings interpreted as first-century C.E. synagogues have been excavated at Masada, Herodium, Magdala (Tarichaea on the west shore of the Sea of Galilee), Gamala in Gaulanitis (the modern Golan Heights), and perhaps Chorazin.[6]

The early Palestinian synagogues were utterly plain, without murals or mosaics. There was no raised platform for reading the Torah, no Torah shrine for its storage, no images of objects such as the menorah. The space was functional, with nothing to distract the worshiper. The Diaspora synagogue in Delos also seems to be without Jewish symbols. Sixty lamps were found that have no Jewish markings, although some have pagan ones, including deities. These early buildings thus differ from later synagogues from the third and fourth century C.E. with their many mosaics and paintings of animals and humans.

The prayer called *shemone esre* ("eighteen benedictions") was given set form at Jamnia, the center of rabbinic education after the first war. Before 70 C.E. these benedictions were worded in various ways by the officiant; even later, when the wording was set, there were several versions. Several texts in the Apocrypha mention morning prayers (Psalms of Solomon 6:4–5), and Qumran texts assume prayer twice a day (Manual of Discipline—1QS 10.11).

Both Philo (*On the Special Laws* 2.62) and the rabbis present the reading and interpretation of scripture as the most important event in synagogue meetings. Apparently there was no fixed sequence for reading the books of Moses.[7] Jesus (Luke 4:17) and Paul (Acts 13:15) are pictured interpreting prophetic texts that had been read. Paul converted some leading women at the synagogue in Thessalonica (Acts 17:4); no ancient source mentions their segregation from the men. Acts (13:16; 17:17) and Josephus (*Antiquities* 14.110) refer to "God-fearers" in the synagogue, non-Jews who attended but had not converted and become proselytes.

Immigrants to Jerusalem were attracted to synagogues frequented by others from the same homeland (Acts 6:9), but in smaller towns, the synagogue would belong to the whole community. The head of the synagogue is mentioned often (Luke 13: 14–15).

From early times Jews prayed toward Jerusalem and built synagogues facing the holy city. Many synagogues in Galilee faced the south; this seems to have become even more important later, when Constantine Christianized the empire.[8]

### *Holy Days: Sabbath and Annual Festivals*

These meetings at the synagogue and the accompanying Sabbath rest from work were the most well-known symbols of Judaism in this period. The few biblical texts on the Sabbath were extended by rules that attempted to ensure rest; the rabbis compared these rules to mountains hanging from a hair. As with any such core symbol, there were sectarian differences: Jubilees (2:17–18; 50:6–13), the Essenes (Josephus, *Jewish War* 2.147), the early *hasidim* (1 Macc. 2:35–41) and, later, Karaites were stricter than the rabbis; the Jewish Christians (Matt. 12:1–14; 24:20) and Paul (Rom. 14:5–6) were more lax. Philo's discussion (*Moses* 2.209–220; cf. 3 Maccabees 7) reveals the conflict evoked by these powerful identity symbols. Torah was studied on the Sabbath, and the family ate a festive meal together, which included wine sanctified by the *kiddush* prayer. Friday was called the Day of Preparation, but this did not include an evening meeting in the synagogue, a later custom.

The Passover feast celebrated Israel's freedom from slavery in Egypt. The central ritual was a meal together before the fifteenth of the springtime month of Nisan. The necessary elements of the Passover meal itself were the prayer sanctifying the day, four cups of wine, the recitation of the *hallel* (Psalms 115–118), and the eating of bitter herbs. Fifty days later came Pentecost (Shavuoth). This feast, unlike Passover, was focused on the Temple in Jerusalem and the offering of firstfruits.

New Year (Rosh Hashanah) during the month of Tishri (September–October) was the time when everything living was judged by God. On the tenth of the same month came Yom Kippur, the Day of Atonement. This day was observed even by those who did not strictly keep other customary rituals (Philo, *On the Special Laws* 1. 186). It was a day of repentance for sins. The Feast of Tabernacles (Sukkoth) was celebrated on the fifteenth of Tishri. Processions with a bundle of palm branch, willow, myrtle, and an ethrog (a citron) moved through Jerusalem each of the seven days of the feast. Jews built and sat in leafy huts, booths reminiscent of Israel's tents in the wilderness.

Purity and impurity were major issues in the temple era and in early rabbinic times. Sadducees tried to restrict the concern for purity to the priests; Pharisees encouraged all Jews to make purity a priority. Scripture listed several sources of impurity, and the oral law added contact with a non-Jew (M. Pesahim 8.8; John 18:28; Acts 10:28), the land outside Israel (T. B. Shabbath 14b), and idolatry (M. Abodah Zarah 3:6; Acts 15:20, 29; cf. 1 Cor. 8:10).

**Languages**

There were four primary languages used in Palestine in the first century C.E.: Latin, Greek, Aramaic, and Hebrew. John mentions that Pilate put a sign on Jesus' cross "in Hebrew, in Latin, and in Greek" (John 19:20). However, little Latin was spoken in Palestine.

The situation for Greek may be typified by the coins struck by rulers. The Hasmonaeans used exclusively Hebrew until Alexander Jannaeus, who began to use bilingual (Hebrew and Greek) coins in addition. His grandson was the first Jew to issue coins with only a Greek identification. The Herodian princes and Roman procurators also issued only Greek coins.[9]

A letter written perhaps by Bar Kokhba himself reads, "Now this has been written in Greek because a desire has not been found to write in Hebrew."[10] From Jerusalem there is the famous first-century synagogue inscription of Theodotus, a priest and archisynagogos who built the synagogue and a guest house for visitors from abroad and supplied them with water. There are many ossuary inscriptions from Palestine, two thirds in Greek alone, one tenth in Greek and Hebrew (or Aramaic).[11] Since sepulchral inscriptions probably best indicate the language of the common people, it is significant that the vast majority of those published are in Greek. Books were written in Greek by persons from various social strata and religious parties in the two centuries B.C.E.: 1 Maccabees, Tobit, the additions to Esther, and the additions to Daniel. Many scholars today conclude that Greek was widely used in first-century Palestine by Christians as well as other Jews.

Whether more Greek or Aramaic was spoken in Palestine is debated. It used to be thought that Aramaic was on the wane in the Seleucid pre-Maccabaean period, but more evidence for Aramaic has accumulated recently. The finds at Qumran reveal that literature was still being composed in Aramaic in the first century before and after Christ. Examples are the Genesis Apocryphon, the Testament of Levi, a Targum of Job, and a text which refers to "the Son of God" and to "the Son of the Most High."

There are also legal documents and letters in Aramaic found in the Cave of Letters of Wadi Habra and at Murabba'at. In examining this material, Joseph Fitzmyer concludes that there is little evidence for Greek influence on Aramaic, but that Aramaic clearly affected the Greek used by Jews.[12] In fact, he argues that Aramaic was the most commonly used language in Palestine in the first century C.E.

Although there is not as much evidence for Hebrew as for Aramaic, there are epigraphic and literary indications that Hebrew was written in Jesus' time and still used in certain oral activities such as midrashic sermons, halakic teaching, and legal discussions. The Qumran texts written in Hebrew far outnumber those in Aramaic, but they are early, from the last two centuries B.C.E. The *pesharim*, or commentaries, were written in Herodian script and are probably first-century-C.E. compositions. Otherwise, the evidence for Hebrew in the century in which Jesus lived is sparse.

## Hellenistic Culture and the Cities

Greek culture was influential in several ways in Palestine, perhaps most pervasively in religious worship. Indigenous pagan cults were transformed by Greek elements. Herod the Great built several *caesarea* (shrines dedicated to Augustus) in Samaria, Panias, and Caesarea (Josephus, *Jewish War* 1.407), and they contained statues, one of Augustus modeled after Zeus and another of Rome modeled after Hera.

Festival games were often connected with these cults. Theaters and amphitheaters were built, by Herod in Caesarea, for example, and even in Jerusalem, where various kinds of games were celebrated: gymnastic and musical games, chariot racing, and animal baiting (Josephus, *Antiquities* 15.267–291).

Palestine also produced famous persons in Greek literature. Ashkelon educated the Stoic Antiochus, an influential tutor of Cicero. Damascus produced Nicholas, who became Herod's trusted counselor. The Epicurean Philodemus of Gadara was a well-known contemporary of Cicero whose writings have been found in the Italian town of Herculaneum.

The Hellenistic architecture of public buildings was prominent in all Greek cities. Each had its temples, theaters, gymnasia with arcades, stoa, agora, aqueducts, baths, fountains, and colonnades in the Greek style. Herod sponsored much of this (Josephus, *Jewish War* 1.422–425) and built his own palace in Jerusalem (Josephus, *Jewish War* 5.176–183). Much of the Temple in Jerusalem was itself built in Greek style (Josephus, *Jewish War* 5.184–227).

In one area of aesthetics, Hellenistic standards gave way to the demands of the second commandment (Deut. 4:15–19; 5:8), which forbids images of humans and animals. Even Herod the Great, that great Hellenizer, avoided such images in the mosaics, murals, and statues of his Greek buildings, with only one or two exceptions (Josephus, *Antiquities* 15.267–291; 17.151). The prohibition seems stricter than at any other time in Jewish history; nothing but floral and geometric designs are found on the tomb facades, decorated ossuaries, and sarcophagi of this period.[13]

The influence of Hellenism was most effective in the sphere of trade and industry. Political organization was another of the most important ways Hellenism affected Palestine. Many cities were founded that were—or were transformed to be—ruled by a democratically elected council. The council ruled not only the city but also all the villages and towns belonging to its often extensive territory. There were thirty-three such cities in or near Palestine, a few of which will be sketched below.[14]

First, a caution about the Gospels: Few of the parables of Jesus reflect the world of Hellenistic-Roman cities. Judea and Galilee were administered by the Ptolemaic system of villages grouped into districts known as "toparchies." A village clerk, an official of the central government, administered the village, and a commandant controlled the toparchy.[15] These two types of official are never mentioned in the Gospels, although they are related to the tax collectors. In contrast to this system, the number of true Greek cities was very small. In Galilee, only Tiberias and perhaps Sepphoris qualify. Even Jerusalem may not have had a council, and it was supervised by a royal *stratēgos* who was appointed, not elected (Josephus, *Antiquities* 17.156, 209–210; *Jewish War* 1.652; 2.8). Palestinian villages did not rule their own territory. Jesus' parables of the kingdom accurately represent the world beyond Galilean village life as one of kings and princes whose ministers are slaves. The parable of the marriage feast, in which a king sends his hosts to destroy a recalcitrant village (Matt. 22:2–14), is the world of Herod the Great, Archelaus, and Antipas (see the characterization in Mark 6:17–27!), not the world of Greek democratic cities. It is a world of the very rich and the poor, the king and the peasant, of only two social classes.[16] There is only a single merchant in all the Galilean parables (Matt. 13:45–46). Religious scribes, not professional bankers, devour the estates of widows (Luke 20:46–47).

Over against this world, there were Greek cities important to first-century-C.E. Judaism. Jamnia in the south had its own harbor and territory. After the war against the Romans, it became a center of Jewish learning under Johanan ben Zakkai. Joppa, with the best harbor on the Palestinian coast, became Jewish when the Maccabee Simon established a garrison there, forcing the Gentiles to leave the city (1 Macc. 13:11). Herod rebuilt Caesarea (Josephus, *Antiquities* 15.331–337; *Jewish War* 1.408–414) between 21 and 9 B.C.E., and in 6 C.E., if not before, it became capital of the kingdom, which means that the high priests of Jerusalem lost significant civil power. Herod lavishly disguised his intentions by reconstructing the Temple in Jerusalem between 18 and 10 B.C.E. The Roman prefects, before and after the reign of Agrippa I, lived in Caesarea, and Agrippa I died there (Acts 12). All twenty thousand Jewish inhabitants of the city were massacred in one hour at the outbreak of the rebellion in 66 C.E. (Josephus, *Jewish War* 2.457; 7.362).

There were also independent Greek cities in the Decapolis (Matt. 4:25; Mark 5:20; 7:31), clustered near the Sea of Galilee. It used to be supposed that these cities were a political confederacy, but now most scholars interpret "Decapolis" simply as a loose geographical term. Damascus was one of these cities (Acts 9:2; 2 Cor. 11:32). An uncertain textual tradition makes Gadara the location where Jesus exorcised two demoniacs (Matt. 8:28). A third city of the Decapolis was Pella; at the beginning of the war with Rome, the Christian community from Jerusalem is said to have fled there (Eusebius, *Ecclesiastical History* 3.5.2–3).

Herod the Great settled six thousand colonists, including soldiers, at Samaria and gave them estates. He built a temple to Augustus and renamed the city Sebaste in honor of the same emperor. Soldiers from Samaria served Herod and the Romans against the Jews.

After Pompey's conquest of Palestine, Gabinius divided the Jewish area into five districts with councils (57–55 B.C.E.), and the council of Galilee met in Sepphoris. It was a center of the rebellion that followed Herod the Great's death, which might be explained by its priestly Hasmonaean loyalties. It was burned and its residents sold as slaves, but Herod Antipas rebuilt it, making it an "ornament of all Galilee" (Josephus, *Antiquities* 18.27). In the war against Rome, although the citizens were predominantly Jewish, the city supported Rome. Josephus captured it, but Vespasian later garrisoned it with his soldiers at the request of its Jewish citizens.

Herod Antipas founded his new capital on the Sea of Galilee and named it after the emperor, Tiberias. The population was mixed, but the majority were Jewish. The constitution of the city was Greek, so there was a council of six hundred members, elected officials, and a mint for city coins. It passed into the control of Agrippa I, then to Roman procurators of Judea, then, about 61 C.E., to Agrippa II. Josephus describes the factions in the city at the beginning of the war (*Life* 32–42). The revolutionary party won, but when Vespasian advanced, it offered no resistance (Josephus, *Life* 352).

Most of these cities were self-governing *poleis* with councils of several hundred citizens, territories, and their own coins, although this cannot be proved for all. Most were predominantly Gentile, but in Jamnia, Joppa, Sepphoris, and Tiberias, Jews had equal rights and outnumbered Gentiles. Jerusalem is the only city where Gentiles were excluded from civic rights.

## Peasants

Peasants worked the land as their ancestors had always done; their lives were spent in small villages where kinship and loyalty were primary values. The Hasmonaeans seem to have distributed conquered lands to such Jewish peasants, freeing them of taxation by the Seleucids, in exchange for the peasants' serving in the army in times of crisis. The Hasmonaeans also kept some of the conquered territories as royal lands, which they leased to tenants to cultivate.

Pompey's destruction of the Maccabaean state had disastrous consequences that contributed to the social disorder leading to the first Jewish war against the Romans. When the Roman general separated the Greek cities of Samaria and Transjordan from Judea, he made a considerable number of Jewish peasants landless. This happened when the population of Judea had already reached its peak,[17] so that some of the Jews went to Judea but others migrated into the Diaspora around the Mediterranean (see 1 Macc. 15:16–24).

When Herod received some of this land back from Augustus, much of it remained royal land, and he expropriated the lands of his political opponents. There was a trend in the direction of large holdings by the rich, whose lands were cultivated by tenant farmers. This trend excited the savage hostility between landlords and renters typified in Matthew 21:33–41 and Josephus, *Jewish War* 2.427. Small landowners and tenants often were forced to ask for loans. The pressure for these loans was so intense in Herod's reign that Hillel found a legal way out of the remission of debts every seventh year required by Deuteronomy 15:3. Economic strains that caused such a grave change in Mosaic legislation produced deep antagonism between the owners of large rural properties and their tenants or debtors. These owners often lived in the cities, sometimes foreign ones (see Josephus, *Life* 422, 425, as typical).

Taxes fell heavily on these peasants. They not only had to pay tribute to Rome but also had to support Herod's lavish building in Judea and in various Greek cities as far away as Antioch. The peasants paid taxes, rent, and then principal and interest on loans, if they were fortunate enough to have land on which to eke out an existence. Philo (*On the Special Laws* 3.159–162) gives a narrative from the 30s C.E. of what peasants in the Roman empire experienced when they could not pay. This struggle for scarce land was one factor that stimulated the revolutionary cause of Hezekiah and John of Gischala in Upper Galilee, a marginal zone where Jewish and non-Jewish populations clashed.

## Galilee

### *Regionalism*

The reader of Matthew might get the impression that northern Galilee is geographically, socially, religiously, and politically remote from southern Judea. For example, when Joseph "heard that Archelaus reigned over Judea in place of his father Herod, he was afraid to go there, and being warned in a dream, he withdrew to the district of Galilee" (Matt. 2:22). And when Jesus "heard that John had been arrested, he withdrew into Galilee" (Matt. 4:12), a region which is then referred to as "Galilee of the Gentiles" (Matt. 4:15, quoting Isa. 9:1). Despite his denial, Peter's accent betrayed that he had been with "Jesus the Galilean" (Matt. 26:69, 73). This sample raises the questions whether there were significant differences between Galilee and Judea and how one might characterize the culture of the two regions.

Some scholars claim that Galilee was relatively isolated, the people living together in small villages detached from the scattered urbanized communities.[18] The Ptolemies and Seleucids had founded a few cities in Galilee in the Hellenistic period, and later the Herods established two Greek cities: Sepphoris, near Nazareth, and Tiberias, on the Sea of Galilee. Sepphoris was a priestly city, populated by wealthy Jewish landowners who favored the Romans during the Jewish wars; when Josephus captured it on behalf of the rebels, the Galilean villagers took out their rage on this city, which they detested (Josephus, *Life* 375). Tiberias was founded between 17 and 20 C.E. by Herod Antipas, who accepted settlers from everywhere, Jewish and Gentile, rich and poor. The palaces contained representations of animals and thus violated the commandments. On several separate occasions Galilean peasants attacked the city, and eventually they succeeded in burning the palace and massacring the Greek minority (Josephus, *Life* 65–68, 381, 384). Unlike those of Sepphoris, the Jews of Tiberias remained loyal to Jerusalem against the Romans, and two thousand of them fled to Jerusalem for protection before the advance of the Roman general Vespasian (Josephus, *Life* 354). In both cases, however, there are sharp differences of life-style and attitude between the peasants of the Galilean countryside and the wealthy landowners of the cities.

It may appear logical to argue that, since the Jews of Sepphoris were hellenized, their rural Jewish peasant antagonists were not, but the conclusion does not follow. Socially, the peasants may have been hellenized in a different way (e.g., economically but not intellectually) or at a slower rate; either process would have created and maintained social and religious alienation between city and country.

Galilee was not geophysically isolated.[19] Trade routes connect the cities of lower Galilee with the Greek cities of the costal plain. The same valley connects Tiberias and Sepphoris to the Mediterranean. Two valleys connect Tarichaea on the Sea of Galilee to the coast. Chorazin and Capernaum sent and received goods from Akko-Ptolemais via the Wadi Beth ha-Kerem. All these towns, where the Gospels locate Jesus' career, were Greek-speaking and cosmopolitan, located on busy trade routes connected to Roman administrative centers. The same is true of Arav, near Sepphoris, where Johanan ben Zakkai is said to have spent eighteen years; it was not isolated. A case for topographic and cultural isolation can be made only for upper Galilee, and even there trade was carried on with the Phoenician coast, especially with Tyre. There were severe cultural tensions between the cities and the peasants of the countryside, but that social alienation must have been maintained not by geography but by symbols: for example, by the "representations of animals" in houses or by the absence of such "idols." Both kinds of house were built in lower Galilee, where Jesus and Johanan taught.

### *Galileans on Pilgrimage*

"Three times in the year shall all your males appear before the Lord" (Ex. 23:17; 34:23; Deut. 16:16). The rabbis took this as an action to be encouraged, not one to be considered binding for each Passover, Pentecost, and Tabernacles. Rather, such a journey was made once a year (Luke 2:41), once after several years (Acts 20:16), or once a lifetime. Philo mentions making such a pilgrimage only once (*On Providence* 64), though he may have gone more often. Mark

(10:1, 32) narrates only one journey to Jerusalem by Jesus; John (2:13; 5:1; 7:2, 10; 10:22; 12:1) tells of many.

A highly stylized list of places from which pilgrims came is given in Acts 2:5, 9–11 (cf. Philo, *On the Special Laws* 1.69). Acts 6:9 lists synagogues in Jerusalem organized by Jews from different countries. And the famous Greek synagogue inscription of Theodotus mentions a hostel in Jerusalem for needy travelers from foreign lands. Even the Gentiles would go up to feasts in Jerusalem (Josephus, *Antiquities* 3.318; John 12:20; Acts 20:4, 16).

Josephus mentions the roads pilgrims traveled, usually through Samaria, a three-day journey that avoided the valleys and hills of the other routes (*Life* 269; *Jewish War* 2.232; see John 4). They also came by way of the coastal plain or through Peraea east of the Jordan (Mark 10:1, 32).

Rabbinic sources stress the spiritual aspect of the visit, but Josephus emphasizes its social and political role, especially for Galileans, one example of which is the conflict after the death of Herod the Great in 4 B.C.E. (*Antiquities* 17.149–167, 213–218). At the following festival of Pentecost, thousands gathered for the religious observances, formed into three groups, and attacked the Romans (*Antiquities* 17.254). One must be careful when discussing the rebelliousness of the Galileans at the festivals, for in this text Josephus names Galileans, Idumaeans, Transjordanians, and Judeans, stressing that the Judeans were the most eager rebels. The possibility, even the expectation, of such conflicts is often noted (Josephus, *Antiquities* 20.105–112; Mark 13:2; see Luke 13:1). The story of Jesus cleansing the Temple (Mark 11:15–17) and the charge at his trial that he spoke against the Temple (Mark 14:58) might be viewed in this social context.

Various motivations for the pilgrimage to Jerusalem, by both the peasants and aristocrats of Galilee and by Jesus, have been suggested. Some scholars, reading Josephus, suggest that Zealot political ideology is of primary importance. Others, reading the rabbis, see spiritual motivations. Alternatively, it has been suggested that the Galileans' attachment "was based on the belief that the God of the Temple in Jerusalem was the one who provided them with the necessities of life from the land" as promised in the Mosaic covenant,[20] a suggestion which has the virtue of recognizing that the Galileans were more concerned with agricultural production (see Josephus, *Jewish War* 3.42–44) than were the Judeans. The discussion about the motivation of these pilgrims will continue, but the social fact of their importance demonstrates the religious and cultural loyalty of Galilean Jews to the Temple of Jerusalem.

## Judea and Jerusalem: Holy City and Temple

### *Herod's Jerusalem*

Despite the great crowds that followed Jesus in Galilee (e.g., Mark 2:13; 3:7; 4:1; 5:24; 6:34) and proclaimed his entrance into Jerusalem (Mark 11:8), he died forsaken by his disciples and the crowds (Mark 14:70–71; 15:9–14, 21) "outside the gate" of the city (John 19:20; Heb. 13:12). Near its walls, Jesus ate his last supper, was tried by the high priest and by the Roman prefect Pilate, and was crucified. His success in the small towns of Galilee dissolved into failure in urban Jerusalem.

The sources of Jerusalem's attraction were not economic. Brigands infested the roads to the city. There is no natural east-west passage through the mountains; only the north-south route along the watershed is a natural road. The surrounding land is poor for agricultural purposes. The high ridge on which Jerusalem is located acts as a rainmaker, which means that it is also a rain barrier for points east. Only Herod's building activity and the Temple explain the (imported) commerce. The result was that a highland city with little water, poor soil, and dangerous roads had flourishing trade and commerce, all oriented to the sacred Temple.

There are both literary and archaeological sources to help clarify the nature of this ancient holy city (Josephus, *Jewish War* 5.136–247; Tacitus, *Histories* 5.11–12; Aristeas 83–120; and the Mishnah, especially the tractates of Middot and Tamid). In the twentieth century, there have been more than twenty important excavations in the city. "It was built, in portions facing each other, on two hills separated by a central valley (the Tyropoeon), in which the tiers of houses ended" (Josephus, *Jewish War* 5.136, tr. Thackeray in Loeb Classical Library). The Upper City was built on the higher, western ridge; the Lower City contained the Temple on the eastern, crescent-shaped hill (its name, Ophel, means "hump"). The two hills were separate fortresses. Pompey occupied the Upper City in 63 B.C.E. but still had to besiege the Temple. In the Seleucid period, Syrian troops and hellenized Jews settled the Upper City as "Antioch-at-Jerusalem" (2 Macc. 4:9, 19),[21] so the two areas were hostile to each other. Herod strengthened both parts; the fortress of Antonia dominated the Temple in the Lower City, and Herod's palace with its three huge towers dominated the Upper City.

Herod doubled the size of the Temple Mount, cutting away high rock in the northwest and buttressing it with walls and vaults in the southeast. The walls around the mound supporting the temple area enclose 35 acres. The masonry is Herodian. The master course of stones below the southern gates has a height of six feet; the cornerstone of this course measures 23 by 6 feet and weighs over 100 tons.

Coming west over the Mount of Olives, one would descend through the Kidron valley and come up through the Golden Gate in the walls supporting the Temple Mount, perhaps the same as the Beautiful Gate of Acts 3:2, the setting of the story in which Peter heals the lame man. Crossing the Court of Gentiles on the Temple Mount, one would enter the temple area on the east through the Corinthian Gate, so named because its Corinthian bronze exceeded the value of gold and silver (Josephus, *Jewish War* 5.201). Continuing westward, one would cross the Court of Women; passing through the Nicanor Gate, one would come to the Court of Israel and from there proceed to the Court of the High Priests and the high altar before the holy Temple itself. The porch in front was about 165 feet wide, but the Holy of Holies behind it only 115 feet wide. No one passed beyond the double veil into the Holy of Holies, of course, except the high priest, who entered annually on the Day of Atonement.

To the northwest was the fortress Antonia, built by the Hasmonaeans, who had named it Baris; Herod strengthened it and renamed it for Mark Antony. A tribune with his soldiers and centurions ran downstairs to arrest and protect Paul, who addressed the people from its steps (Acts 21:32, 35).

In the northwest corner of the Upper City, Herod built his own palace with two large banqueting halls and quarters for a hundred guests. There were pools with flowing fountains inside the palace gardens. He reinforced the north side of his palace by constructing three huge towers, naming one after his brother Phasael. Philo (*On the Embassy to Gaius* 299) relates that Pilate lived in Herod's palace during the Jewish feasts, and Josephus tells about two prefects who addressed Jewish crowds from the platform of Herod's palace, Pilate in 30 C.E. and Florus in 66 C.E. (*Jewish War* 2.175–176, 301, 308). When Jesus was tried by Pilate, he was sitting on a judgment seat (Matt. 27:19) before chief priests and crowds (Luke 23:4), probably outside. John notes (19:13) that the final verdict was given from the judgment seat at a place called the Pavement and, in Hebrew, Gabbatha ("the raised place"), which may have been Herod's palace, not Antonia.[22] Festus would have heard accusations against Paul in the same palace (Acts 25:1).

Nahman Avigad excavated a street in the Upper City that was built over the remains of a house occupied in Herod's reign. City improvements meant that the family was evicted for Herod's new construction, which John Wilkinson convincingly suggests was a rectangular grid of streets oriented by the palace platform.[23] Jerusalem as rebuilt by Herod was not a chaos of narrow, crooked alleys but a city with a plan like Antioch. The Upper City was the residential quarter of the rich. The houses were Hellenistic, with a central court surrounded by rooms and with underground cisterns and pools. One observer called the result "by far the most famous city and not of Judea only" (Pliny the Elder, *Natural History* 5.14, tr. H. Rackham in Loeb Classical Library).

The Lower City was more popular and oriental, densely populated by the poor. It contained the municipal building and the archives, which were burned early in the war against the Romans by rebels, who succeeded in destroying bills of debt. The houses were built of small stone, crowded together with little garden space, although they too had an inner court protected by a wall. Scholars differ over whether the streets in the Lower City were unplanned or were another rectangular grid formed around the Temple.

The population of Jerusalem caused a water problem, and Herod needed more water for the fountains in his palace. He more than doubled the length of the aqueduct bringing water to the city from the south (from 14 to 42 miles). Again, scholars differ over whether this enabled a doubling of the population of the city from 35,000 to 70,000 or whether the new complex simply doubled the water requirements of the city, so that the population would have remained around 40,000.

### *Sadducees and Priests*

Despite the power and influence of the Sadducees, not a single text of theirs survives. We know them only through the eyes of their religious, social, and political enemies (1 Enoch 91–104; Psalms of Solomon 4; Assumption of Moses 7). Josephus is the main source of information, with some references occurring in the New Testament and in later rabbis.[24] Josephus' earliest statement says they deny Fate, the immortality of the soul, and eternal rewards after death and accept free will (see Matt. 22:23; Acts 23:8); socially, he describes them as behaving like aliens to their peers (*Jewish War* 2.164–166). Describing political tensions between Pharisees and Sadducees under the Maccabee Hyrcanus, Josephus explains that the Pharisees give the people certain regulations not recorded by Moses and that the Sadducees reject these (*Antiquities* 13.297; see 18.16–17). In these controversies, the Sadducees have the support of the wealthy, not the populace, while the Pharisees have the support of the masses (*Antiquities* 13.298). However, one common opinion, that the Sadducees accepted only the five books of Moses as authoritative, rejecting the prophets (an opinion found in Origen, 185?–254 C.E.), is not supported by Josephus and is probably erroneous.

The Sadducees were aristocrats. Some were priests, but not all; many belonged to the lay nobility.[25] Their name is probably derived from Zadok, who held priestly office under Solomon. Although Sadducees and priests are not to be identified, they were closely related, and the priestly aristocracy were the political leaders in Judaism as early as the Persian period. This political and cultural contact with foreign rulers resulted in their Hellenization, as is clear in the books of the Maccabees. Under Hyrcanus, Aristobulus, and Alexander Jannaeus, Sadducees were powerful. The interval of Pharisaic dominance under Alexandria (76–67 B.C.E.) was brief. In the Herodian and Roman periods, some of the high priestly families were Sadducean (Acts 5:17; Josephus, *Antiquities* 20.199). However, when the state was destroyed in 70 C.E., the aristocrats disappeared too.

The priests' power resulted from the fact that they had the exclusive right to sacrifice (Exodus 28 to 29; Leviticus 8 to 10; Numbers 16 to 18). To help clarify the social situation in Palestine during Jesus' time, it is crucial to discuss priestly dues: i.e., taxes.[26] Modern historical criticism has made possible a correct understanding of the growth of the final Priestly strand of the Pentateuch and, with it, the growth of the wealth of the priests themselves. In pre-exilic times, and as late as Deuteronomy, the sacrifices were given to priests only on the occasion of cultic ritual in the Temple; after the animal was burnt on the altar, most of it was eaten by the offerer, some by the priest. But the Priestly Code introduced tithes (Num. 18:20–32) and the firstborn offering (Num. 18:15–18) as taxes, and by the time of Nehemiah these were exacted. The people began to give a tenth of fields and orchards; one isolated text demands a tenth of the cattle (Lev. 27:32–33)—not only of animals sacrificed but of any animals slaughtered. In addition to the earlier Levitical sacrificial practice, the tithe of the Priestly Code was simply added as a "second tithe." Power and taxes shifted from the kings to the priests. The "firstfruits" of the seven kinds of crops listed in Deuteronomy 8:8 were given as taxes to the priests. In addition, the "heave" offering *(terumah)* was given of every other sort of produce from field and tree, the most important being wheat, wine, and oil, in the amount of about one fiftieth of one's annual income. The heaviest of all was the tithe, which the Gospels make clear was calculated scrupulously

(Matt. 23:23; Luke 11:42). Whatever food the ground produced was tithed and given to the Levites, who gave a tithe of what they received to the priests. There was also the half-shekel tax, another post-exilic addition (Ex. 30:11–16), which Jesus paid (Matt. 17:24–27; see Josephus, *Jewish War* 7.218). Finally, the Temple received many voluntary donations, ranging from the gold given by Alexander the Alabarch of Alexandria and brother of Philo for the temple gates to the mites of poor widows (Mark 12:41–44).

Some of the aristocracy, not necessarily Sadducean, were called "elders." They were not educated sages but heads of families, wealthy persons, those who had been public leaders. In addition to the Sadducees, the elders were a second element in the Sanhedrin, though a declining one in this period. References to them are found in Josephus (*Antiquities* 4.218) and in the New Testament (Matt. 27:1, 20, 41; Mark 15:1).

### *Scribes and Pharisees*

The third element in the Sanhedrin were the teachers of the Torah, scribes, a professional bureaucracy (see Ben Sira's book in the Apocrypha). Their knowledge of the Torah gave them influence. Persons from all social classes became educated scribes: for example, the important priest and captain of the Temple R. Hananiah (M. Aboth iii.2); the priest and general Josephus (*Life* 8–9); the tentmaker Paul (Acts 18:3); a day laborer, Hillel; and a merchant, Johanan ben Zakkai.[27] These scribes taught students and advised the Sanhedrin on judicial matters by interpreting the Torah. Many stories are told about the growing esteem in which the people held the scribes. The status and power of the high priest, in contrast, was continually undermined by the Seleucids, Herodians, and Romans when they dismissed and appointed high priests at will. Although their power was diminishing over against the scribes, the priests remained the ruling element in Judea until the war destroyed their political and religious function.

The increasing power of the scribes aided the Pharisees, although the two were not the same kind of group. The scribes were professional scholars of the Torah; the Pharisees were sectarians concerned with strict legality, especially in relation to dietary laws and purity regulations. They were "the most accurate interpreters of the laws" (Josephus, *Jewish War* 2.162). Paul was "as to the law a Pharisee, . . . as to righteousness under the law blameless" (Phil. 3:5–6). "According to the strictest party of our religion I have lived as a Pharisee," Paul claimed (Acts 26:5; cf. 22:3). The name (*perushim* in

Hebrew) means "the separated." Certainly they separated themselves from unclean things, as Leviticus demands, but this also involved separation from unclean persons—women after childbirth, lepers, women and men with bodily discharges (see Leviticus 12 to 14)—and from the dead (Numbers 19). The apostle Peter separated himself from (Christian) Gentiles in Antioch (Gal. 2:12). But this kind of separation was characteristic of all Jews (see Tacitus, *Histories* 5.5: "they sit apart at meals"). The name came from a separation in which other Jews did not participate; their stricter interpretation of purity meant that they separated themselves *from other Jews.* They were separate from the uneducated and from the *am ha-arez,* who did not keep the commandments so strictly (M. Haggadah 2.7), and the commandments involved are especially those prescribing kosher food and purity. The Jewish people in general were observant (Josephus, *Against Apion* 1.42–43; 2.227–228, 232–235, 272–273; Rom. 9:30 to 10:4), although not always according to the oral Torah of the Pharisees. "Of the 341 individual Houses [of Shammai and Hillel]'s legal pericopae, no fewer than 229 . . . approximately 67 per cent of the whole, directly or indirectly concern table-fellowship."[28] Pharisees maintained their identity in Hellenistic urban culture by strict adherence to these core symbols centering around table fellowship.

In Leviticus (7:20–21; 15:31; cf. Num. 19:13, 20) the Israelite is to be pure *while eating a sacrifice in the Temple.* Jacob Neusner stresses that the Pharisees reinterpreted Torah to "lay stress upon universal keeping of the law, so that every Jew is obligated to do what only the elite—the priests—are normally expected to accomplish."[29] They shifted the focus from eating sacrifices in the Temple in Jerusalem to eating everyday meals in lay Jewish houses everywhere. This reinterpretation of the biblical Priestly Code in favor of the priesthood of all Jews enabled Judaism to survive the burning of the Temple, which had been the central institutional symbol before 70 C.E. After the fall of the Temple, the rabbis combined three pre-70 elements: (1) the Pharisees' emphasis on every Jew keeping priestly purity, (2) the scribal stress on the study of Torah and the centrality of the learned scholar, and (3) the conviction that the community, the people of Israel, now stood in place of the Temple.[30]

The traditions of the Pharisees as the rabbis remembered them after the fall of Jerusalem are amazingly ahistorical.

> If we were confined to only the rabbinical traditions about the Pharisees, we could not have reconstructed a single significant public event

> of the period before 70—not the rise, success, and fall of the Maccabees, or the Roman conquest of Palestine, or the rule of Herod, or the reign of the procurators, or the growth of opposition to Rome, or the proliferation of social violence and unrest in the last decades before 66 A.D., or the outbreak of the war with Rome.[31]

But contrary to the later rabbinical traditions about the Pharisees, they had once been more political. They first appear in Josephus' account of the Maccabaean queen Alexandra, who listened to them with "too great deference," so that they eventually became "the real administrators of the state" (Josephus, *Jewish War* 1.111). During this period they executed their opponents, which endangered the aristocratic citizens (*Jewish War* 1.113–114). Earlier, the Pharisees *may* have been the hostile faction opposed to Alexander Jannaeus, who crucified eight hundred of them (*Jewish War* 1.97, 113), but Josephus does not name the opponents. He does name the Pharisees as opponents of Herod the Great, to whom they refused to take an oath of loyalty; he fined them, an amount promptly paid by his brother Pherora's wife.

> In return for her friendliness he (a Pharisee) foretold—for they were believed to have foreknowledge of things through God's appearances to them—that by God's decree Herod's throne would be taken from him. (Josephus, *Antiquities* 17.43; cf. 15.4, 370, and Acts 23:8–9)

Herod killed these Pharisees and many in his court who approved.

The early Pharisees were a political party. Josephus names one Pharisee, Saddok, as a cofounder of the revolutionary party (*Antiquities* 18.4, 9). But the later sources, the New Testament and rabbinic literature, do not refer to them as such a political party. Therefore, sometime after Herod killed many of them and during the time of Hillel, the character of Pharisaism changed from a political force to an alienated sect focused more intently on purity, separation, and table fellowship, although they were still influential in urban circles (Josephus, *Antiquities* 18.15), perhaps including the settlements along the waterfront of the Sea of Galilee such as Tarichaea, Chorazin, and Capernaum (Josephus, *Life* 134–135, 158; *Antiquities* 20.43; Luke 7:36; 11:37). It is exactly over these eating habits and the reinterpretation of the Torah involved that the Pharisees and Jesus came into conflict (Mark 2:15–17; 7:1–23). Further, the former Pharisee Paul was most intense in conflict when rejecting his own earlier custom of separating from the impure at table (1 Cor. 10: 23–33; Gal. 1:13; 2:11–18).

### *Crafts and Trades*

Besides the religious and social groups just characterized, there are professionals active in certain occupations. "A man will not teach his son to be an ass-driver or a camel-driver, or a barber or a sailor, or a herdsman or a shop-keeper" (M. Kiddushin 4.14). A Babylonian list also negates becoming a shepherd, tax collector, or customs collector (T. B. Sanhedrin 25b). As the finds at Beth Shearim make clear, there were also Jewish sculptors by the second century C.E. In contrast to these "base crafts," there were also "required crafts," and many of the early rabbis were employed in such occupations: sandal makers, bakers, perfumers, carpenters, leatherworkers, professional scribes.[32] These skills were often passed from father to son. And at times, whole villages were employed in a particular occupation; for example, Beth-saida has its name from the fishing industry.

Trade was carried on in certain centers, in Jerusalem, Tiberias, and Tarichaea, for example. The names of items of commerce were often transliterated from Greek into Aramaic or Hebrew. There was significant local trade, especially in pilgrimage seasons. And there was some foreign trade. Wine and cattle were exported from Sharon, olive oil from Judea, grain from Galilee.

## Ecology of the Jesus Movement

Jesus formed a renewal movement in this society that was influenced by ecological, political, and cultural factors. "Economic factors were responsible for the most striking phenomenon of the Jesus movement: the social rootlessness of the wandering charismatics."[33] Peter (Mark 10:28) and others (*Didache* 11.3–4) are said to fit this pattern. Parallel responses to economic deprivation are found in the resistance fighters, prophets like Theùdas (Acts 5:36), emigrants, and robbers (Luke 10:30). The causes of these economic dislocations were overpopulation, the concentration of possessions, and competing tax systems.[34] The country was so heavily populated that all the land was cultivated. The pattern of repeated warfare meant that each new conqueror took some land and confiscated more. But the most painful economic pressure came from taxes, which both the Romans and the priests demanded. The priests' claim to this revenue was supported by the final Priestly source in the Mosaic Torah and by the Sadducees and Pharisees (Matt. 23:23; Luke 18:12). A strict interpretation of the relevant commandments was in the self-interest of both groups.

Ecological factors influencing the Jesus movement have to do with the interplay between humans and nature, especially the relationship between cities and rural areas. Jesus traveled through the small, often anonymous towns of Galilee. Citizens of Sepphoris, Tiberias, the coastal plain, and the Decapolis heard none of his sermons. When Jesus did enter the territory of cities in the Decapolis, he remained outside the walls (Mark 5:1; 7:31; 8:27). As we have seen, the parables usually reflect rural images, only once picturing an urban merchant (Matt. 13:45–46).

But two realities modify this popular sketch of the Jesus movement as confined to country areas. It was in tension with another important Jewish renewal movement, the Pharisees, who were an *urban* group. Josephus observes (*Antiquities* 18.15) that Jews living in "cities" practice the Pharisees' way of living. They took the concept of the primacy of law from the polis world with the constitutions of the Hellenistic cities as models,[35] a significant shift of emphasis from an earlier understanding of Torah as "a story *(mythos)* with law *(ēthos)* embedded in it," Haggadah with Halakah embedded in it.[36] They adopted deductive modes of reasoning and interpretation that were found in Hellenistic education, not in the Pentateuch. Hillel's seven rules of interpretation are found earlier in Cicero (*On Invention* 2.40.116). In tension with the Pentateuch, which excluded Ammonites and Moabites from the congregation of God, Pharisees accepted proselytes (Matt. 23:15); as Athens hellenized the world, so Pharisees would admit admirers from other ethnic groups into Israel. The Pharisees' fundamental distinction between *degrees* of impurity allowed urban artisans and shopkeepers to continue their daily tasks, not ritually pure enough to enter the Temple but not so impure that they would pollute their tools.[37] The rural population rarely obeyed these purity laws. Jesus' tension with this sect needs explanation. Can the controversy between Jesus and the Pharisees be explained by rural–urban tensions? Or did the two come into contact in towns around the Sea of Galilee like Capernaum, Chorazin, and Tarichaea? As noted earlier, the last two towns are among the few where contemporary archaeologists have uncovered first-century-C.E. synagogues, buildings that may suggest moderate prosperity and the local influence of Pharisees.

Second, how does one characterize the women wandering around Galilee with Jesus and following him to Jerusalem (Mark 15:40–41; Luke 8:1–3; 24:10)? Joanna, the wife of Chuza, Herod's steward (Luke 8:3) belongs to Lucan redaction (Luke 24:10 adds her to Mark 16:1), so it is problematic to claim a woman from the tetrarch's court in Tiberias as Jesus' disciple. But if the motif that these women financially supported Jesus and his followers is not anachronistic, it follows that they were not simply rural peasants. Women following Jesus was "an unprecedented happening in the history of that time,"[38] and the consequence was that one of them, Mary Magdalene, not Peter, was the first to witness Jesus' resurrection from the dead.[39] Such unconventional social relationships stimulated negative reactions that led to Jesus' death on a cross, but the positive reaction to the new social possibilities requires social explanation. The apocryphal book of Judith, written in Palestine, reflects a social context in which the stories about Jesus' feminine disciples might be possible,[40] but we know neither the language nor the century in which it was written. We do know that Jesus' follower Mary from Magdala is from a town probably to be identified with Tarichaea, and the name indicates that the Hellenistic fishing industry was prominent there (see Josephus, *Jewish War* 635).

The early Palestinian Christian community which produced Q (the sayings source found in Matthew and Luke) understood Jesus as a prophet for the heavenly Sophia, "Wisdom" (Luke 7:33–35; 11:31). Perhaps in Q (Luke 10:22) but certainly in Matthew, Jesus was identified with Sophia herself.[41] Some scholars think the stories about Sophia were modeled on the myth of Isis and could result in social relationships of equality between men and women.[42] But we do not know that Jesus himself connected an understanding of Sophia with his practice of encouraging women followers. Another source might have been the eschatological suspension of the social distinctions between men and women (Mark 12:25), but this may not be early.[43] The sources of Jesus' practice of calling female as well as male followers remains a historical puzzle.

The simple rural ecological context of the Jesus movement has been somewhat overdrawn. It remains true, however, that the Jews living in the towns of Capernaum and Tarichaea were alienated from the Jews in the Greek cities of Sepphoris and Tiberias, and that Jesus could characterize the Temple in Jerusalem as having become a "den of robbers" (Mark 11:17 quoting Jer. 7:11).

Several other prophets in Palestine were also critical of the powers in Jerusalem. Judas the Galilean and Theudas are mentioned in Acts (5:36–37; Matt. 24:4–8). They and the Essenes, who had retreated into the wilderness near the Dead Sea, demanded hatred of outsiders (Manual of Discipline—1QS 1.10), an attitude rejected by Jesus (Matt. 5:43–47). Several incidents make it clear that Jews and Gentiles in Palestine had great difficulty living together. At the beginning of the war against the Romans, Jews were massacred in many city-states (Josephus, *Jewish War* 2.456–458, 477–480, 559–

561); likewise, the Jews of Tiberias killed the Gentiles (Josephus, *Life* 67). The actions of Roman soldiers, often recruited from Hellenistic cities like Samaria, were highly offensive during Passover festivals (Josephus, *Jewish War* 2.224, 229). When Agrippa I, who was favorably disposed toward the Jews, died, the Gentiles of Caesarea placed statues of his daughters on the roofs of local brothels (Josephus, *Antiquities* 19.357). Integration was not working in Palestine in the first century C.E.

The political conflicts just enumerated resulted at least in part from the fact that the cultural identities of both Jews and Greeks in Palestine were threatened. The Hellenization of Judaism, which had occurred in language, economics, politics, and even in the interpretation of the Torah, threatened to continue. And in a cultural situation where a minority group is under heavy pressure from a dominant society, acculturation occurs at different rates; the norms that are relaxed and those that are intensified vary within the minority group. This kind of variation occurred within the Jewish minority, with mutual alienation resulting between Pharisees, Sadducees, Essenes, and Jesus' disciples. The tragic result was that the attempt to preserve Jewish identity by intensifying selected norms led to a loss of identity with the whole group, since various sects intensified different norms.[44] For example, the Pharisees' extreme stress on purity in everyday life with the accompanying social and religious separation from both Romans and Jewish *am ha-arez* was related to this potential loss of self-identity. It was in these cultural circumstances that Jesus' followers, as a Jewish renewal movement, experimented with inclusive community.

However, the popular "Cynic interpretation" of the Jesus movement harmonizes the Gospels under the slogan of "lack of possessions."[45] This picture of wandering charismatics does not appear outside the Gospels—for example, not in Acts, where the apostles, except Peter, remain in Jerusalem. Paul is not a wandering beggar but earns his living. The lack of possessions is a Lucan redactional emphasis (see Luke 6:24–25; 16:19–31; Acts 4:36–37), not a historical description of the Jesus movement in Palestine. Mark 10:28–30 is not concerned with temporary support for wandering prophets; it promises a substitute social family for *located converts* whose families had rejected them. There was no ethic of homelessness freely chosen by wandering charismatics but, rather, a politically and economically caused rootlessness experienced by many in Palestine. Luke 14:26, which includes a "wife" among those left by Jesus' followers, is also Lucan redaction. The exhortation "Do not be anxious" (Matt. 6:25) reveals that the concern of the wandering prophets reflected in Q is similar to that of many: How could one survive? Again, Luke utilizes these stories as a criticism of rich Christians, a criticism whose goal is to reduce social tensions within located congregations (Luke 5:28; 12:33; 14:33; 18:22). These sayings function as advice to Greek churches outside Palestine, not as historical description of the Palestinian Jesus movement, which included wealthy and married persons.

Nevertheless, the Jesus movement was socially located in the rural village culture alienated from Greco-Roman cities. This alienation may be related to Jesus' rejection of some social structures "by envisioning a different future and different human relationships."[46] For example, in Mark 10:15, a saying Bultmann judged authentic, Jesus taught that "whoever does not receive the kingdom of God like a child (slave) shall not enter it." Two texts promise the new convert other brothers, sisters, and mothers, but omit (Roman patriarchal) fathers (Mark 3:31–35; 10:28–30). Matthew 23:9 develops this as a criticism of leadership in the congregation: "Call no man your father on earth."

Jesus' omission of "fathers," his valuation of a child, and his practice of calling women followers differ significantly from the patriarchal structures and values of Greco-Roman cities. However, within a decade or two after the crucifixion of Jesus, the movement had crossed the most fundamental division in Greco-Roman society, the gulf between village and city, between Capernaum and Corinth, and had absorbed urban attitudes toward fathers, children, and women very different from those of the earliest traditions.[47]

# 5
# City Life

The larger towns and the cities of the Roman empire were situated on highways, at river crossings, and at natural harbors. A traveler on the road leading to a city passed farms, orchards, and huts where farm workers lived. The arches of an aqueduct delivered water to the city; tombs stood along the way, including separate buildings for individual families. As the road approached a gate penetrating the city wall, there were shops, shrines, and wells.

## Physical Environment

Outside and inside the gates people crowded closely together: traders, innkeepers, peddlers, beggars, slaves shopping or fetching water. The gate itself was large, broad enough to accommodate draft animals and carts; it was ordinarily opened at sunrise and shut tight at sunset. (One of the large doors that were swung shut in this way usually had a smaller door in it, which could be opened when necessary to allow an individual to enter. The doors of great houses were similarly designed, and Jesus may be alluding to this when he urges his followers to enter by the narrow gate rather than the broad one, Luke 13:24.)

Inside the walls, our traveler might find an informal, haphazard arrangement of streets or, in more modern Greek towns and in Roman colonies, a formal grid of streets crossing at right angles. Often the main thoroughfares were marked off with special paving, although most of the streets and alleys offered plenty of dust to be shaken off angrily (Matt. 10:14; Mark 6:11; Luke 9:5; 10:11; Acts 13:51) or, once inside a house, to be washed off and the feet anointed solicitously (Luke 7:38–46; John 12:3; 13:5–15).

### *Dominant Landmarks*

Some cities, especially in the east, showed off their wealth and importance by building colonnades along the main streets, which offered a covered sidewalk, with protection from sun or rain as well as from passing animals, vehicles, and litters. These main streets generally led from the gate to a public square dominated by large buildings of impressive materials.

In an oriental city, the major monuments were the temple of the guardian deity and the palace of the ruler, which in the empire was usually taken over by the chief Roman administrator. During the reigns of Hellenistic kings and later the Roman emperors, oriental cities like Palmyra and Jerusalem took on some of the characteristics of Greco-Roman cities.

In a Greek city, the central agora functioned as marketplace and civic center: shrines and temples stood all around, colonnades gave shelter to merchants and money changers, the *bouleutērion* ("council house") provided a small roofed space for meetings of the council, the *prytaneion* ("town hall") housed a central sacred hearth, and statues of gods and heroes and statesmen had places of honor. Scattered about the city were the precincts of other temples. Each Greek city also had its *gymnasium,* where the young people went to school and exercised and where adults came to watch and to join in the events, and its theater, where religious festivals were celebrated with musical and dramatic performances.

In a Roman colony, the *forum* usually contained a temple to Jupiter (alluding to his great temple on the Capitoline Hill in Rome), a *curia* where the town council met, a *basilica* where law cases and business deals could be conducted under a sheltering roof, a smaller temple or two, and honorific statues of distinguished citizens and of the emperor and his family. Other temples could be found throughout the city, scattered along the streets or set off in individual precincts. Roman towns typically also had public baths, a modified version of the Greek theater, and often a large amphitheater for gladiatorial games.

### *Public Spaces*

In the hot, dry climate of the eastern Mediterranean, people naturally moved outdoors into public places. They gathered outside and inside the city gates, along the streets with their shops and colonnades, in small squares at wells and fountains, and in specialized market or bazaar areas. They met in the main square for political meetings, audiences with governmental authorities (Acts 18:12), and trials and lawsuits. In eastern cities, the town elders gathered outside the main gate to discuss events and make local decisions. Crowds gathered in public squares and at the entrances to temples; you could find children there (Luke 7:32) and beggars and cripples (Acts 3:2). People went to temple precincts to pray or simply to sit and pass the time. They gathered in public baths and (in cities with a strong Greek tradition) in gymnasia. On festival days they came together in theater, amphitheater, and circus. Urgent public meetings, like the one at Ephesus (Acts 19:29–41), might also be held in the theater.

### *Houses*

Lining the streets of every town were the walls of private houses. In the east, these were usually of adobe brick and turned a plain facade to the street, penetrated only by a door and perhaps by a few narrow windows, more often than not on an upper story. The houses looked inward, to a small garden at the back or to a central courtyard. The wall facing the street might be plastered and whitewashed, which gave Paul a handy epithet to hurl at the high priest (Acts 23:3). In Palestine and Syria, the houses tended to be single-storied, although crowded cities like Aradus and Tyre (Pomponius Mela 2.7.6; Strabo, *Geography* 16.2.13, 23) had tall buildings of several stories that were worth comment. Roofs were flat, which provided additional space for living, sleeping, or praying (Acts 10:9).

The wealthy residents of Greek cities lived in large houses dominated by a central courtyard; they entertained in dining rooms paved with mosaics, combining the coolness of tile with the color and intricate designs of carpet. Normally rainwater was collected in cisterns, or servants were sent out to public fountains to fetch it. Where water was available from a public aqueduct and the householder had enough influence and money to arrange a connection to it, one wall of the columned courtyard might well be filled by a display of flowing water. Some of these houses were quite large and could accommodate considerable groups of people—such as the house of Philemon at Colossae, where Christians and other guests could gather (Philemon 2, 22), and that of Gaius at Corinth, which could hold "the whole assembly" of Christians (Rom. 16:23). In more crowded cities, houses had several units and several stories, like the large upper-class residential complexes that have been excavated at Ephesus[1] or the house at Troas where Paul was preaching when a boy fell out the third-story window (Acts 20:9).

In the old cities of Italy, the traditional upper-class form of house was dominated by a central room known as an *atrium,* a semipublic reception room in which the busts of distinguished ancestors were displayed. Usually the atrium was roofed, with a rectangular hole in the middle to allow light to enter and rainwater to fall into a shallow pool in the center of the floor. The door, guarded by an attendant, was open to the street, and private living quarters were arranged around an open courtyard in the back. By the time of the Principate, however, fewer wealthy families were living in such traditional houses; instead they lived in roomy villas on the outskirts of town or else in suites on the lower floors of apartment houses. Sitting and dining rooms, often with high ceilings and mosaic floors, opened directly onto an inner courtyard that served as a light well; sleeping rooms and slaves' quarters opened off corridors.

The less affluent lived in similar but smaller apartments, usually higher up in the same buildings. In typical apartments at Ostia, the port of Rome, a main room received light through windows overlooking the street or a central courtyard. Beside it was at least one sitting room; behind it, away from the light, were several sleeping rooms. Often such apartments were occupied by several people, who shared the main room and kept individual sitting or sleeping rooms for their private use. Other poor people lived in tiny rooms on the very top floors of tenement buildings, or in single-roomed *tabernae,* or in small lofts above their workshops.[2]

## Class and Status

In terms of power, influence, money, and the perceptions of the time, we can divide the population of the Roman world into two main categories, those with influence and those without it, the "honorable" and the "humble," those who governed and those who were governed, those who had property and those who did not. The upper category was very small, the lower one very large.

### *Upper Classes*

At the peak of the socioeconomic pyramid was the single figure of the emperor, supported by the other members of the imperial household and by the officials of the central administration in Rome. Just below was the senatorial order, which during the Republican period consisted of former magistrates, representing the most distinguished families of the Roman city-state. Under the Principate, the composition changed; although some emperors tried to encourage the traditional aristocracy, others tried to root it out, and nearly all of them appointed favorite individuals to the Senate as a means of reward and as a way of making the Senate more compliant. By the end of the first century C.E., individual senators were descended from families in Gaul and Spain and North Africa and took their responsibilities very seriously: They commanded the armies, administered some of the provinces, contributed to social and cultural projects, and fulfilled ceremonial priesthoods. There were about six hundred of them, and they were by definition fabulously wealthy; each had to own at least 100 million sesterces' worth of property.

A larger group was known as *equites* ("equestrians" or "knights"). According to traditional Roman custom, these were the wealthy landowners who could afford to ride to battle on horseback. By the end of the Republic they were the richer Roman citizens who had not entered the public world of politics and the army. Under the Principate, the order of the knights became an intermediate elite, with certain status symbols and with responsibility for certain duties in the government of city and empire.

On a lower level, the local aristocracies in the provinces and cities had acquired wealth and influence through inheritance, business, or appointment. They exercised political authority by serving as decurions—members of the local council—in cities and towns throughout the empire. They were the landowners, the manufacturers, the merchants and traders. Their civic duties included collecting taxes, supervising harbors and markets, and undertaking embassies to governors and kings (Plutarch, *Old Men in Public Affairs* 794a).

The women of the upper classes—mothers, wives, and daughters—were expected, both in Greek and in Roman tradition, to be modest and unobtrusive and to lead uneventful and unexciting lives.[3] Their marriages were often arranged to suit the political convenience of their families, they were often married quite young (twelve was a normal age), and they remained under the authority of their fathers even after marriage, unless they had been specifically married in a rare old Roman ritual. Nevertheless, many fine stories were told of strong Roman women operating behind the scenes, influencing their menfolk to take some public action: The message of Pilate's wife to her husband (Matt. 27:19) fits into a pattern of anecdotes about aristocratic Roman women, who were often more successful than she. Upper-class Roman women were frequently reminded of exemplary models of feminine behavior who remained steadfastly faithful to their husbands, even after they had been widowed—an ideal was the *univira,* the woman who had been married to only one husband. In conflict with this ideal, however, was the legislation of Augustus, part of a program to encourage upper-class fecundity and discourage celibacy, which required every woman between the age of twenty and fifty to be married, under pain of losing most of her rights of inheritance and many other privileges. (This law was later rescinded by the Christian emperor Constantine, because it also conflicted with the virtue of celibacy.) Roman women were ordinarily prohibited from inheriting more than 10 percent of their husbands' estates, although some of them were able to become rich through inheritances from their fathers.

The members of these upper classes were relatively few, but they were conspicuous because they controlled the wealth and political power of the empire. We meet them occasionally in the pages of the New Testament: Roman governors like Pontius Pilate, the procurator of Judea; Sergius Paulus, the proconsul of Cyprus (Acts 13: 7–12); Annaeus Gallio, the proconsul of Achaia (Acts 18:12–17); or members of local aristocracies like Dionysius in Athens (Acts 17:34) and Erastus in Corinth (Rom. 16:23), both of whom are represented as Christian converts.

### *Lower Classes*

Below this aristocracy, the great mass of the population lived its lives. A large intermediate level consisted of the small landowners, craftsmen, and shopkeepers and also the middle and lower ranks of Roman citizens in the army, from centurions down to ordinary legionary soldiers and veterans. These were people of some moderate substance, and most of the Christians who are named in the pages of the New Testament seem to belong to this group: the tentmakers Aquila and Prisca, for instance, or Lydia, the dealer in luxury textiles (see chapter 3). Celsus in his anti-Christian polemic could still in the third century C.E. sneer that Christians' rites were performed in the shops of shoemakers and fullers.

Below these merchants and craftsmen were the really poor, who had no property and supported themselves by piecework at the docks, in construction, or on farms. If they were Roman citizens in Rome they could claim their portion of the monthly grain dole, and there were special provisions made to feed the poor in some other cities (Strabo, *Geography* 14.2.5). One strategy by which a poor man could survive was by attaching himself as a client to a more powerful patron. Another was to steal or beg. Among the beggars were the sick, the blind, the lame, and the lepers, who play so important a part in the Gospel accounts of Jesus' ministry.

Under some circumstances foreigners were also thrust to the edges of society, the victims of prejudices that tended to be more cultural than racial. Many Romans, for instance, considered Greeks effete, glib, and unreliable. Easterners in turn found the Romans brutal, dull, and haughty. Greeks and Romans alike were suspicious of the peculiar customs of the Jews, and occasional hostility could break out in violence as we have seen, often politically motivated. For the most part, however, the cities of the Roman empire accommodated people of different races, cultures, and classes with little overt trouble.

The lowest legal status of all was the slave's. Greek philosophers considered him something less than human. Roman law regarded him as a piece of property, and the thousands of slaves who worked as chattel gangs on ships, farms, road construction, or mining were treated as nothing but a commodity. On the other hand, the obvious fact that many slaves were intelligent, resourceful, clever human beings made somewhat ambivalent the position of those who were entrusted with the supervision of a farm or an urban workshop, with entertaining the family or educating its children. They had certain legal rights to make contracts, and some of them had their own money to administer and spend. Some of them were given considerable responsibility and independence; one example is Onesimus, who apparently was traveling on some assignment of his master's when he decided to run away (Philemon). In trying to understand the psychology of a slave, we should probably distinguish between the slave born in captivity, usually within a family in which slaves participated to some extent in the social life, and the freeborn person who was captured and reduced to slavery, uprooted from home and family by war, pirates, or slave hunters, and cut off from everything that ordinarily provides support structures to a human being.[4]

### *Social Mobility*

The upper classes enjoyed great privileges, and they guarded them vigilantly. They could not be sued by their social inferiors, they received more lenient penalties if convicted of crime, they could claim the front seats at shows, they had the right to wear and display certain symbols of their status, and when the state distributed money or food or wine they were entitled to a bigger portion than the poor who needed it more. "To him who has will more be given, and he will have abundance" (Matt. 13:12; Mark 4:25; Luke 8:18) was an ineluctable principle of ancient Roman society. The "honorable ones" regarded the "humble" with disdain and without apology across the great gulf fixed between them (Luke 16:19–31). Classical literature is filled with upper-class sneers, unrelieved by any sense of compassion, at the disgusting laziness and squalor and servility of the poor. Legal barriers emphasized the gulf between the orders. These were informal but real: Members of the senatorial aristocracy were forbidden to marry former slaves, separate courts tried the upper classes and the lower classes, and separate punishments were decreed. Peter Garnsey argues that these distinctions originated in administrative prejudice and convenience rather than in theory,[5] but that did not make the barriers any less real in the perceptions of both upper and lower classes. Even at meals, whether private dinner parties to which a rich patron invited some of his clients or public banquets given by an aristocrat for his fellow citizens, your place and even what you got to eat depended strictly on your status; the invitation to "come up higher" would never be extended to one of inappropriate status, although some Roman authors thought that everyone at a dinner should eat the same food and be accessible to each other. According to Gerd Theissen, the dispute at Corinth with which Paul is concerned (1 Cor. 11:17–34) may well reflect this situation: The host at a Christian *agapē* feast is acting like a patron at an ordinary banquet, making distinctions between the guests with higher status and those with lower status.[6]

Social standing and privileges were carefully guarded, but the barriers between classes were not completely impermeable. Opportunities for social upward mobility existed, and we know of many who found a way to a higher station; many of them left proud accounts of their careers on inscriptions. In nearly every case the step upward owed something to the talent and aggressiveness of the beneficiary, but also in nearly every case it owed a great deal to connections, to the favorable sponsorship of someone in authority. The emperor, for instance, promoted prosperous or promising provincials to the equestrian order or even made them members of the Roman Senate. In the municipalities, certain members of the community could rise to the local aristocracy. In Italian towns like Pompeii in the first century C.E. the citizens elected their own magistrates. Outside Italy, and later within it, promotion to the local aristocracy usually came by appointment. On the recommendation of an influential acquaintance, the emperor or his governor would enroll the candidate in the local council, or else (as in the case of the farmer of Mactaris in chapter 3) he was elected by the members of the local council in recognition of his achievements and his donations for the good of the city.

Another way in which the system worked to elevate an individual was in the acquisition of Roman citizenship. This could be granted by the Senate, by certain generals, or by emperors, to individuals or to whole communities. A non-Roman could also acquire citizenship by serving in the army; after his years of service in the auxiliary legions, the soldier was given citizenship upon discharge, which his children could also claim. The pride that citizenship called forth, and the status it conveyed, is well shown in the dialogue between Paul and the tribune (Acts 22:26–29).

The most common and also the most dramatic rise in status came about in the manumission of slaves. Roman citizens set their slaves free in remarkably large numbers, and each manumitted slave became not only a *libertus* or *liberta* ("freedman" or "freedwoman") but also a Roman citizen. The freedman was bound to his former master (who now became his patron) by certain legal obligations, and even the most successful freedman carried with him a certain stigma of his servile origin: His name proclaimed his status as a freedman; he could not hold public office or rise to the status of an equestrian; he could not marry a member of the senatorial aristocracy. On the other hand, any children born after manumission enjoyed complete social freedom and could even rise into the aristocracy. The sorts and conditions of freed slaves were as varied as those of the rest of the population. Some barely managed to get along and were as dependent as ever on their former masters. Others earned a comfortable living by working hard at a craft or trade, either under their patron's sponsorship or with a good deal of independence. Through inheritance, luck, or acumen, others managed to become very rich.

Such rises in status could often be abrupt, and they were often isolated from other marks of status. A freedman, even a freedman of the emperor, remained a freedman, with all the liabilities of that condition, and he was vulnerable to the sneers and jibes of his social betters. So the freedman Trimalchio (see chapter 3) is depicted as hopelessly boorish and incapable of any but the most vulgar and maudlin sentiments. In the same way, a woman who had gained wealth through inheritance or investment was in a position of influence and power, even though society expected women to have a subordinate position. Many of the women mentioned in the Pauline books of the New Testament seem to be in this position: the mother of Mark (Acts 12:12), Lydia (Acts 16:14, 40), Prisca (Acts 18:2–3;

Rom. 16:3–4; 1 Cor. 16:19), Phoebe (Rom. 16:1–2), the mother of Rufus (Rom. 16:13), and Chloe (1 Cor. 1:11).[7]

There were thus many different categories of upward social mobility. For all of them, however, the system rewarded faithful service and devotion to the ideals of the society.

Not all cases of social mobility are success stories, of course. Senators or equestrians could fall from favor and be removed from their order by the emperor, wielding his power as supervisor of the census. (A Christian senator, for instance, who declined to burn incense to the emperor's image in the course of normal duties might well fall from favor.) Rich men and women could always lose their fortunes—shipwrecks or prolonged droughts or bad investments might ruin a family financially—and this would involve demotion to a lower census category. (Emperors were known to help favorites in such difficulties by giving them the money needed to maintain their status.) Criminal convictions involved loss of property and, sometimes, citizenship. A free woman who cohabited with a slave could become a slave of his owner; we hear of some women doing this willingly—marrying a prominent slave of the emperor's, for instance, or becoming a prostitute. Free men and women, usually not Roman citizens, could become enslaved through conviction in a criminal proceeding, through capture by slave dealers or in war, or through selling themselves into slavery, presumably to avoid the even harsher fate of total poverty.

## Work

### *Upper-class Attitudes*

The aristocracies of the Greco-Roman cities despised manual labor; indeed, any labor that was subject to the orders of another person. This was one more way in which the upper classes emphasized and reinforced the distinction between themselves and the rest of society. The need to work, our literary (and thus upper-class) sources tell us over and over, prevents a person from living a fully satisfying life of leisure. Plato said, for instance (*Republic* 6.495d–e), that the minds of manual workers are stunted by their work, mentally as well as physically, and Aristotle said (*Politics* 3.1278a) that the man who must work for his livelihood will not have the time or disposition to attain to virtue; he will never be self-sufficient, because he must depend on the patronage of others to buy the goods or services he offers. Among the Romans, Cato considered retail trade an unworthy occupation for a gentleman because of its meanness (*On Agriculture*, preface), and Cicero (*On Duty* 1.150) clearly distinguished between the "liberal" pursuits of a gentleman and the mundane cares of earning a living by manual labor.

This is not to say, of course, that the upper classes were inactive. They could enjoy leisure on their inherited estates but they also had their proper work, in politics, law, and war. Cicero himself led a frenetic life of political activity in the first century B.C.E., later serving as an elder statesman, defending friends, prosecuting enemies, serving a term as governor of the province of Cilicia in Asia Minor, advising political allies, and also withdrawing to one or another of his country villas to think, to read and write, and to entertain in an atmosphere of cultured leisure. At the end of the first century C.E., Pliny the Younger in his *Letters* gives us another example of a conscientious member of the aristocracy devoted to his duties of public service (chapter 3). The upper classes took great pride in this service, and on their tombstones they listed the offices held, commissions undertaken, public buildings erected, and public games sponsored.

### *Small Businesses*

Every main street in an ancient city was lined with shops, some run by slaves or freed for a rich entrepreneur but many run by people who had achieved some modest success through good sense and skill and who themselves, with perhaps a few slaves and some hired help, operated a small business or two. These were the bakers, butchers, greengrocers, barbers, fullers, cobblers, auctioneers, moneylenders, and innkeepers. They trained their sons and daughters to follow them and were much less reticent about their trades than their social superiors may have thought they should be. In the eyes of the upper classes they were common and servile, but they took pride in their successes and accomplishments. As in modern America where people tend to ask new acquaintances "What do you do?" so, in the ancient world, small entrepreneurs tended to identify themselves by their occupations. On their tombstones they boasted of their professions and even their business addresses. The New Testament reflects this in its tendency to identify characters as "the carpenter's son" (Matt. 13:55), or "Jesus the carpenter" (Mark 6:3), "Matthew the tax collector" (Matt. 10:3), "Simon, a tanner" (Acts 9:43), "Cornelius, a centurion" (Acts 10:1), "Lydia, a seller of purple" (Acts 16:14).

Members of this class contributed to the community where they lived. The more successful ones even managed to join the local aristocracies: the freeborn as magistrates and decurions, the freedmen as ministers of the imperial cult.

### *Working Conditions*

The small independent merchant, the freed person or slave working on behalf of a wealthy patron or master, the apprentice under contract to an artisan—all worked long hours in small shops. In general the workshops were single rooms where work was done, supplies stored, wares displayed and sold; often the shopkeeper and the family (including slaves and apprentices) slept and ate there as well, in the back or on an elevated mezzanine. Bits of scattered evidence seem to imply that tradespeople gathered together in the same neighborhood; there are references to the Street of the Harnessmakers, for instance, or the Fishmongers' Forum.[8] This concentration allowed the shopkeepers to take advantage of common sources of supply and suggests that the atmosphere was one of amiable sociability rather than cutthroat competition, with much visiting back and forth during the long working day. The day lasted from sunrise to sunset, if we can extrapolate from the apprentice contracts preserved on Egyptian papyri; there were many opportunities for conversation. Several stories about Socrates in Athens take place in the cobbler's shop of Simon the shoemaker, where people gathered to discuss philosophy and politics. We can also imagine that in the leather shop of Prisca and Aquila in Corinth, Paul found occasional work and used the time to discuss the Christian gospel.[9] Work often claimed much of the time of Jewish teachers, who like Paul may well have conducted lessons on the job and also met with their disciples at night, on the Sabbath, and at festivals.

## Play

### *Leisure Time*

To the neighbors of urban Jews, it seemed a foolish and wasteful habit to maintain one day of enforced leisure out of every seven. But even though they did not observe a regular weekly Sabbath, the pagan residents of the cities managed to find some time off from work. The young and wealthy could afford to spend long hours exercising in the gymnasia of Greek cities, and the public bath was a characteristic feature of most Roman cities. After a long morning of work, many Romans could take the time to exercise, socialize, and wash in the baths, which in the summer offered a welcome refuge from midday heat and in winter offered sociable warmth. All through the day there were opportunities to stop and talk, to indulge the Mediterranean need to move out into the streets and visit with other human beings, to see and be seen. You could lean out an exterior or courtyard window and gossip with neighbors, or chat with customers or the shopkeeper next door, or recline for a proper business lunch with colleagues at a restaurant, or sit on a tavern stool to drink wine and chat with friends, or strike a pose in the public square to watch the passing crowd. Dinnertime came several hours before sunset and was an occasion to visit and entertain. Ancient literature tells us about a number of dinner parties that went on long into the night, but most people tended to go home early—the streets in most towns were not safe, and nocturnal pedestrians risked being mugged by robbers or beaten up by the police patrols.[10]

### *Holidays*

On special occasions, celebrations offered relief from the normal routine. Dignitaries might celebrate their assumption of a new magistracy or the dedication of a new public building by inviting all their fellow citizens to a banquet. Aristocratic families might observe the coming-of-age of a son, or the marriage of a son or daughter, by inviting the whole city to a banquet or by making presents of money to all the residents. (This custom sometimes got out of hand; as governor of Bithynia, Pliny the Younger was moved to ask the emperor whether he ought to curtail the practice in some way; *Letters* 10.116.) This kind of special feast day might well have been more welcome to the poor unemployed folk in the streets and lands of the city than to the prosperous farmers and merchants with business to attend to (Matt. 22:2–14; Luke 14:16–24).

Religious festivals gave additional opportunities to vary the pattern of daily life. On the day of a god's annual festival, the people decorated the temple, threw open the doors, made sacrifices, and held processions. Enterprising workers pitched tents and booths, sold food and souvenirs, sang, and told fortunes. In rural villages and smaller towns, the annual festival of the local god often had the look and feel of a country fair, with eating, singing, and dancing that could go on through the night.

In some of the Greek cities, the so-called sacred games were major attractions and industries. The prize in such games, as Paul points out (1 Cor. 9:25), was a simple and perishable crown of greenery, but even so, the prize in a sacred game brought great prestige, and when the victor returned to his hometown he received a hero's welcome. Sacred games brought great prestige to the few cities that were entitled to conduct them, but other cities held their own events. Some of these were simple, fairly relaxed events of purely local interest, with competitions for hometown boys and girls. Elsewhere, larger prizes attracted competitors from longer distances, and the ancient sources (mostly inscriptions recording success stories) give the impression of a kind of specialized tour, in which the same ostensibly amateur competitors would turn up over and over at the various festivals. These would have been mostly upper-class youths, whose families could afford to support their careers.

The local religious festivals of Italy were similar to those of Greece, but by the time of the late Republic and Principate, the Romans had developed a distinctive pattern of games in honor of the gods. They began with several days of theatrical shows, sometimes revivals of Greek or Latin classics, sometimes more modern pantomimes or farces, often crudely suggestive in their plots and staging. Sexuality was a widespread theme in plays and dances, in statues, in rumors of excesses in the emperor's palace; and the disapproval of a Paul is matched by that of pagan moralists like Seneca (e.g., *Moral Epistles* 14.1–2; 95.24; *On the Shortness of Life* 12.8; 16.4–5).

One or more days of chariot races followed. At their grandest, in the Circus Maximus at Rome, for example, hundreds of thousands of spectators watched in rapt anticipation for the starting signal, then broke into roars of approval or dismay at the way the race progressed. The excitement was heightened by the fans' rooting for their favorite team or charioteer, by money bet on the outcome, and by the possibility of a crack-up and the danger to horses and men.

Gladiatorial shows were held at irregular intervals. They were never as popular as chariot races, but during the Principate they attracted immense crowds. Even the Greek cities of the East built new amphitheaters or rebuilt old theaters to accommodate them. Skilled gladiators were almost always professionals, as popular as rock stars are today. They were trained to specialize in one of several forms of fighting, and the crowd got its thrills by appreciating the various skills of the gladiators as they hunted wild beasts imported from the corners of the empire, or (at the climax of the days' events) as they fought in equally matched pairs, usually with different weapons. The blood, the smells, the threat of death added a unique excitement, and the sponsors of the games—usually the emperor himself, in Rome, and the most important magistrates in the other cities—were unstinting in their efforts to obtain talented, aggressive fighters for the spectators' enjoyment.[11] One or more executions might be included on the day's program; when this was a straightforward matter of giving a gladiator or soldier a weapon with which to despatch the unarmed criminal, there was not much entertainment value for the crowd, and such executions were scheduled at midday, during the lunch break. More imaginative executions were also staged, however: The convicted criminal might be thrown unarmed into the arena with one or more hungry wild beasts or might be dressed up as some mythological character for a hideously realistic performance of his gruesome death. In reaction, we hear that there were limits to how bloodthirsty some crowds were. Cicero for example remarks (*Letters to His Friends* 7.1) that the crowd was moved to sympathetic indignation when Pompey butchered 600 elephants at the dedication of his new theater in 55 B.C.E.

## Education

### *The Gymnasium*

The most distinctive institution of Greek cities in the Hellenistic-Roman period was the gymnasium. (When for instance the books of Maccabees make the point that the Hellenizers in Jerusalem had gone to the extreme in adopting Greek customs, they say that they built a gymnasium, 1 Macc. 1:14; 2 Macc. 4:9, 12.) This was a public institution, maintained by the city. The building usually consisted of an open courtyard *(palaestra)* surrounded by a colonnade; along one side were rooms for bathing and meeting. The meeting rooms were suited to classes; boys and girls together came for instruction at the hands of a *grammatistēs* (a specialist in reading and writing). In some cities the parents had to pay the teachers; in others they were paid at public expense through special endowments. Instruction relied heavily on the copying and memorizing of certain anthology selections, which eventually became more or less standardized, forming a basic core curriculum concentrating on the epics of Homer, the tragedies of Euripides, the comedies of Menander, and the speeches of Demosthenes but including other passages from classic and more contemporary (Hellenistic) authors as well. One result was that in all Greek cities the content of education was similar. All educated people had not only read the same standard passages, they had copied them, recited them, memorized them, and shared a common sense of culture. They all knew the more familiar mythological tales, and they all recognized standard quotations when they heard them in the theater, in speeches, in philosophical discourses, and in letters. It seems likely that his audiences would have recognized the passage to which Paul alludes from Menander (1 Cor. 15:33), and possibly those from Epimenides (Titus 1:12) and Aratus (Acts 17:28) as well.[12]

### *Rhetoric and Philosophy*

More advanced training took various forms, but typically a young man who wanted to participate in public life would attach himself to a *sophistēs* (a teacher of rhetoric). Rhetorical technique was the chief content of higher education, and it permeated every area of public life. The rhetoricians taught the parts of a well-constructed speech and with the help of standard textbooks produced models of speeches, as well as commonplace passages (which could be inserted into any speech as needed) and lists of possible ways to say anything about any topic. The most characteristic form of instruction was the public lecture, which made available to the general population a sense of the standards by which to judge an oratorical performance.

Rhetoric was so pervasive in the educational and cultural environment of the first and second centuries that even the philosophers, who were the sophists' competitors and critics, were unable to resist its allure. The four most important philosophical persuasions—the Platonists, the Peripatetics, the Stoics, and the Epicureans—were based in Athens, which was the intellectual capital of the Greeks long after it had lost its political power and was the appropriate location at which the Christian gospel could confront the old pagan wisdom (Acts 17:15–34).

There are indications in the New Testament that Paul and other early Christian leaders were being judged on their rhetorical abilities and that some of their audiences were comparing them as if they were engaged in an oratorical competition: Paul's response was to label such rhetorical pretensions as foolishness, but to do it with a ringing sarcasm to show that he too knew how to play the game of rhetorical vituperation (2 Corinthians 10 to 13). It is difficult for us to know the exact level of rhetorical training and sophistication among the Christian communities to which Paul's letters were addressed, but the allusions to rhetorical and philosophical commonplaces that are scattered throughout remind us that the average resident of a Greek city had a basic acquaintance with the classics, with tales of mythology, and with rhetorical principles, reinforced by the plays and mimes and recitations of bards at festivals, and by the lectures and discussions of rhetoricians and philosophers in marketplaces, gymnasia, and street corners.

### *The Jewish Pattern*

We have very little information about the education that was conducted in the synagogues of the Jewish Diaspora. There is no indication that Hebrew was taught, since the scriptures were translated into Greek, and Jewish inscriptions of the Diaspora tend to be written in Greek or Latin. On the other hand, children and proselytes did clearly receive scriptural instruction; the writings of the New Testament, addressed to Christian groups in Greco-Roman cities that included Jews, clearly presuppose a knowledge of the Jewish texts.

## Family and Household

Greco-Roman political writers understood the household to be the basic building block of the state. Cities, they observed, are composed of households; the state constitution, then, must regulate relationships in these smaller units (Aristotle, *Politics* 1; Dionysius of Halicarnassus, *Roman Antiquities* 2.24–27).

Some political philosophers, who might also be called sociologists, gave the discussion of the household a specific form; Aristotelians and Neo-Pythagoreans were concerned about the relationships of authority and subordination between three pairs: husbands and wives, fathers and children (mothers often are not mentioned), and masters and slaves.[13]

The households structured according to this form were upperclass. Legal marriages were possible only for citizens, a small minority. Children born to slaves were illegitimate according to civil law. Furthermore, most lower-class households did not include slaves, even though approximately one third of the population of Roman Italy and of an Asian city like Pergamum were slaves.[14]

### *Husbands and Wives*

The growing economic power of some women in these centuries brought greater legal and domestic independence, changes that produced tensions in Greco-Roman cities and households. Juvenal resented and satirized these developments (*Satires* 6). Plutarch's *Advice to Bride and Groom* is more moderate, but he clearly insists that the husband rule and the wife be subordinate (142d–e).

Unlike Cleopatra, wives were to worship Roman gods and goddesses, not those of Egypt or the East. Romans feared sedition when their wives followed the barbarian Dionysus, Queen Isis, the lawgiver Moses, or Jesus. These foreign religions experienced persecution by the Roman state partially because Romans feared a restructuring of the Roman patriarchal household.[15]

### *Fathers, Mothers, and Children*

Roman fathers had extraordinary power over their children, and texts often are concerned with them, not with mothers. They were so severe that "Greeks regarded the Romans as cruel and harsh" (Dionysius of Halicarnassus, *Roman Antiquities* 2.27.1). A Roman master could only sell a slave once, but if a Roman father sold his child and then the child attained freedom, the father could sell him or her again. The appellation "father" had very different cultural meanings in these centuries for Roman, Greek, and Jew.[16]

### *Masters and Slaves*

There were more slaves in the Roman empire than in any previous society. Although there had been slave rebellions in the first two centuries B.C.E., there were none in the first century C.E. Surprisingly to a modern person, there were not many political tensions between masters and slaves in the century of Jesus and Paul. There were debates about how slaves should be treated (Seneca, *Moral Epistles* 47) but hardly any about slavery as such. Jews and Christians initiated ethical exhortation addressed *directly* to slaves, instead of reflecting about them in the third person, as had been the practice.[17] Normally, household slaves were considered a part of the extended family and had a share in its religious practices. Romans were offended when their slaves converted to Judaism or Christianity and refused the traditional rites.[18]

## Clubs

### *Types and Purposes: Membership*

In the Greek and Roman cities of the Principate, in addition to the natural group of the extended family, people organized themselves into many forms of voluntary associations for social purposes —a sacrifice to a god, an occasional meal, a drinking party, an exchange of different political views or a confirmation of shared ones.

In the Greek tradition, groups of *orgeōnes, thiasōtai,* and *eranistai* are known. In Roman cities, groups were often referred to as *collegia.* The potential of even the most social group to take on a political coloring led the authorities to limit such organizations to three main types of organizations under the Principate.[19]

First, the professional collegia were composed of businessmen of a common trade, such as the shippers, porters, warehousemen, bakers, merchants of livestock, carpenters, and the like. These clubs had considerable money and influence, although they seldom exerted any political or economic pressure. The imperial authorities expected them to provide the necessary economic services to their city, and this they were apparently happy to do. Inscriptions from such collegia show us the honors with which they rewarded generous members of the organizations, the grateful resolutions passed in honor of the reigning emperor, and the admission of new members, by election of the group as a whole on the recommendation of an admissions committee. Each group set its own limits on size and qualifications for membership and chose a god to preside over its meetings and receive sacrifices at its banquets.

Clubs of the second category, *collegia sodalicia,* were devoted to the worship of specific gods. Often such groups were made up of foreigners and were devoted to a god from their home territory. The Jewish synagogues in each city probably appeared barely distinguishable from other collegia of this category. Other groups with some natural social affinity, like fullers or wool workers or veterans, who had no public charge like the collegia of the first category, often organized themselves as collegia sodalicia; by adopting some patron divinity they took advantage of a loophole in the law and presented themselves as a club whose primary purpose was religious, even though the social pleasures of the monthly meeting were probably more important to most members.

The third category, the *collegia tenuiorum,* consisted of clubs composed of the poor. The law specifically permitted them to form societies in order to provide themselves a decent burial. Members paid an initiation fee and a small monthly membership fee. (Individuals who were too poor to be able to afford even that were simply carted to a common paupers' grave and dumped into it without any proper ceremony.) Each member could then count on a proper funeral, with the surviving members present to provide an appropriate procession outside the walls to a simple grave among tombs owned by the organization. The collegia tenuiorum not only provided their members with peace of mind about their eventual burial arrangements, their main impact was in the regular meetings, which provided significant social contact. Documents of such clubs show that alongside the freeborn members were freedmen and slaves and that the monthly dinner was a time of high-spirited fellowship, which needed to be regulated by certain rules.

### *Organization, Finances, Meeting Places*

The organization of a collegium, which was recorded in a charter, tended to reflect the civic organization of towns and cities. The membership body was frequently divided into smaller groups with names reflecting a military or political model: *centuriae, cohortes, decuriae.* In larger groups we find references to some sort of executive board, called *ordo decurionum* or *gerousia,* reflecting the local aristocratic council of Roman and Greek cities respectively. The chief officer was called *magister* or (in Greek contexts) *archōn.* Other officials included treasurers, secretaries, legal officers, priests, and stewards.

Many groups also had one or more wealthy members who fulfilled the role of patrons: They were especially important in the collegia tenuiorum, in which the contributions of a sponsor would be crucial to the well-being of the group. Income to the club's treasury included the contributions of members, proceeds from fines levied on members who disobeyed the rules, gifts of patrons and benefactors, and return on the group's investments. The group spent its resources on the purchase and maintenance of a meeting place, regular banquets, sacrificial victims and materials, funerals of deceased members, and gestures of honor and gratitude to the ruling emperor and to special patrons.

Smaller groups met in an area of a public temple, or in a rented hall, or in a private house; groups that could afford to do so, however, built their own meeting place. This normally had a small temple dedicated to the group's patron divinity, an open courtyard for meetings, dining rooms for the common meals, and various kitchens and service rooms.

### *Government Attitudes Toward Groups*

Professional groups had existed in Rome from the earliest times, but by the late Roman Republic they had become centers of political activity. Certain public figures used these organizations as political action groups, and their activities often included violence and physical intimidation. As a result, the Senate twice abolished such groups during the first century B.C.E., and Julius Caesar sponsored a law between 49 and 44 B.C.E. that suppressed all clubs. This law continued in effect under the Principate, which was always more concerned with the security of the state than with the individual rights of its subjects to assemble. Still, the tendency to form associations was too strong to be resisted, and although Augustus and Claudius reaffirmed the law suppressing them, certain exceptions were made that permitted some clubs to exist. These exceptions were the three categories just outlined.

## Cults

### *The Olympian Gods*

The public worship of the official gods permeated the social life of Greek and Roman cities. Their temples were the major landmarks, their festivals provided the major holidays, and their sacrifices dominated a large part of the economy.

Many of the Greek gods were agricultural in origin: Zeus was a sky god who sent the rain; Demeter produced the grain from the earth; Dionysus caused the grape to grow and the sap to flow in trees; Aphrodite was concerned with the process of reproduction and fertility; Artemis was associated with the monthly cycle of the moon; local demigods inhabited rivers, trees, and woods and protected those who lived near them. Some of the gods presided over more urbanized activities, such as Athena, with her interest in politics, war, and industry; Hephaestus the blacksmith and craftsman; Hermes the merchant and messenger; Ares the sponsor of war. A general term in Greek for such a god or demigod was *daimōn,* which has come into English by way of medieval Latin as "demon." The early Christians tended to concede that these gods, these *daimones,* did indeed exist, but they interpreted them as spirits of the Antichrist rather than creatures of the true God, which explains the modern meaning of "demon" (1 Cor. 10:20–21; James 2:19; Rev. 16:14; 18:2).

These were the gods of Greek mythology, and the tales about them formed the stuff of Greek education, theater, literature, and art. They were good, exciting stories, which often depicted the gods as physically overwhelming but subject to all the passions and emotional weaknesses of human beings; deceptions, lies, seductions, and rapes formed the subject matter of many of the myths, and many pagans realized that the stories about the gods presented them as very improbable models for moral behavior. One tendency among intellectuals was to debunk the myths; another was to reinterpret them in allegorical terms. The early Christian apologists lost few opportunities to point out the weakness in any theology based on the traditional myths and constantly made fun of the behavior of the gods in the old stories.

The susceptibility of the gods to human motivations and passions meant that they sometimes visited the towns and cities of human beings. In myths, gods often came to visit human lovers in the form of humans (or sometimes animals). There were also stories of special epiphanies, in which a god appeared to one or more people. Myths told how gods had appeared in disguise to Lycaon and he had fed them human flesh and been gruesomely punished, or how Baucis and Philemon had entertained Zeus and Hermes without knowing who they were; they were richly rewarded (Ovid, *Metamorphoses* 8.626–724).

As for the Romans, they conceived of their gods in a less anthropomorphic way than the Greeks, but they were no less resourceful in discovering the whole range of existence in which the divine operated. The farmer's boundary stone, with its power to control the actions of neighbors on both sides, was regarded as a divine force. So was the mysterious majesty of the sky or a large grove of trees, as well as the farmhouse storeroom, which was responsible for preserving the food and seed in usable condition, and the rust that appeared out of nowhere to spoil tools and crops. Eventually, when the Romans met the Greeks and were overwhelmed by the facile charm of their culture, this straightforward but rich religion of the soil was overlaid with tales from Greek mythology. The Roman Jupiter was identified with the Greek Zeus, Juno with Hera, Minerva with Athena, Vulcan with Hephaestus. At the same time, however, a specifically Roman genius persisted in the prayers and rites that were conducted by the official priests of the state. This assumed, in common with most polytheism, that there was always room in the pantheon for another god, that human knowledge had not succeeded in discovering all the divine beings that existed. It also assumed that the welfare of Rome and of its empire depended on the continued goodwill of the gods.

The characteristic form of worship, public and private, was the sacrifice. Just as certain specified victims were offered on the altar at the Jewish Temple in Jerusalem, so the Romans made sacrifices on the altars in front of temples of their gods. Depending on the nature of the deity and the solemnity of the occasion, the offering might consist of a bull or cow, a pig, a sheep, a bird, a specially baked cake, or a piece of incense. When a living victim was offered, it was sprinkled with barley meal, bedecked with ribbons, and stunned with a hammer blow; its throat was slit and the entrails were examined to make sure it was acceptable to the divinity; and certain inedible parts were laid on the altar to be consumed by fire. The remaining parts were normally cooked and eaten as a meal in honor of the god; leftovers were transported to a meat market for sale. This was a major source of supply for these markets, and the question of eating meat that had been offered to idols was a real one for residents of a pagan city with as much cultic activity as Corinth (1 Cor. 10:25–31).

The sacrifices were accompanied by prayers. In both the Greek and Roman traditions, the purpose of prayer was to strike a bargain with the divinity. The prayer usually began with an invocation, a reminder of past benefits or an allusion to the god's great power to confer benefits, and then moved on to the statement of the request, nearly always accompanied by a promise to do something for the god in return. If the prayer was granted, the petitioner was then obligated to do whatever he or she had promised; this might be as simple as the offering of a sacrifice of thanksgiving or the dedication of a small commemorative plaque, or it might be as elaborate as the construction of a new temple. The Romans were particularly scrupulous, with a typical finesse and a mind for legal detail, in making sure that the god understood their petition. If there was any doubt as to the name by which the divinity wished to be called, they would add, after the invocation, the saving clause "or by whatever name thou dost wish to be called," and the terms of the request and of the promised thank offering were spelled out in careful detail. Official prayers of the Roman magistrates were written down and repeated without any variation; if one syllable or one ritual gesture was performed incorrectly, the prayer might well be invalid, and the texts of many prayers preserved for us contain archaic Latin forms that had gone out of use centuries before the prayers were written down. The contrast with early Christian worship, where the officiant improvised the prayers and avoided the Roman kind of repetition (whether vain or not), would probably have been evident both to Christians and to any pagans who were present at their rituals.[20]

These Olympian gods and goddesses were chiefly worshiped as the protectors and defenders of public life. Their festivals and sacrifices were occasions for general public celebration, they affirmed the solidarity of the city and the success of the empire, and they satisfied the need for pageantry, ceremony, and religious awe.

But private individuals also had ways of expressing their personal devotion to these great gods. People would occasionally stop at the open door of a temple to say a quick prayer or make a small offering. Or they might have a statue of a favorite god at home, or salute a god's image in the street by hanging a garland on it or by touching their fingers to their lips and extending them toward the image (Minucius Felix, *Octavius* 2). There were customary invocations as well, as when potters invoked the name of Vulcan as they were removing pots from the kiln (Varro, *Satires* frag. 68, ed. Buechler). Such casual expressions of traditional polytheistic piety were unavoidable in the normal cultural world of the cities in the first and second centuries C.E. They were as common as the statues of gods, the paintings of mythological scenes, the street-corner shrines, the fragrance of incense, the smell of burning flesh emanating from temple altars.

On the other hand, for centuries intellectuals had been questioning the existence of these official gods or allegorizing them into lofty abstractions; they turned to skepticism or philosophy to express their deeper religious needs. Ordinary men and women tended to concentrate their devotion on more accessible gods, like the protectors of the household, the divine spirit in the hearth, the tutelary divinities of the pantry, or the spirits of departed ancestors. Country dwellers practiced the traditional rites to local divinities of fields, streams, and woods, which in some parts of the Mediterranean are still addressed by their descendants to rural saints and spirits. Many people in time of need turned to the cult of Asclepius (or Aesculapius), whose temples functioned as hospitals.

### *Ruler Cult: The Augustales*

One alternative to the traditional gods during the first centuries C.E. was the cult of the reigning emperor. This cult served a religious purpose in its veneration of palpable uncontested power, a political purpose in focusing allegiance to the empire and its ruler, and a social purpose in the way it involved wealthy freedmen in the responsibilities of the cult administration.

The traditional religion of Rome had been directed to unseen but perceptible powers: in the clear or stormy sky, in the boundary stone, in the seed grain, in the rust that settled on crops and spoiled them. In a similar way, the cult addressed to the emperor was directed to power that could subdue nations through the armies it commanded, move mountains through its engineering skill, exercise control of life and death over individuals and whole populations through the utterance of a word, and hold a defensive shield between the people and the horrible specter of civil war.

The civilizations of the eastern Mediterranean had venerated their rulers as gods for millennia. In Egypt, the pharaoh had been regarded as the living incarnation of the god Horus. In Greek legend, Heracles had become one of the Olympian gods, and another category of demigods known as "heroes" received sacrifices and prayers. Such "heroic" honors were also extended to contemporaries in Greece during the fifth century B.C.E., and by the end of that century a living general (Lysander of Sparta) set up altars to himself. Alexander the Great, incorporating both these traditions as conqueror of Egypt and superhuman general of the Greeks, was hailed as a god by several Greek cities, and this example was followed by many of his successors—not only the Ptolemaic dynasty of Egypt but also the Seleucids in Syria. The trappings of this kind of Hellenistic ruler cult also appear in Acts (12:20–22), where Herod Agrippa appears before the people at the hellenized city of Caesarea. Roman generals during the Republic had generally resisted this sort of adulation, but Julius Caesar was intrigued by its possibilities. After his death his heir, Augustus, declared Caesar a god and erected a temple and altar in his honor in the Roman forum. In his own honor, however, Augustus permitted altars and temples to be erected only in some of the cities of the Greek East where this kind of cult had already become a routine form of homage to the ruler. In Rome and Italy, he decreed that worship should be directed not to himself, but to his *genius,* the divine spirit which presided over his life and from which his power emanated. In this he was acting like the father of a normal Roman household, to whose genius the family regularly offered incense. During the next century, the cult of the living emperor became an accepted feature of public life. Oaths were sworn by the genius of the emperor, whose divine power was then involved in enforcing the oath. The term *kyrios* ("lord") was used to refer to the emperor Nero, as we see in the language of Festus (Acts 25:26). Vespasian was acknowledged as *sōtēr* ("savior"), and so was his son Titus. His other son, Domitian, expanded the conception of the divinity of the emperor and demanded to be acknowledged as *dominus et deus* ("lord and god"). This, like previous attempts of Caligula and Nero, was viewed after his death as un-Roman presumption, and under the emperors of the second century the cult of the emperor served, in a lower key, as a kind of pledge of allegiance to the empire.[21]

Devotion to the living emperor could be expressed by sacrificing a bull or offering incense to his image. Ordinarily this was a public ritual performed by magistrates or priests, although we know that Pliny the Younger when governor of Bithynia in the early second century C.E. required individuals to perform the ritual as a way of affirming allegiance to the emperor and of identifying Christians, since they would refuse to participate (*Letters* 10.96).

The ministers of the cult were often the imperial or municipal officials appointed as magistrates or priests. But from the time of Augustus, special collegia were established to tend the cult of the emperors; these were the Augustales, composed of prominent freedmen in each town. From their number a board of six was chosen each year to preside over their activities, and the whole organization served an important function in integrating these freedmen into society. They were barred from being elected to the Senate in Rome or the local councils in the municipalities; but, as we have seen, many of them had money and influence. Through service as Augustales, however, they could gain dignity and recognition; it gave them an important duty in the public life of the community and put them in a position where their wealth could be channeled into public service.

### *Mystery Cults*

The "mysteries" provided another form of religious expression. Originally local Greek agricultural festivals, during the classical period they had already developed a more universal appeal. Unlike the state and family cults, to which one belonged by virtue of citizenship and birth, these cults invited individuals to become voluntary participants in their secret ceremonies. They promised a special intimacy with the divinity and a carefree immortality beyond the grave, which they delivered through a symbolic ritual in which eating, drinking, and revelations assured the initiate of salvation, of communion and intimacy with the deity.

The Eleusinian mysteries, in honor of Demeter and Persephone, owed their importance partly to the fact that Eleusis was a suburb of Athens, that most prestigious of Greek city-states, but also to the spectacle that surrounded the rites and allowed them to be interpreted in many ways by different initiates through the centuries. They were based on the myth of the rape of Persephone by Pluto, and they commemorated the annual cycle in which the seed grain is buried in underground silos, dies and, then is planted in the earth and comes to new and nourishing life again. The ceremony included preliminary washing in the sea, an examination to ensure moral and ritual purity, a solemn procession from Athens to Eleusis, symbolic reenactments of the myth, a late-night ceremony in which a sudden flash of bright light revealed some ineffable mystery (which modern scholars, basing their guesses mostly on hostile indications in Christian critics of the rite, assume was an ear of wheat), and breaking a long fast by eating a special mixture of barley and wine and eating unnamed "sacred things." Aristotle (*Fragmenta* 15, ed. Rose) had said that the appeal of the mysteries in his time (the fourth century B.C.E.) consisted not in any specific knowledge that was communicated but in the ritual, which put the initiate into a spiritually receptive frame of mind. By Roman times, this mystery cult at Eleusis represented a high point in spirituality for the more philosophically inclined, and it was eagerly sought out by all levels of society: Roman emperors, Athenian aristocrats, even freedmen and slaves.

The mysteries of Dionysus, who was also known as Bacchus, were even more influential and widespread. They celebrated the god of the lifegiving fluid element in plants and animals, who after wintertime dormancy sprang to life in the spring and promised his devotees bliss both on earth—communicated chiefly through his gift of wine and its capacity to remove a person's cares—and in the afterlife. The ceremonies of the mystery cult included nocturnal initiations, food and drink, ecstatic dancing, and recitation of hymns. The cult comes to our attention in the classical period of Greece (Euripides, *Bacchae*) as an enthusiasm of women, although in the later Hellenistic period its devotees included the male members of theatrical troops known as Artists of Dionysus. It was introduced into Italy in its Hellenistic form as a rather staid society of upper-class women, meeting three times a year, but in the late third or early second century B.C.E. a charismatic Campanian woman, Paculla Annia, re-formed the cult into the more vigorous type of spirituality that it claimed as its origin. According to Livy (39.9–13) she initiated men and young people under twenty, substituted night for day as the time of meeting, and increased the number of meetings to five times a month, all of which look like ways of increasing the appeal of the cult and making it more important in the lives of its members.[22] What Livy tells us about the membership of these Bacchic cults in Italy and even in Rome itself implies that the cult was particularly popular with freed slaves, and that before initiation the candidates had to abstain from sexual contact for ten days, after which they joined in a banquet and were washed with pure water before being led into the sanctuary for the ceremony. Alarmed by the growth of the cult and by the rumors of debauchery and scandal that surrounded it, the Roman Senate in 186 B.C.E. severely restricted its size and the number of cult meetings. It was not, however, within the spirit of polytheism to abolish it altogether. In time, with the growing cosmopolitanism of the Roman empire and the eclipse of the old Roman traditions, Dionysiac cult groups were tolerated and seem to have become eminently respectable. In the second century C.E., for example, we have a membership list of a Dionysiac association from a suburb of Rome: At its head is Agrippinilla, wife of a Roman consul and in her own right the member of a noble family from the Greek island of Lesbos; other high cult offices, all with Greek titles, are held by her relatives; the lower ranks of functionaries seem to be filled by slaves and freed men and women of the family, all of whom (there were between 400 and 500 names on the list) are initiates or candidates for initiation and participate in the procession and ceremonies. This and other inscriptions of the Roman period show an elaborate hierarchy of priests, priestesses, bearers of torches and other sacred objects, wearers of special vestments, teachers, wardens, candidates for instruction, and the like. The details of offices and personnel vary from place to place, although many of the associations have members from a wide range of social groups, and at least some of them, like Agrippinilla's, seem to be a kind of house society made up of masters and slaves.[23] The traditional connection of Dionysus with ecstatic dancing and the drama permitted members of the cults to give public or semipublic performances of pantomimes; ancient pagan critics occasionally complain (Seneca, *Natural Questions* 7.32.3) that even highborn men and women participated in these shows, which were often suggestive and lewd. On another level, the popularity of Dionysus among the wealthy in the second and third centuries C.E. is demonstrated by elaborate burial sarcophagi decorated with Dionysiac symbolism.

### *Oriental Cults*

The appeal of the Greek mystery cults during the Hellenistic and Roman periods is paralleled by the popular devotion paid to several groups of divinities from the Near East, especially Egypt, Syria, Asia Minor, and Persia. They encouraged two general religious trends of the early Christian period and also satisfied the needs generated by the trends. One was toward syncretism, the process by which similar gods of different peoples were identified or were viewed as essentially the same divine being (chapter 2). Another trend was a tendency toward a closer emotional involvement with the divine, and these oriental cults provided an exotic outlet for such religious needs. This led to some resistance: to the Greeks, legitimate *eusebeia* ("piety") involved a fairly staid respect for the gods and rational standards of conduct, whereas the derogatory term *deisidaimonia* ("fear of daimones") could easily be applied to a person who sought out new gods to worship; to the Romans proper *religio* was level-headed, even legalistic, in contrast to *superstitio,* which tended to get out of control with its emotional appeals often loaded with foreign barbarism.[24]

In general, these oriental cults had both a public and a private aspect. In their homeland, they were official state cults. In Greek and Roman cities their rites were frequently incorporated into the official religious calendars, and public sacrifices were held in their temples. In addition, private associations of devotees, with their own special hierarchies, initiations, and ceremonies, met there as collegia. Many of them had stringent sets of rules for behavior and ritual purity.[25] As far as we know, there was not any central religious authority to regulate doctrine or procedures to the individual cult associations, although in some of them we find particular priesthoods that required some special commitment or special knowledge. As with most cult associations, those of the oriental gods drew their membership from all social classes. They exercised a special appeal to more wealthy members of society, however, who spent huge sums on initiations and dedications.

In the Egyptian cult, the central figure was the goddess Isis with her consort, Osiris or Sarapis. Isis was the great mother, who protected her consort and all those who turned to her. Osiris was the god of the underworld, whose death and revivification were celebrated each year (Plutarch, *Isis and Osiris* 377b–c); manifested as Sarapis, he was a fatherly figure who appeared to his devotees in dreams, healed them, and rescued them from difficulties. These two gods were attended by others from the Egyptian pantheon, including Horus or Harpocrates, the divine child, often shown being suckled at Isis' breast, and Anubis, the jackal-headed guide of the souls of the dead into the underworld.

Public ceremonies, adapted from the rituals of the great temples in Egypt, included daily morning and evening services in which incense was burned, water from the sacred Nile was scattered about, and hymns were chanted in the gods' honor. At some temples priests from Egypt presided, distinctive with their shaven heads and white linen robes. Processions through the streets were also held, the devotees carrying emblems and wearing masks of the gods. In addition to this public worship, individuals were initiated into several grades of mysteries, which were accepted in a spirit of mystical possession; for example, after fasting, study, and the payment of a large initiation fee, the hero of Apuleius' novel *The Golden Ass* is "reborn" (11.16, 21), washed, and purified (11.23); he sees the celestial and infernal gods (11.23), eats a cultic meal, and prays

(11.24), all of which results in his deliverance from fate, misery, and the fear of death (11.1, 12, 15). References in other Latin authors, as well as numerous inscriptions, show us that Isis appealed to women of all social strata: She was the giver of all good and perfect gifts, including marriage, language, and civilization, and she was celebrated in hymns as having given equal powers to men and to women.[26] Inscriptions show us that, like other collegia, devotees of Isis or Sarapis met once a month. A characteristic form of meeting was the banquet of Sarapis, to which special invitations were issued and at which the guests felt that the god was spiritually present at their meal.

An inscription from Thessalonica casts light on a cult society in honor of the Egyptian god Anubis. It met in a house built by a Roman citizen, and nine of the fourteen functionaries mentioned were also Roman citizens; they were called "companions at table" and "bearers of the sacred objects." The inscription reveals a group of Romans of high status active in the public cult of the Egyptian gods at Thessalonica in the first half of the second century C.E.[27]

Isis was not the only important goddess at home in the eastern Mediterranean. Artemis at Ephesus is one example, with her celebrations of fertility. The Syrian goddess with her consort Adonis, whose death was mourned and resurrection celebrated each year, is another. But the most famous of all was Cybele, or Kubaba, worshiped at Pessinus in Phrygia as the "Great Mother of the Gods." Her sacred totem was a black stone, tended by a professional priesthood whose members had pledged their eternal devotion by undergoing ritual castration. In this they imitated the story of the goddess's consort Attis, who emasculated himself in ecstatic rage and remorse after being unfaithful to the Mother. By the Roman period, shrines of the Great Mother were common in all cities of the empire. They were often served by one or more eunuch priests, known as Galli: conspicuous in their yellow robes, they celebrated their goddess with wild shouts and dances and flagellation, accompanied by pipes and tambourines and clashing cymbals. But it was not unusual for a group of more respectable members of society to meet in the temple and conduct its meetings, sacrifices, and dinners there in a way parallel to that of any other collegium. In the second, third, and fourth centuries C.E. we have evidence, both in literary descriptions and in commemorative inscriptions, about a rite called the Taurobolium. It was celebrated not by the eunuch Galli but by one of the prominent members of the collegium, who descended into a trench while a bull (or, in more economical versions, a ram) was sacrificed in such a way that its blood poured down into the trench and soaked and coated the person there. The inscriptions show that members from the very top of Roman society, who would probably be the only ones who could afford it, were the participants in this rite. Its effect, according to these same inscriptions, was to renew the life of the participant, to cause him or her to be reborn *(renatus):* The earlier examples indicate that the rebirth lasted for twenty years; a later example, perhaps influenced by the Christian doctrine of baptism, claims that the effect of the rite lasted into eternity.[28]

The cult of Mithras differed from the others in that it was limited to men and had a more highly regulated organization. It also offered a more highly developed theology, a legacy of speculation by Persian magi working in a tradition of strict dualism. In its mythology and in its ritual, the cult of Mithras emphasized the opposition of good and evil, of light and darkness. The heroic figure of Mithras was born from the primordial rock and in a great duel killed the bull of heaven, whose carcass released the potent forces needed to produce life on earth. This myth, in which Mithras overcame the powers of evil, spread from Iran across the Roman world during the second and third centuries. The worshipers were organized into associations that met in small cult rooms arranged to look like caves, with a central aisle leading to a sculptured image of Mithras slaying the bull and flanked on both sides by long low couches on which the worshipers could recline. The meetings included daily prayer services and more formal periodic gatherings with cultic meals of bread and wine. Initiation was a long and elaborate process and could include various ordeals: exposure to heat and cold, branding, fasting, and flagellation. The preliminary grades of Raven, Bridegroom, and Soldier could be followed by initiation into the higher orders of Lion, Persian, "Sunrunner," and Father. These seven degrees of initiation corresponded in some way to the seven levels of the planetary spheres and apparently represented the progressive purification of the soul and its journey into the next world. Only men could join the Mithraic cult, in keeping with its quasi-military organization. It was especially popular with soldiers; outposts on the edges of the empire often had their temple of Mithras.

# 6

# Christianity in the Cities of the Roman Empire

The early Christian churches are similar to other institutions in the Greco-Roman city. None of these other organizations are exact parallels, but some are close enough to aid in understanding those churches and to provide a glimpse of how Greeks and Romans—indeed, the Christians themselves—would have perceived the churches.

## Christian Adaptation of Urban Social Forms

Certainly the Christians were careful to distinguish themselves from the standard religious institutions of their social environment. The Christian group calls itself an *ekklēsia* ("assembly"), a word borrowed from the political assembly in the Greek cities. It systematically rejects the vocabulary of the pagan cults; there is no temple, no priest, no sacrifice, except Jesus himself. The terminology of the ruler cult is avoided; even the epithet *sōtēr* ("savior") is not applied to Christ until relatively late. In the same way, the Christians are careful not to use vocabulary that would suggest the various pagan mystery cults.[1]

### *The Household*

Most early churches met in Greco-Roman households. Writing from Ephesus, Paul sends greetings from Aquila and Prisca "together with the church in their house" to the church in Corinth (1 Cor. 16:19). Three other passages use a similar formula (Rom. 16:5; Philemon 2; Col. 4:15). Paul notes that he had baptized the "house of Stephanas" when in Corinth (1 Cor. 1:16; cf. 16:15–16). Similarly, the Christians mentioned in Romans 16:14–15 may well be members of three household congregations.

Luke too gives the household a central place in his narrative of early Christianity. Missionary and apologetic sermons are preached in public, but the life of the church occurs in houses. After Jesus' ascension, the eleven, the women, and Jesus' mother and brothers assemble in an "upper room" (Acts 1:13), in the same "house" (2:2) where the choice of Matthias (1:26) and Pentecost (2:1) occur. Luke thinks of this as the house of Mary, the mother of John Mark, a congregational meeting place to which Peter returns after being freed from prison (12:12), a house with its own gate (12:14). The "Hebrew" James was not present for worship in this "Hellenistic" household (12:17); "many" gathered there, but not the whole church in Jerusalem. Rather, they broke bread in various houses (2:46), where they heard the teaching of the apostles (2:42). Some who "were possessors of . . . houses sold them" (4:34) and took the money to the apostles, who in turn distributed it to those in need, according to Luke's narrative (cf. Luke 5:11; 18:28–29). As a persecutor, Saul enters "house after house" and drags Christians to prison (Acts 8:3). As convert and missionary, Paul accepts hospitality in the house of Judas in Damascus (9:11, 17), from Jason's household in Thessalonica (17:5), from various houses in Ephesus (20:20), another in Troas (20:8), from Philip in Caesarea (21:8), and from Mnason's household in Jerusalem (21:16). Acts concludes with Paul in his own hired dwelling at Rome (28:30), preaching and teaching.

Other texts mention the conversion of entire households (Acts 11:14; 16:15, 31–34; 18:8). While many entire households converted, in the early decades many slaves and wives converted when the patriarch (master and husband) did not (1 Peter 2:18; 3:1). Conversely, the conversion of the head of the household did not always mean the conversion of the slaves (e.g., Onesimus in Philemon 10), although typically their conversion may be assumed.

The image of Paul accepting hospitality in Christian households and the stories of households converting correspond to Jesus' commission in Luke 10:5–9: The itinerant missionary is to enter a house and remain, eating and drinking what they provide, while healing and preaching. But Christians "of corrupt mind and counterfeit faith" (2 Tim. 3:8) found acceptance in some households (3:6). The author of the Pastorals was especially concerned about some wives and widows who would gad about "from house to house . . . saying what they should not" (1 Tim. 5:13; cf. Ignatius, bishop of Antioch, *Letter to the Ephesians* 7; *to the Magnesians* 6; *to the Philadelphians* 4; *to the Smyrnaeans* 8; Hermas, *Visions* 2.3.1; *Similitudes* 7.1–7). This reflects the fact that these household-based groups were distinguished from the whole church in a city, which might also come together (Rom. 16:23; 1 Cor. 14:23). They were also distinguished from the one international church (Col. 1:18; 4:15).

These house churches were the basic cells of the growing church, at a time when significant social tensions surrounded the household in Roman society (chapter 5). It is not surprising, then, that much early Christian ethical exhortation is addressed to households, beginning with Colossians and 1 Peter. This is continued in Ephesians, chapters 5 to 6; the Pastorals; 1 Clement 21; Ignatius; and Polycarp 4–5.[2]

This Christian mission based in the household may have significant antecedents in Jewish households and synagogues of the Diaspora. At Passover, "every dwelling house is invested with the outward semblance and dignity of a temple" (Philo, *On the Special Laws* 2.148, tr. F. H. Colson in Loeb Classical Library). Among pagan cults, also, worship was sometimes conducted within households, especially before a public temple was built.

### Clubs and Voluntary Organizations

The thiasoi that met in Greek cities and the collegia in Roman cities resembled Christian communities in several significant ways.

They all worshiped some god. The professional, social, and burial societies all adopted a patron deity, to whom sacrifice was made as a central ceremony of the regular (usually monthly) meeting. In accordance with normal pagan practice, the meat from such a sacrifice was then shared by the members as part of a common banquet. These could often become raucous events, and the group was sometimes compelled to include in its bylaws some regulations against inappropriate behavior.[3] Some of these regulations recall Paul's criticism of the worship of the Corinthians (1 Corinthians 11).

Most of these societies depended on the generosity of one or several patrons to supplement the more modest contributions of ordinary members. These patrons were expected to provide more elaborate banquets, for example, or to pay for the construction of a new temple. The hosts of Christian house churches functioned in a way analogous to that of such patrons. At Corinth, Stephanas seems to have been such a patron (1 Cor. 16:15–18), and at nearby Cenchreae, Phoebe is identified as *diakonos* and *prostatis* (Rom. 16: 1–2). The latter term probably denotes a woman who functions as patroness to some society.[4]

Christian apologetic writers, arguing that they should not be singled out as objects of persecution, could make the claim that they were legitimate funerary collegia entitled to assemble. In the third century, Tertullian (*Apology* 38–39) made an elaborate argument that Christian groups were entitled to the protection rather than the persecution of the authorities. Among his arguments is the claim that the groups exist for funerary purposes and, as required by the law, require a monthly contribution from each member and eat a common meal together. An anecdote shows that at least some emperors recognized the validity of such claims: On one occasion a public place was sold or rented to a group of Christians and a group of tavern owners made a counter claim to use the space, but Alexander Severus ruled that it was better for the place to be used for religious purposes, no matter what god was worshiped (Scriptores Historiae Augustae, *Severus Alexander* 49.6).

On the other hand, there were important differences. The Christian groups were totalistic in a way paralleled only in Judaism; other loyalties became secondary. Further, the Christian groups were more inclusive socially than were the voluntary associations. Some of the latter did include slaves and freeborn persons, both men and women, but usually they were associations of socially homogeneous people. In addition, the Christian groups were more conscious of a dynamic connection with a worldwide society of like-minded believers, to a much greater degree than the pagan collegia.[5]

### *Synagogues*

Socially and religiously, the existence of Jewish synagogues in Greco-Roman cities was crucial for the success of the early Christian mission. Christians appropriated many of the activities of the synagogues: scripture reading and interpretation, prayers and common meals. Jewish communities in Hellenistic cities were legally constituted as collegia, and Christians claimed this same legal status (chapter 5). Both synagogue and church provided charity to the poor, the widows, and the orphans among their members, and both synagogue and church had the sense of belonging to a broad international entity, the people of God. The synagogue loosed Jewish ties to a temple cult, and Christians in turn proclaimed their independence of temples and priests. Furthermore, Christians seldom forgot their origin as a Jewish sect. Even when the Christian sect had developed its own identity, and observation of the Jewish Law became optional, some Christians apparently continued to observe their traditional Jewish customs; in the second century there is evidence that many Christians were observing kosher restrictions in their food (Eusebius, *Ecclesiastical History* 5.1.26;

3.1–2; Minucius Felix, *Octavius* 30.6; Tertullian, *Apology* 9.13).

But there are a surprising number of differences between synagogue and church. The organizational terminology of Judaism is not used in the earliest church. The role of women in some early Christian churches is significantly greater than in contemporary Judaism. And distinctively, the ethnic community no longer forms the boundary for most Christian churches, although some Jewish Christian groups continued to exist in the earliest centuries.

Jewish synagogues were tolerated within the law because they could be viewed as funerary collegia and also because they had been granted special permission for assembly by Julius Caesar (Josephus, *Antiquities* 14.213–216). At first, Christian groups seem to have enjoyed this same permission, because the authorities did not make any distinction between them and the Jewish synagogues out of which they came. But when the authorities became aware of the distinction between them, which Jews and Christians alike were making, the Christians no longer fell under this rubric.

### *Philosophical Schools*

Philosophical or rhetorical schools may be models for understanding parts of the New Testament. Noting that ten passages in Matthew cite the Old Testament in a distinctive way, Stendahl proposed that they reflect an advanced study of the scriptures in the "school" of Matthew.[6] Matthew's scribes and Paul himself did teach, of course, like the philosophers, although Paul was itinerant. In the Hellenistic age, each philosophical school had its distinctive way of life. Ethics was central. Each school had adherents who accepted the previous heads of the school as authorities. There were rivalries between the schools and even conversion stories (see Diogenes Laertius 4.43 and chapter 2). In the confusing world after Alexander the Great, the philosophical schools encouraged individuals to choose some values and ways of life and reject others.

The Pythagoreans formed a close community which shared all things in common and in which diet and clothes were strictly regulated, a description that has close parallels to the earliest Jerusalem church described in Acts (chs. 2; 4 to 5).

The Epicureans organized communities of devotees living together as a household and bound together in communal love. Cicero comments (*About the Ends of Goods and Evils* 1.65, tr. H. Rackham in Loeb Classical Library) on "what companies of friends Epicurus held together in one small house, and what affections and sympathy united them!" And this still continued among the Epicureans of his own day, in the first century B.C.E. Epicurus stimulated intense loyalty in his disciples and bitter opposition in his critics. He and his household lived austerely, as sectarians withdrawn from the rest of the city and its culture. As Paul did later, Epicurus wrote letters to his communities, which honored him as a god. No later leader arose in the school to match his importance, with the result that the school changed very little. Epicurus valued pleasures, the most important of which was friendship. This emphasis on friendship reflects a strong cohesion among adherents to the Epicurean way of life. It is not surprising that critics should associate Christians and Epicureans (Lucian, *Alexander the False Prophet* 25, 38).

In many ways, Paul and other wandering Christian teachers like Apollos and Barnabas must have appeared to their contemporaries as very similar to the philosophers and rhetoricians. They spoke in public and in private, in synagogues and in homes—and there was already a tendency to view Jewish communities as a type of philosophical sect, a tendency that Philo exploited in many of his writings in which he interpreted Judaism for the benefit of educated pagan contemporaries.[7]

### *Wandering Moralists*

Among the travelers on Roman roads and ships were the philosophical itinerants, Cynics, wonder-workers, and priests. They addressed the sense of uncertainty among many in this Roman world of change by presenting appeals to be believed rather than philosophical arguments to be followed. We meet such itinerants in the orations of Dio Chrysostom, who wandered about in obedience to an oracle's command, teaching on moral themes in the tradition of Socrates and Diogenes (e.g., *Orations* 3.12–24; 4; 13.9; 72; 80); in Philostratus' *Life of Apollonius of Tyana,* with its laudatory picture of an unselfish, conscientious miracle worker; in Lucian's *Alexander the False Prophet,* which lashes out with an exposé of a false oracle (Alexander planted tablets in a temple of Apollo which foretold that the healing god Asclepius would take up residence in Alexander's hometown of Abunoteichus; he feigned divine madness; he "found" a goose egg—in which he had previously inserted a large snake fitted with a false human head—which would prophesy and answer questions for a fee; he sent messengers abroad to proclaim that the god gave oracles, caught fugitive slaves, healed the sick, and even raised the dead); in Lucian's *Passing of Peregrinus,* which treats with skepticism the career of a Cynic preacher who had connections with various Christian communities and who immolated himself in spectacular fashion at the Olympic festival in 165 C.E.; and in Apuleius' *Golden Ass,* which depicts debauched eunuch priests of the Syrian goddess (8.27), as well as virtuous priests of Isis who guide the hero of the tale to a deep committed relationship with the goddess (book 11).

Such wandering moralists attracted disciples and conducted discussions and lectures in public and private. The Cynics affected a life-style of poverty and simplicity, and in contrast to the flowery speeches of the rhetoricians, both they and the Stoics cultivated a special type of discourse, the *diatribē,* a homily that made a straightforward moral point and illustrated it with parables and stories. In some, satiric accounts of social foibles helped give the impression of a decadent and naughty world. They reflected and encouraged a widespread contemporary impression that the world was a bad place. An effective philosophical teacher, whether Cynic, Stoic, or Epicurean, might well inspire his hearers to turn their backs on this decadence and vice and take up a style of life more appropriate to philosophical contemplation (Epictetus, *Discourses* 3.23.37 and Seneca, *Moral Epistles* 6.1; 108.3–4). Paul uses the style of the Stoic-Cynic diatribe frequently, especially in his letters to the Corinthians and the Romans.[8]

It was usual for such teachers to take associates with them on their travels. The Cynic-Stoic philosopher Musonius Rufus (*Discourse* 11) suggested that young men work with their teacher on a farm in the country. Dio Chrysostom traveled without any pupils, but Apollonius of Tyana had many disciples (Philostratus, *Life of Apollonius of Tyana* 4.34, 36–37, 47). Both Jesus and Paul traveled with numbers of associates (e.g., Acts 20:4; 2 Cor. 8:19).

Women traveling with such preachers were viewed with suspicion. Lucian for example claims (*Runaways* 18–19) that Cynics carry off wives on the pretense of making philosophers out of them and then share them around with their associates, all the time condemning drunkenness, adultery, lewdness, and covetousness. The Midrash tells of a wife who irritated her husband because she habitually went to hear Rabbi Meir preach in the synagogue on the Sabbath (*Midrash Rabbah to Lev. 9:9*). Jesus and the women who followed him about the countryside were slandered (Mark 15:40–41; Luke 8:2–3). Women were also among Paul's associates (Rom. 16:1–3, 6–7; cf. Acts of Paul 3.7).

Financial support might come from several sources: begging, lecture fees, working, or support from the group of disciples. Begging brought Cynics a bad reputation, and so did charging a fee for services; Lucian makes fun of a preacher who charged an exorbitant rate for a lecture on frugality (*The Dead Come to Life* 34). In contrast, Musonius, Dio Chrysostom, Paul (1 Thess. 2:9), and some rabbis supported themselves by their own labor. The religious community was normally expected to support Christian missionaries (Matt. 10: 11; Mark 6:10; Luke 9:4; 10:7; 22:35; 1 Cor. 9:4–12; 3 John 6; cf. *Didache* 12:2; 13:1). In this way the Christian missionaries could point to a clear distinction between themselves and the Cynic beggars.

In the context of the many other wandering moralists, early Christian preachers sought to avoid being identified with them and to project a better image. Dio Chrysostom distinguished himself from others in relation to his appearance (*Oration* 72), and Philostratus tried to distinguish Apollonius from fraudulent religious figures in many respects. Philostratus and Luke wrote to project a praiseworthy image of Apollonius and Paul; and Paul himself was forced to be concerned with such distinctions in 1 Thessalonians 2 and 2 Corinthians 11.[9]

## The Major Centers

The social forms outlined above were experienced by Christians in specific urban centers. Jerusalem is described in chapter 4. Christians were soon active as well in Antioch of Syria, then in Asia Minor, Macedonia, and Achaea, and very soon in Rome itself and in Alexandria.

### *Syria: Antioch*

The oldest story preserved about the church of Antioch in Syria presents a dilemma that remained typical for the Christians of this city:

> But when Cephas came to Antioch, I [Paul] opposed him to his face, because he stood condemned. For before certain men came from James, he ate with the Gentiles; but when they came he drew back and separated himself, fearing the circumcision party. And with him the rest of the Jews [i.e., Jewish Christians] acted insincerely, so that even Barnabas was carried away by their insincerity. (Gal. 2:11–13)

The Fourth Book of Maccabees, written by a Jewish author in Antioch about the same time as this dispute, is also concerned with Jewish–Gentile relationships as symbolized by the traditional Jewish dietary laws. The Gospel of Matthew, which was probably written in Antioch, alludes to this dispute too (ch. 15), as does Ignatius, the bishop of Antioch around 100 C.E. (*Letter to the Philadelphians* 5–9).

Jewish power and influence in the city is best seen in the great central street paved with marble by Herod the Great in honor of Augustus. This central street, among the earliest of its kind, was two Roman miles long and constituted one of Antioch's claims to fame in antiquity. According to Josephus (*Against Apion* 2.39), Antioch included Jewish residents from its very beginning. The Christian Hellenists, expelled from Jerusalem, at first preached "the word to none except Jews. But there were some of them . . . who on coming to Antioch spoke to the Greeks also" (Acts 11:19–20).

The juxtaposition of different cultures reflected in these texts was partially a result of the policy of the Seleucid kings of Syria. When Seleucus I founded the city in 300 B.C.E., he built one quarter for the Greeks and another for native Syrians and surrounded the separate quarters with walls. The city was laid out from the beginning on a strict gridiron plan common to Hellenistic cities of this period. It occupied a wide plain between the Orontes River on the west and a mountain range on the east. From this Greek city, urbanization and Hellenization radiated into all parts of the Hellenistic kingdom of Syria, including Palestine.

Seleucus situated the capital at Antioch for good reasons. It controlled the land routes that connect Asia Minor, the Euphrates, and Egypt. It enjoyed an unrivaled water supply from the springs at the suburb of Daphne 4 miles to the south, and an agriculturally fertile plain. It offered the security of some distance (14 miles) from the sea, while remaining only a day's journey from one of the best harbors in the Mediterranean. On the other hand it suffered from torrential winter rains, and the Orontes River often flooded. And Mount Silpius, which towered over it, made it difficult to fortify and defend.

The city's patron deity was the goddess Tyche, depicted as a robed goddess wearing a crown made like a city wall, holding a sheaf of wheat in her right hand, seated on a rock symbolizing Mount Silpius, and resting her foot on a swimming boy representing the Orontes. Tyche ("Fortune," "Lady Luck") represented the capricious swings of fortune that governed the careers of Hellenistic kingdoms, the fertility of the fields, and the security of a city subject to earthquakes, attack, and floods.

When the Roman general Pompey occupied Antioch in 64 B.C.E., he granted *libertas* to the city, a freedom which in theory meant that the city might have its own constitution, be free of a military garrison, and be exempt from the payment of tribute. Caesar confirmed this freedom when he arrived in 47 B.C.E. Roman merchants swiftly established themselves and brought increasing prosperity. Caesar undertook a comprehensive building program, which both enhanced Roman prestige and introduced the Roman way of life to the city. During the reign of Augustus, Antioch became the capital of an imperial province, the headquarters of the legate of Syria, who controlled three or four legions to protect both the Parthian frontier and the trade routes. Its position as an international thoroughfare is illustrated by the sight of ambassadors from India passing through on their way to see Augustus (Strabo, *Geography* 15.1.73). Augustus himself visited the city twice, in 31–30 and in 20 B.C.E. Throughout the Principate, Antioch continued to receive the patronage and protection of the emperors. It was a great intellectual center as well as a center for travel and commerce.

The Jewish community at Antioch was probably as old as the city itself (Josephus, *Against Apion* 2.39; *Antiquities* 12.119). The first Jewish residents may have been mercenaries in the army of Alexander the Great (*Against Apion* 1.192, 200). A century and a half later, Jews in the city were affected by the events of the Maccabaean revolt in Judea. Maccabaean martyrs are sometimes associated with the city; some sources speak of a "captivity" of the Jews at Daphne under Antiochus IV. Later, important developments in the Jewish community are associated with the frequent visits of Herod the Great to the city. His visits and his building activity enhanced the prestige and importance of the local Jews. Their wealth increased; they sent expensive offerings to Jerusalem (Josephus, *Jewish War* 7.45), and Jewish Christians were able to send famine relief to Christians in Judea under Claudius (Acts 11:27–30). A significant number of "Greeks" were attracted to the synagogue, to the discussion of the Torah, and to the Jewish way of life (Josephus, *Jewish War* 7.45), for example Nicolaus, who later was attracted to the Christian way (Acts 6:5). Hellenistic culture influenced the culture of the Jews, as seen in 4 Maccabees, written in Antioch, and in Galatians.

The influence and wealth of the Jews declined significantly around the middle of the first century C.E. According to the sixth-century church historian John Malalas, about the year 40 there was a pogrom in Antioch in which pagans attacked the Jews, killed many, and burned their synagogues. This may have been connected with the pogrom in Alexandria two years earlier, and the resistance of Antiochene Jews to Caligula's decree in 39–40 C.E. that a statue of himself be placed in the Temple in Jerusalem (chapter 1). It was during this time that Jewish Christians began to preach to and eat with pagans in Antioch (Acts 11:19–20, 26; Gal. 2:11–13).

After two and a half decades of comparative quiet, severe tension between Jews and non-Jews was aroused in every city of Syria by the revolt of Judea against Rome. At Antioch, however, the strong hand of the Roman governor maintained tranquillity, except for two disturbances. In 67 C.E., Antiochus, a son of the archon, or ruler, of the Jewish community, claimed that the Jews planned to burn the city. This resulted in an attack on central Jewish symbols, including Sabbath privileges and their refusal to sacrifice to pagan deities. Those accused by Antiochus as responsible were burned to death in the theater (Josephus, *Jewish War* 7.47). Near the end of the war, a fire did break out, and Jews were again endangered. After taking Jerusalem, Titus arrived in Antioch amid cries urging the expulsion of the Jews. He refused to expel them, however, observing that since Judea had been destroyed, Jews had nowhere else to go (Josephus, *Jewish War* 7.100–111). He left the status of Jews in Antioch as it was before the war.

Much of the subsequent history of the Jewish community in this city is obscure. In the urban population there were Jews among the curial ruling class, among the shopkeepers and artisans, and among the slaves. There was a Jewish settlement at Daphne, the fashionable suburb south of the city, and Jews also probably lived in the fertile plain to the north.

The crucial story of the history of early Christianity in Antioch can only be sketched in outline. Power struggles ensued during the transition from Jewish ways of life toward Gentile customs and thought. Controversy developed early over the initiation of Gentiles into the church (Acts 15; Gal. 2:11–13). The tension centered on whether these Gentiles needed to accept the central cultural-religious Jewish symbols, especially circumcision and dietary laws. The heated discussion of table fellowship is reflected in the Antiochene sources of 4 Maccabees and Matthew. Paul himself insists that he never accepted any compromise of his "freedom" from these sectarian customs. Contemporary scholars suspect that Paul's clash with Peter was over more than personality differences. It was rather a fundamental crisis of authority concerning the relationship between Paul and Antioch as well as between Antioch and Jerusalem. Paul was resisting the attempt of Jerusalem "orthodox" Christians to extend their authority to Antioch, and he lost.

Acts 13:1 gives a glimpse of the leaders in the church at Antioch: Barnabas, Symeon the Black, Lucius the Cyrenaean, Manaen the childhood companion of Herod Antipas, and Saul. All five names are Semitic except Lucius.

Acts 11:26 gives more important information: "In Antioch the disciples were for the first time called Christians." The source of this name is intensely debated, but it may be that the simplest explanation is still the best. The disciples were called "Christus-people" by pagans "because it was in Antioch that they first stood out from Judaism as a distinct sect."[10]

In summary, eastern and western cultures were in contact and conflict here. The relationship between Jews and Gentiles in the church was debated and tentatively decided. Antioch, an urban center, had centers of education and produced exegetical schools for the early church in the evangelist Matthew, the apologist Theophilus, and the preacher John Chrysostom. As the Seleucids hellenized the eastern Mediterranean from Antioch, as Caesar romanized the province from this city, so Christian missionaries like Paul and his opponents set out from this city to christianize the *oikoumenē* ("inhabited world"). Augustus made Antioch a center of power. James and Peter introduced new patterns of organization and power among Christians in the same city. Matthew retold the story of Jesus in a way that has influenced its retelling ever since. Eventually, the concept of the monarchical episcopate, vigorously defended with theological arguments by Ignatius, bishop of Antioch, may have originated here as well. The ethnic diversity, culture, education, power, trade, and religion of this city enabled the Christians there to make unique contributions to the development of earliest Christianity.

### *Asia Minor: Ephesus and Other Cities*

"God did extraordinary miracles by the hands of Paul" in Ephesus (Acts 19:11–20), including driving evil spirits out of the sick. Jewish exorcists attempted the same but were beaten, so that fear fell on all the residents of the city. Acts then pictures a huge bonfire in which books of magic are burned. Luke has placed the scene in the appropriate place: A number of ancient writers refer to such books as "Ephesian tales" (e.g., Plutarch, *Table Talk* 7.706e).

But the primary story in Acts 19 concerns the riot that breaks out when the makers of silver statues of Artemis—devotional aids and tourist trinkets—object to Paul's missionary activity. This goddess was closely identified with the city in which her temple, the largest and most lavishly decorated in the Hellenistic world, was one of the major attractions. She was a form of the Mother Goddess indigenous to Asia Minor, recognized as far more ancient than the Greek inhabitants (Pausanias 7.2.6–8), who eventually identified her with their own Artemis. When the author of Acts describes the riot, he depicts their interest in the "idols" of Artemis as commercial. But what religious appeal lay behind the passion of those crowds who chanted, "Great is Artemis of the Ephesians"? One clue may be found in the statue itself, a stiff upright figure resembling the trunk of a tree or a mummy, covered with sculptured animals and plants, including twenty-four or more rounded objects on the goddess's chest. It used to be taken for granted that these were exuberantly multiplied breasts of the great fertility goddess. More recently, some scholars have identified them as ostrich eggs, which also signify fertility and are found today in many Greek village churches. Others insist that Artemis was not a fertility goddess at all but the mistress of destiny; the objects are stars or planets.[11] In an essay in her honor from late antiquity, she is praised as one who has remained a virgin, loves women, helps them to hunt and to capture men in war, helps them in childbirth, and even protects the civilized urban Greeks from the wild forest (Libanius, *Oration* 5). Hellenistic writing about Artemis of Ephesus concentrates, typically, on her role as a savior (Strabo, *Geography* 14.1.22; Achilles Tatius, 7.13 to 8.14). Among her benefits to humans is her ability to rule over cosmic powers, symbolized by the zodiacal signs on her statues (cf. Eph. 1:21; 3:10; 4:8; Col. 1:16; 2:8, 15, 20).

Her temple was a bank where persons from all parts of the world deposited money; it would be safe there since no one would dare to violate the holy place. The temple also loaned money and received legacies and private donations. It owned revenue-producing property with sacred fish and herds of deer (Dio Chrysostom 31.54; Strabo, *Geography* 14.1.29). It was an asylum for debtors and for the helpless (Achilles Tatius 7.13).

Missionaries carried the cult of the goddess throughout the world; she it was "whom all Asia and the world worship" (Acts 17:27; cf. Libanius, *Oration* 5.29). Strabo (*Geography* 4.1.4) tells how the goddess, in a dream, commanded a woman to take her statue along on a colonizing expedition, so that in many cities reproductions of her Ephesian statue were known and worshiped. This story is strikingly similar to the stories from the Egyptian cults, and might be compared to the story of Paul's vision in Troas (Acts 16:9).

Paul came into conflict not only with exorcists and with silversmiths making silver statues of Artemis but also with persons in the synagogue (Acts 17:17; 19:8–9, 33–34). In 14 B.C.E. Agrippa wrote a letter to the magistrates and people of Ephesus that the Jews of Asia should be able to collect sacred money to send to Jerusalem and that they should not be forced to appear in court on the Sabbath (Josephus, *Antiquities* 16.167–168; cf. 14.262–264). In contrast with other cities of Asia Minor, the Jews in Ephesus have left little physical evidence: A single carving has been discovered, a menorah scratched into one of the stones of a library erected in the second century C.E.

Ephesus was an important commercial center, jealous of its prerogatives as one of the leading cities of the Roman province of Asia. When the last Hellenistic king of Pergamum died in 133 B.C.E., he bequeathed his kingdom, which included Ephesus, to the Romans. The Ephesians joined Mithridates VI of Pontus in rebelling against Rome, and literary sources report that Sulla devastated Ephesus. Pompey defeated Mithridates in 67 B.C.E., after which the city experienced an economic boom accompanied by extensive building activity. In general during the first century B.C.E., however, Ephesus was both politically and economically weak. All the cities of Asia Minor had suffered severe extortions from Roman governors and soldiers (Appian, *Roman History* 12.7.48), and during the civil wars following the death of Julius Caesar, Antony asked the province to give him in one year taxes for the next ten (Appian, *Civil Wars* 5.5; cf. Plutarch, *Life of Antony* 24). Augustus' victory brought peace and prosperity to Asia and Ephesus, and the resulting urban development left monuments that are still striking in their ruined state. When the disturbance against Paul moved to its raucous "hearing" in the theater of the city (after a remodeling in 66 C.E., it could accommodate about 24,000 spectators), the town clerk reminded the crowd that they were risking a charge of rioting (Acts 19:40) and suggested that they take any complaints to the courts or Roman officials.

Because they benefited from the peace and prosperity of the Principate, cities in Asia Minor competed for the honor of building each new emperor's temple. This was the most active region in the whole empire in enthusiasm for the cult of the emperor, and that brought the Christians into frequent collision with the authorities (1 Peter 2 to 4; Revelation 2 to 3). Ephesus was permitted to erect two temples to Augustus, which made it the chief city in the province. Tiberius, however, after significant hesitation allowed Smyrna, a rival city to the north, to build his temple, and Ephesus lost her preeminence; it also saw this emperor reduce the asylum rights of the temple of Artemis. Gaius favored still another city, Miletus, to the south of Ephesus. It was in the reign of Gaius's successor, Claudius, that Paul preached in Ephesus, a city still embroiled in competition for imperial favor with its neighbors. Under Domitian and again under Hadrian, Ephesus was named *neōkoros,* warden of the emperor's temple. Throughout the second century C.E., Ephesus enjoyed a golden age in education, art, and architecture.

In this city, Paul knew several Christian households. He taught in the "hall of Tyrannus" (Acts 19:9), and a Deutero-Pauline author remembers the household of Onesiphorus, which refreshed Paul in Ephesus despite his chains (2 Tim. 1:16–18; Acts of Paul 7 also refers to an Ephesian imprisonment).

Ancient tradition associates not only the Pauline school but also Johannine Christianity with Ephesus. Eusebius (*Ecclesiastical History* 3.1, 23; 5.8) quotes Clement, Origen, and Irenaeus concerning John's activity in Asia, and John's Gospel may well have been written here. The Apocalypse (Rev. 2:6) expresses concern about the evil effects in Ephesus of the Nicolaitans, who seem to be among those who "eat food sacrificed to idols and practice immorality" (Rev. 2:14–15). The specific churches singled out for comment (Revelation 2 to 3) are within easy communication from Ephesus.

In the second century, Ignatius (*Letter to the Ephesians* 7:1) has negative images of some Christians here. They have "evil doctrine," which has corrupted some families (16:1), against which Ignatius cites a triadic formula referring to the Father, Jesus Christ, and the Holy Spirit (9:1). Knox has pointed out parallels in chapters 2 and 3 of this letter to phrases in Paul's letter to Philemon; since the name of the bishop of the Ephesians is Onesimus, he suggests that this is the same person who was Philemon's slave and who had been active in collecting Paul's works.[12] In the same letter, Ignatius refers to Paul, "who in every letter makes mention of you in Christ Jesus" (12:2).

Paul passed through Ephesus several times (Acts 18:19; 19:1), and its central location made it a natural focus of Christian life in Asia Minor. He also touched at other old Greek cities along the western coast, which formed the Roman province of Asia. At Alexandria Troas, a major port at the northwestern corner of the province, he set sail for Europe and may have founded the Christian community (Acts 16:8–11; 20:6; 2 Cor. 2:12), which was still strong in the early second century when Ignatius passed through on the way to martyrdom in Rome (Ignatius, *Letter to the Philadelphians* 11:2; *Letter to the Smyrnaeans* 12:1). Paul also landed at the port town of Assos, south of Troas (Acts 20:13–14), and at Miletus, the next large port city south of Ephesus (Acts 20:15–17).

Several of the Seven Churches of the Apocalypse are on or near the coast. Ephesus (Rev. 2:1–7) takes first place, as the largest center of Christianity in the region. Smyrna (2:8–11) was an old Greek city, with a proud history and prosperous present, which constantly disputed Ephesus' claim to preeminence. Pergamum (2:12–17) was the old royal capital of the Attalid kingdom; among its many monuments was the "throne of Satan," presumably the famous altar of Zeus on the citadel. Thyatira to the north (2:18–29), Sardis to the southwest (3:1–6), and Philadelphia to the southeast (3:7–13), occupied the territory of the ancient kingdom of Lydia. Thyatira, which seems to have preserved some form of its old Lydian organization throughout the years of Hellenistic kings and Roman domination, was a large commercial center on the river leading to Smyrna. Inscriptions there show intense activity on the part of guilds of many craftspeople, including dyers, wool makers, and linen weavers, which recalls Lydia, the dealer in fine textiles from Thyatira (Acts 16:14). Sardis was the ancient Lydian capital; it enjoyed a good location and continued to be a prosperous center within the Roman province. Its large and prominent Jewish population shared in the general prosperity (chapter 2). Philadelphia, which had been founded by Attalus II Philadelphus, controlled a large rural area. The Apocalypse (Rev. 3:9–10) implies that a significant number of Jews lived there and that they had come into conflict with the small Christian community. Farther south, along the Maeander River, which flowed into the sea at Ephesus, a series of important cities led up into the central highlands of Asia Minor. Laodicaea (Rev. 3: 14–22) dominated the wool-making industry of the whole region, and its products were widely known. Paul (Col. 2:1; 4:13–16) greets the Laodicaean church and singles out Nympha, the patroness of a house church; the Apocalypse describes the Christian community there as rich and comfortable. Near Laodicaea, and participating in its successful wool trade, were Hierapolis (whose name, "Holy Town," shows that it owed its original importance to a temple of one of the native deities) and the much less important Colossae. The Letter to the Colossians reveals Paul's concern over the inroads in this area of a group opposed to his teachings, whose "angel worship" may reflect external influence (Persian, Gnostic, and Essene influences have been suggested by different scholars) or local influence from one of the native cults of Asia Minor.[13]

All these cities lay within the Roman administrative province of Asia. To the east, cutting across the central highland plateau of Asia Minor, lay the province of Galatia. It is rugged terrain, cold in winter and hard to farm. Acts tells how Paul brought the Christian gospel to the southern part of the province, the lands inhabited by races who went back long before the coming of the Hellenistic Greeks. He came from Cyprus and passed through the coastal territories of Pamphylia and Pisidia, where he preached in the important local centers of Antioch, Iconium, Lystra, and Derbe (Acts 13:14 to 14: 24; all were Roman colonies), as well as in the surrounding rural countryside (14:5–7). Local languages, like Lycaonian, were still heard in the first century C.E. (14:11). Landowners included descendants of the old native aristocracies, Roman citizens of Italian origin who had come to Asia Minor as colonists in one of the romanized cities and had acquired land through investment, and also wealthy Romans of the equestrian and senatorial class, like the family of Sergius Paulus, whom Paul encountered as governor of Cyprus (13:7) and whose family is known to have had extensive landholdings in Pisidia. It has been suggested that Sergius Paulus may himself have provided Paul with introductions to the aristocracy in Pisidian Antioch, which had the status of a Roman colony.[14] The northern part of the province was the proper homeland of the Galatians, a vigorous nomadic people related to the "Gauls" of modern France, who had arrived in Asia Minor in the second century B.C.E. Most scholars think it was to congregations in this area that Paul addressed his Letter to the Galatians. Here, rural tribal settlements predominated, although a few scattered cities had been founded by the Roman authorities as civilizing centers within the highland countryside, which produced grain and wool.

On the northern coast of Asia Minor, facing the Black Sea, the Romans combined the two kingdoms of Pontus and Bithynia into a single province. Paul does not enter this area (Acts 16:7), but we know that there was a strong Christian movement there, spread widely throughout the country as well as in the cities, by the beginning of the second century. As mentioned in chapter 2, our source is the famous description of Pliny (*Letters* 10.96) as he reports on the prevalence of Christianity in the province to the emperor Trajan.

Throughout Asia Minor, a characteristic form of native religion was an ecstatic devotion to the great Earth Mother, manifested as the Artemis of the Ephesians, or Cybele of Phrygia, or one of many other local fertility deities (Strabo, *Geography* 10.3.6–23). The enthusiastic possession, which was typical of local cults, finds a counterpart in the prophetic sect that gathered around Montanus in the middle of the second century C.E.: Its impact was among a large rural population of Christians, and it stressed an ecstatic experience of the spirit. Asia Minor is also the setting of the story of Baucis and Philemon, who entertained gods without recognizing them (Ovid, *Metamorphoses* 8.618–724). There may be some connection with Acts 14:8–18, in which the people of Lystra in Lycaonia greet Barnabas and Paul as Zeus and Hermes.

### *Macedonia: Philippi and Thessalonica*

Paul's mission in Macedonia is a pivotal event both in Acts and in Paul's letter to the Philippians. Paul begins the "second missionary journey" in Acts 15:41, then proceeds according to the confusing itinerary in Acts 16:6–8. Despite special guidance by the Spirit, there is no missionary activity, although Luke's narration suggests that the move to Europe and to the Gentile mission was God's will.

Sailing from Troas, Paul lands at Neapolis, then travels along the Via Egnatia to the Roman colony of Philippi. Luke seems to have wanted a Roman city to be the first mission point on European soil. Beyond Philippi, Paul continues on the Via Egnatia, the crucial east–west route for trade and politics, to Amphipolis, Apollonia, and Thessalonica (Acts 16:12; 17:1). Then he leaves it, smuggled off to Beroea (Acts 17:10) rather than traveling on to the west.

Some years later (ca. 55 C.E.), Paul visited this area again (1 Cor. 16:5; Acts 19:21; 20:1–2), and he may have traveled farther west. In Romans 15:19 Paul claims to have preached the gospel "as far round as Illyricum," a province at the western end of the Via Egnatia even more thoroughly latinized than Philippi and Corinth.

To Luke and Paul, Philippi was the gate from Asia and Europe. It was located on a Macedonian hilltop next to a broad plain through which the main road from Europe to Asia passed. It received its name in 356 B.C.E. in honor of King Philip of Macedon, father of Alexander the Great. Here, in 42 B.C.E., Antony and Octavian, as the avengers of Julius Caesar, defeated his assassins; they then gave it the status of a Roman colony and settled it with veterans of the battle. As a colony, Philippi was a miniature Rome; half the names mentioned in inscriptions are Latin. Augustus granted it the *ius Italicum,* which meant that the colonists, depending on their civil status, enjoyed the same rights of proprietorship as if their land were part of Italian soil.

Political officials were drawn from the descendants of these Roman colonists, and perhaps from the few native families which were sufficiently powerful and loyal to Rome to be granted Roman citizenship. The highest officials in a Roman colony were the two *duumviri,* corresponding to the consuls in Rome and referred to in Acts by the Greek terms *archontes* or *stratēgoi* (16:19–39). Their official attendants were the *lictores* ("rod bearers," the *rabdouchoi* of Acts 16:35, 38), responsible for arresting and scourging persons.

When they arrived in Philippi, Paul and his companions went on a Sabbath day "outside the gate, to the riverside, where we supposed there was a place of prayer [*proseuchē*]" (Acts 16:13). A mile west of the city there is a stream, which may be the one referred to in Acts, but this poses problems if we translate *proseuchē* as "synagogue." Why was a Jewish place of prayer so far from the city, a long way to travel on the Sabbath, and why did they find nobody there except women? We do not have much independent evidence for Jews in Philippi, and *proseuchē* here may not refer to a synagogue at all.

Luke tells one story of local piety by telling about a "slave girl who had a spirit of divination and brought her owners much gain by soothsaying" (Acts 16:16). Roman religion was official from the time of the founding of the colony, and Greek gods played only a small role. On the other hand, local Thracian cults were persistent, and some oriental cults were becoming influential. We know of dedications to Jupiter, Juno, Minerva, Mercury, and Mars; to Victoria Augusta and old Italian fertility gods like Liber and Silvanus; to the Thracian goddess Bendis, represented as a huntress and underworld deity represented with symbols of immortality; to the Thracian horseman, a divine hunter who was worshiped with the title Savior; and to Isis and Sarapis, who were worshiped in a small private shrine.[15]

After leaving jail in Philippi, Paul traveled west to Thessalonica, where he would have noticed striking differences. Like Philippi, Thessalonica was on the periphery of Greece, and founded relatively late, about 315 B.C.E., by Cassander, king of Macedonia. It was named for his wife, a half-sister of Alexander the Great. Cassander had chosen a site where two roads cross: the east–west Via Egnatia and the road leading from the Aegean north across the Balkans to the Danube. The harbor was one of the best in the Aegean. Unlike Philippi, a Roman colony, Thessalonica was a typical Greek city with a Greek type of administration. Its population included handworkers, traders, and orators from Greece, Asia Minor, and Italy, but Greek culture predominated.

When Paul arrived, he found a synagogue (Acts 17:1), but we know very little about the Jewish residents of Thessalonica. One Jewish inscription dated to the mid–first century B.C.E. mentions "the highest god," and scholars disagree about whether the reference is to Yahweh.[16]

After leaving Thessalonica and traveling through Athens to Corinth, Paul wrote the Christians there a letter in which he summarized the gospel to which they had responded: "You turned to God from idols, to serve a living and true God, and to wait for his Son from heaven, whom he raised from the dead, Jesus who delivers us from the wrath to come" (1 Thess. 1:9–10). We know quite a lot about these "idols" that the Thessalonians rejected. Dionysus was worshiped both in a public cult with a state-appointed priest and in private thiasoi. Devotees of Isis and Sarapis, including wealthy Romans of high status, met in a house for religious and social purposes. The cult of the Cabiri, imported from the island of Samothrace, attracted the patronage of members of the city's upper classes by the time of Augustus; in some of its manifestations this cult recalled the violent death of a divine figure with orgiastic dancing and with a commemorative meal.[17]

Luke records that Paul converted several "Greek women of high standing" in Macedonia (Acts 16:14; 17:4, 12). It may be relevant that in Hellenistic times Macedonia was famous for producing aristocratic and royal ladies of outstanding vigor, from Olympias, mother of Alexander the Great, to Cleopatra VII, last of the Greek rulers of Egypt.

Paul left Thessalonica after the city officials took bail from Jason (Acts 17:9) and went south of the Via Egnatia to Beroea, a city "off the main road" (Cicero, *Against Piso* 89), from which he was also expelled. After being expelled from three Macedonian cities and passing through Athens (Acts 17:14–34), he arrived in Corinth, "in weakness and in much fear and trembling" (1 Cor. 2:3).

### *Achaia: Corinth*

In earlier times, from the eighth to the second centuries B.C.E., Corinth had been one of the most important cities of Greece. Its location at the isthmus connecting the Peloponnese to central Greece gave it immense political and commercial power, as it dominated the north–south road along the isthmus, as well as the maritime trade between the Aegean Sea on the east and the Gulf of Corinth on the west. It had been a leader in the resistance to Roman expansion into the Greek mainland in the second century and had been totally destroyed in 146 B.C.E. After a century of abandonment, the strategically important site was resettled in 44 B.C.E. by Julius Caesar as a Roman colony, to serve as the capital of the province of Achaia, which included all of southern Greece. By the time of Paul's visit around 50 C.E., Corinth had once again become a major city. Its walls enclosed an area two and a half times as large as Athens, and its twin harbors, at Cenchreae on the east and Lechaeum on the west, invited large crowds of travelers and merchants. It was the most important administrative and commercial center in Greece and was full of people on the go at all times. Paul seems to acknowledge the preeminence of the church there over the other congregations in Achaia (2 Cor. 1:1).

As Paul approached the city, he would first have seen the imposing mountain of Acrocorinth towering above the city to its south, crowned with fortification walls and a temple of Aphrodite (Strabo, *Geography* 8.6.21). He would have passed through widely scattered suburbs to arrive in the forum, full of reminders of the Roman administration. Latin inscriptions were everywhere. A temple on the western slope of the forum was dedicated to the family of the Julii, and another was dedicated to Livia, the wife of Augustus. At the eastern end, a Roman basilica accommodated the law courts, and at the southern edge, in front of a colonnaded row of shops almost 500 feet long (the largest in the empire!) was the *bēma* ("tribunal"), where the Roman governor conducted official public business (Acts 18:12–17).

If Paul was in Corinth in the spring of 49 or 51 C.E., he might have seen the Isthmian games. These were among the four major panhellenic festivals and were celebrated at the shrine of Poseidon on the isthmus every two years. The reward for winning in these games was a crown of celery, and Paul was moved to comment that these athletes worked "to receive a perishable wreath, but we an imperishable" (1 Cor. 9:25).

Aphrodite was also worshiped with great devotion in this port city. She appeared on Corinthian coins and had temples on Acrocorinth, inside the city, and at the harbor of Cenchreae. Strabo (*Geography* 8.6.20, tr. H. Rackham in Loeb Classical Library) tells the famous story that in her temple "there were more than a thousand temple slaves, prostitutes, whom both men and women had dedicated to the goddess." Most Greeks did not perceive any immorality in prostitution (one exception was Dio Chrysostom, 7.133–137), and Paul's polemic against sexual excess (1 Corinthians 5 to 7) is addressed to Corinthian Christians who had in the local spirit coined the slogan "All things are lawful for me" (1 Cor. 6:12).

Among the archaeological evidence for gods worshiped at Corinth, we find indications that members of many religious groups, here as elsewhere, met to eat a common cultic meal, which recalls Paul's discussions with the local Christians (1 Corinthians 8 to 11). Followers of Dionysus met in subterranean dining rooms, with six couches cut in the rock around a rock-hewn table. Similar dining rooms cut into the rock at the sanctuary of Asclepius could accommodate eleven persons with small tables in front of them. Meals served outdoors in tents were major elements of the ritual at the sanctuary of Demeter and Core. And the cult of Isis, which was popular in Corinth (Apuleius, *Golden Ass* 11.8–12, 16–17 describes a festive spring procession in her honor from Corinth to the harbor at Cenchreae), also included cultic meals in its ritual (Apuleius, *Golden Ass* 11.24).

Isis was also known to her devotees as the goddess "who gave women the same power as men."[18] One wonders whether the power for women proclaimed in Isis' praises was not one of the factors contributing to the remarkable freedom of the Christian women at Corinth (1 Cor. 1:11; 11:5; 16:19; Acts 18:2, 18).

There was money to be made in Corinth, and there were opportunities for the ambitious. A century or two after Paul, Alciphron (*Letters of Parasites* 24.3.16, tr. A. R. Benner and F. H. Fobes in Loeb Classical Library) comments on "the sordidness of the rich and the misery of the poor" and supposes that "the women have Aphrodite, guardian of the city, as their cult goddess, while the men have Famine." Still, some of the Corinthian Christians had enough substance that Paul may refer to their "abundance" (2 Cor. 8:14) in contrast with the Christians in both Macedonia and Jerusalem. Theissen has suggested that this contrast between the rich and the poor in Corinth is one basic source of the disputes in the church.[19] Paul suggests that their manner of celebrating the Lord's Supper will "humiliate those who have nothing" (1 Cor. 11:22). And Paul himself writes to warn them that both he and they will be humiliated if they give sparingly to Jerusalem (2 Cor. 9:4, 6).

In the religious, political, social, and economic environment of this urban center, Paul made contact with a number of Jews. The evidence for a Jewish presence in Corinth is, however, surprisingly sparse. Philo (*On the Embassy to Gaius* 281) includes Corinth in a list of cities having Jewish "colonies." One Greek inscription, crudely inscribed with the words "Synagogue of the Hebrews," documents the presence of an organized Jewish community, although the date cannot be determined.[20] Acts gives the name of a ruler of the synagogue who converted, Crispus (18:7–8; cf. 1 Cor. 1:14), and of another who did not convert but was beaten by a mob, Sosthenes (Acts 18:17). Paul is said to have left the synagogue and lived in a house adjacent to it, a house owned by a Gentile "worshipper of God," Titius Justus (18:7). The leatherworkers Aquila and Priscilla were also Jews (18:2). Paul worked with them and probably used their shop as a place for missionary teaching. The "first-fruits" among the Christian converts in Achaia were the members of the household of Stephanas, who seems to have been the patron of a house church: the Corinthian Christians apparently forgot to pay him the honor due him, and Paul makes a plea on his behalf (1 Cor. 1:16; 16:15–18).

One Roman official mentioned in connection with Paul in Corinth is Erastus, the city treasurer (Rom. 16:23). In 1927 and 1947, different pieces of a Latin inscription were discovered that name an Erastus as donor of the paving east of the theater in Corinth; he offers this pavement "in return for the office of *aedile.*" The aedile was a major magistrate, one of whose tasks was to manage the public games. Erastus therefore belonged to the municipal aristocracy, and this wealthy official may well be the same as the Christian mentioned by Paul.[21]

The kind of spontaneous, emotional civic disturbances illustrated in association with Paul's missionary activity by Acts 18:12 may have been common in the Greco-Roman cities of the Principate, with their context of unemployment and recurrent tension between workers and employers. This particular disturbance resulted in Paul's being brought into the forum to the tribunal of Gallio, proconsul of Achaia, perhaps between July and October of 51 C.E.[22]

Paul repeatedly alludes to the fractious, divisive tendencies within the Christian community at Corinth (e.g., 1 Cor. 1:10–17; 2 Cor. 12:20), tendencies that are not surprising in a place as centrally located, as busy, and as open to outside influence as Corinth.

### *Rome*

Paul arrived in Rome, according to Acts 28:16, as a prisoner; according to scholarly speculation, he arrived in the early 60s; according to pious tradition, he met his death there in the Christian persecutions under Nero. He had already written the Letter to the Romans (between 54 and 59 C.E.), which implies that the church was established there well before his arrival. In Rome, Paul was confronted by a huge, diverse, cosmopolitan population. The streets were filled with people of every nation, speaking a babel of languages, wearing exotic costumes. Public monuments reminded visitors of the power, traditions, and breadth of the Roman empire: Senate house and basilicas, temples of native and imported gods, pyramids and obelisks from Egypt, statues and paintings from Greece, warehouses holding grain and goods from Africa, Spain, Gaul.

The Romans reacted to all this diversity in an understandably complex way. Under some conditions they welcomed the influence, celebrated the diversity, and proclaimed that the uniqueness and strength of their society lay in Rome's ability to absorb many cities, states, and nations under its administration, to adopt and adapt fashions and ideas from the hundreds of cultures they encountered while they were expanding and administering their empire. At the same time a more conservative tendency resisted this kind of cultural encroachment: In 186 B.C.E., the cult of Bacchus was repressed; in 173 and 161 B.C.E., Greek philosophers were banned from the city; in 58 B.C.E., the Senate destroyed altars of the Egyptian gods. Under the Principate, both acceptance and rejection of foreign influence continued, depending on the policies or whims of individual emperors. Indeed, the effects of these individual policies were more immediately and more directly felt in Rome than anywhere else in the empire.

The fortunes of the Jews in Rome indicate how widely official policy could fluctuate. In 61 B.C.E., wealthy Jews ransomed the captives brought back by Pompey from his conquest of Judea. And in 59 B.C.E., Cicero, defending a former governor of Syria accused of maladministration, could appeal to anti-Jewish sentiment as he alluded to their large numbers, their influence, their clannish ways, and their suspicious practice of sending money each year to Jerusalem (Cicero, *For Flaccus* 66–69). On the other hand, Julius Caesar issued a decree granting to the Jews of Rome freedom of worship and permission to send their annual contributions of Temple tax to Jerusalem, and Augustus also granted them special favors. By this time the Jews must have numbered about 40,000, close to 5 percent of the population of Rome. (This figure is based on Josephus—*Antiquities* 17.300–301; *Jewish War* 2.80–81—who tells us that when a delegation came from Palestine in 4 B.C.E. to complain about the conduct of Archelaus, 8,000 Roman Jews, presumably adult males, crowded the precinct of Apollo on the Palatine Hill to demonstrate their support of the ambassadors.)

Jews of every social class lived in Rome or visited there. Herod the Great, for example, was present in 40 B.C.E. when he was proclaimed King of Judea. Agrippa spent many years as a prince in Rome on close terms with the imperial family. Lower on the social scale were small business people like Aquila and Prisca the tentmakers (Acts 18:2–3) or the butcher and the painter we meet in grave inscriptions. Many of the Jews, like much of the population of Rome in the first and second centuries, were poor; they appear in the pagan sources as porters, longshoremen, peddlers, or beggars.

Inscriptions in the Jewish catacombs indicate that about half the Jews had Latin names, which many of them may have gained when they were freed from slavery. Three quarters of the inscriptions were written in Greek, evidence of roots in the Diaspora communities of the Hellenistic world. We know of eleven separate congregations of Jews, and each seems to have had its own autonomous synagogue organization, though between them they shared three exclusively Jewish catacombs as burial places.

Jews were familiar to their Gentile neighbors, although not very well understood. The Roman writers mention the Jews' refusal to eat pork, the practice of circumcision, the Sabbath lights burning in tenement windows, and the abstinence from work on the Sabbath. They also noticed, and resented, the tendency of Jews to seek proselytes; some proselytes and sympathizers were very prominent, including Fulvia, a senator's wife in the reign of Tiberius; Poppaea, the wife of Nero; and Flavius Clemens, a cousin of Domitian.

According to Acts 2:10, Jews and proselytes from Rome were present in Jerusalem on the day of Pentecost, which suggests that the Christian gospel was first carried to Rome by ordinary members of the local Jewish community. This impression is reinforced by Paul's attitude in the Letter to the Romans, for he clearly implies that the church in Rome was not founded by any of the apostles.

The Letter implies a mixed community of Jews and non-Jews. It also implies that there were different parties within the Roman church, each enjoying its own traditions. It seems likely that the first Christians in Rome started within the established synagogues, and there is some good evidence that their zeal caused disputes and trouble with other members of the synagogues. Suetonius (*Claudius* 25) says that in the reign of Claudius (scholars dispute whether it happened in 41, 46, or 49 C.E.) riots broke out among the Jews at the instigation of a certain Chrestus, and as a result the Jews involved were expelled from the city. According to the most plausible explanation of this incident, "Chrestus" reflects a fairly common variant spelling of "Christus," and the disputes between followers of Christ and their Jewish colleagues got out of hand and out of the synagogues, threatening the public order, which was always a concern of the Roman authorities. Once order was restored, the emperor forbade the Jews to hold meetings and exiled the individuals who were responsible; Tacitus says they were all Jews, although some of them may have been Gentile Christians, since to the Roman historian Christians were just another type of Jewish sect. We meet two of these Christian exiles when Paul visits Corinth: the tentmakers Aquila and Prisca, who later go to Ephesus (Acts 18:2; Rom. 16:3). It is possible that these disturbances, and the loss of some leaders among both Christians and non-Christians, was the occasion when the Christians left the synagogues and set up their own organizations, based in the households of people like Aquila, Aristobulus, Narcissus, and Philologus, whom Paul mentions as heads of households (Rom. 16:3, 10, 11, 15).

In any event, when Claudius died in 54 C.E. the exiles were able to return, so when Paul arrived he would have found a large Jewish population, with groups of Christians coexisting either within the synagogues or as separate house churches. He came to Rome as a prisoner, escorted by a centurion, but while in Rome he was permitted to rent his own lodgings and to circulate freely (Acts 28:30–31). At this point, the Christians seem to have been mostly of eastern origin. They spoke Greek, the language in which Paul had written to them, and they derived their instruction, inspiration, and leadership from easterners.

Certainly Paul was not the only Christian preacher to come to Rome; the political and commercial geography of the Roman empire virtually guaranteed that visitors of every type streamed into it every day. A persistent tradition maintains that Peter also came to Rome and, like Paul, was executed there in the persecutions under Nero in 64 C.E. There is no mention of Peter's residence in Rome in either Acts or Romans, but the statement in 1 Peter (5:13) that that letter was being written "at Babylon" can be interpreted as an apocalyptic equivalent to "in Rome." The tradition of Peter in Rome was already strong at the end of the first century C.E., when Clement of Rome refers to it in his letter to the Corinthians (1 Clement 5; Ignatius, *Letter to the Romans* 4:3) and archaeological excavations under St. Peter's Basilica in the Vatican indicate that a memorial of some kind was erected in the second century C.E. to commemorate Peter's martyrdom.

In the century following Nero, people who were Christians came to Rome from every part of the empire. This diversity assured that somewhere in Rome a group of adherents was practicing virtually every variation of Christian faith. This diversity made it relatively difficult for the individual congregations to feel united, and the bishops of Rome (tradition preserves a list of names going back to Peter, Linus, Cletus, and Clement) were frequently faced with fractious resistance to their authority. In spite of that, the prestige of Rome throughout the empire endowed the church of Rome and its bishop with a special respect. We can appreciate the prestige in the tones with which the Roman church addresses the Corinthian church, in the First Letter of Clement, written around 100 C.E., and we can appreciate the respect with which the Roman church was regarded in the tones of the *Letter to the Romans* of Ignatius, bishop of Antioch.

One local custom in the church of Rome, that of the *fermentum,* illustrates an early attempt to bind the diverse congregations together into one fellowship: The bishop, when he celebrated the Eucharist, set aside some of the consecrated bread to be distributed to the several congregations around the city. Then, as the presbyters celebrated the Eucharist in the house churches, they mixed some of this bread from the bishop's table with their own, to unite all households of faith at a single table at which their bishop presided (Eusebius, *Ecclesiastical History* 5.24.14).

For all its diversity, the church in Rome up until the first half of the second century C.E. continued to be a Hellenistic community, speaking Greek and maintaining close contact with the Christian churches in the east. The evidence indicates that some upper-class Romans began to be attracted to Christianity in the first half of the century, but it seems likely that their education and cultural taste made them feel at home in the Hellenistic environment of the church in Rome. It is only around the middle of the second century that we can document any significant conversions among lower-class Romans, who did not speak Greek and would need a translation of the New Testament into Latin.

It had become traditional in Rome to cremate the dead and bury the ashes in communal tombs along the roads approaching the city. Christians, with their belief in the resurrection of the body, needed space to bury their dead without cremation. Wealthy members of the community donated space on their suburban estates, and as the numbers of Christians, both living and dead, increased, they dug down into the relatively soft volcanic rock to produce the long, grave-lined corridors known as catacombs. Like their pagan neighbors, the Christians often built small outdoor dining rooms near the entrances to their tombs, and in time these became shrines to the Christians who had died a martyr's death.

As far as we know, the first time that the Christians in Rome came to the attention of the authorities was during the reign of Claudius, when the disturbances "stirred up by Chrestus" prompted the emperor to expel from the city the people involved, who were evidently (to the Romans) Jews. The Roman Christians gained their greatest early notoriety in 64 C.E., after the great fire, which destroyed nearly half of the monumental center and downtown residential areas of the city. Nero, in search of a scapegoat to assume the blame for the disaster, rounded up Christians, perhaps relying on Jewish apocalyptic literature, which referred with satisfaction to the expectation that God would burn the whole earth and all its inhabitants (cf. *Sibylline Oracles* 2.15–19, 196–213; 3.54). Trials were held, confessions were extorted, and the convicted Christians were thrown to the wild beasts in the circus or nailed to crosses or burned alive. The Roman historian Tacitus calls Christianity a "deadly superstition" but adds that the tortures inflicted on its followers were so grim that the populace of Rome felt compassion for them and resented Nero's cruelty (Tacitus, *Annals* 15.44).[23]

Later tradition remembered the reign of Domitian (81–96 C.E.) as a time of persecution. Under Trajan (98–117 C.E.), we know that Ignatius, bishop of Antioch, was convicted and then brought to Rome for execution; in his *Letter to the Romans,* he asks the Christians in Rome not to intercede on his behalf. In general during the second century, however, the authorities in Rome seem to have paid little attention to the Christians. Their pagan neighbors must have regarded them with a certain amount of suspicion, as vaguely similar to the Jews or to the worshipers of the Syrian gods. The suspicion was mixed in some cases with respect, and we have seen that by the middle of the second century the Christians were having some success in making converts among the Latin-speaking native Romans. The Christians were still of course liable to occasional trial and condemnation, even in those long periods when there was no general persecution. So in 165 C.E. a visitor from Samaria, Justin, known ever since as "Martyr," was accused by a Cynic philosopher and condemned to death. Thereafter, however, all was relatively calm in Rome, and under the dynasty of the Severi we find that the imperial court itself exhibited a lively and sympathetic interest in the variety of religions being practiced in the city. These included Christianity, and we read that the emperor Alexander Severus (222–235 C.E.) had a shrine in his palace with an image of Christ (Scriptores Historiae Augustae, *Severus Alexander* 29.2).

### *Egypt: Alexandria*

Along with Jerusalem, Antioch, and Rome, the city of Alexandria at the northwestern corner of the Nile delta was one of the four greatest centers of Christianity from the third century C.E. on, and from it the gospel spread throughout the northern part of Africa.

We have no evidence at all about how Christianity came to Alexandria. Paul refers to the activity of a certain Apollos at Corinth (1 Cor. 1:12; 3:4–6, 22; 4:6; 16:12; cf. Acts 19:1). Acts 18:24–28 tells of his influence at Ephesus and adds that he was from Alexandria. He was eloquent and well versed in the scriptures, which probably means that he interpreted the Torah allegorically, as did other Alexandrian writers like Philo and Origen.

Alexandria had been founded by Alexander the Great in 331

B.C.E. and as the capital of the Ptolemaic kingdom became one of the largest, richest, most lavishly decorated cities of the world (Strabo, *Geography* 17.1.8–10; Achilles Tatius 5.1–2). After Cleopatra, the last of the Ptolemies, committed suicide in 31 B.C.E., the Romans took it over, and Augustus installed there a prefect, accountable to himself alone, who administered the newly created province of Egypt from the old Ptolemaic palaces in Alexandria.

The Ptolemies had established the "Museum," a royal institute at which the foremost scientists and poets of the world were maintained and encouraged to study and write. Together with the Royal Library, the most complete in the world, the museum gave an intellectual prestige to Alexandria that was matched only by Athens. Under the later Ptolemies and the Roman domination, the museum and library gradually became less important, but Alexandria continued to be a major center of intellectual activity.

The city was consummately cosmopolitan. Founded by a Greek king and organized as a Greek polis, it nevertheless included large numbers of native Egyptians within its population, as well as immigrants from all over the world. They brought with them their gods and goddesses to join the Greek and Egyptian gods already worshiped there; among these was the god Sarapis, a syncretistic deity combining the nature of the Egyptian god Osiris with the outward appearance of a Greek father-god. The city was also one of the most important ports in the world. From here the grain ships set out bearing Egyptian grain to Rome, as well as Egyptian linen and luxury goods. And they brought all the products of the world to Alexandria in exchange.

Among the cosmopolitan population lived a very large number of Jews, who occupied more than one of the five regions into which the city was divided. The central synagogue was fabulously large, and Jews were active in almost every type of work in the city. Their prominence brought them to the attention of their pagan neighbors, and the animosity broke out into serious violence in 38 C.E.; the Roman prefect Flaccus encouraged the Greeks as they plundered Jews' houses, burned synagogues, and flogged Jewish councillors. The story is told by Philo of Alexandria *(Against Flaccus* and *On the Embassy to Gaius),* as part of a hearing against Flaccus in the presence of the emperor Gaius in Rome. Later, conflict between Jews and Greeks again broke out in 55 and 115 C.E.

Philo himself was one of the most important thinkers and writers of the Jewish Diaspora. He stood in a proud tradition of Jewish literary production in Alexandria, which also included the translation of the scriptures into Greek. Philo reflects the syncretistic spirit of the city, interpreting Jewish tradition within the terms of Greek philosophy.

It was in this city that, according to tradition, the evangelist Mark preached and wrote his Gospel, and his tomb was venerated in the city until Venetian traders absconded with the relics to Venice. Tradition becomes history with the appearance of Demetrius as bishop in 189 C.E.; he was patriarch of Alexandria, and the Christian theologian Origen was in constant tension with him. Continuing the intellectual tradition of Hellenistic Jews like Philo, Origen and Clement of Alexandria presided over a Christian school known as the Didaskaleion. These Christian philosophers interpreted the gospel in a broad, syncretistic way. Beside these "orthodox" Christians, Gnostics such as Basilides and Valentinus were active in Egypt. The Gnostic Hermetic books were written in Egypt from the second to the fourth centuries C.E., as were many of the Gnostic texts recently discovered at Nag Hammadi. Alexandria also produced the priest Arius, whose theories about God and Christ were the subject of furious debate at the First General Council of the church, called at Nicaea in 325 C.E. by the first Christian emperor, Constantine.

After Constantine recognized Christianity in 312 C.E., its quarrels and controversies became matters of state. The Christian church had grown into a new phase of its history, but its new trials—battles over doctrine, organization, and discipline—continued to be experienced for the most part in the urban environment, where for almost three centuries the church had been furtively but effectively nurtured.

# Notes

### Chapter 1: Historical Background

1. Victor Tcherikover, *Hellenistic Civilization and the Jews* (Atheneum Publishers, 1970), pp. 126–203; Martin Hengel, *Judaism and Hellenism* (Fortress Press, 1974), vol. I, pp. 267–309.

2. A. N. Sherwin-White, *Roman Society and Roman Law in the New Testament* (Oxford University Press, 1963), pp. 162–171; E. Mary Smallwood, *The Jews Under Roman Rule* (E. J. Brill, 1976), pp. 568–571; Emil Schürer, *History of the Jewish People,* rev. by G. Vermes et al. (T. & T. Clark, 1979), pp. 399–427.

3. Smallwood, *Jews Under Roman Rule,* pp. 351–352.

4. Ibid., pp. 421–427.

5. Yigael Yadin, *Bar Kokhba* (Random House, 1971), pp. 172–183.

6. Peter Garnsey, "The Lex Iulia and Appeal Under the Empire," *Journal of Roman Studies* 56 (1966), pp. 167–189.

7. W. H. C. Frend, *Martyrdom and Persecution in the Early Church* (New York University Press, 1967), pp. 162–169.

8. P. Winter, *On the Trial of Jesus* (Berlin, 1961), pp. 67–90; Smallwood, *Jews Under Roman Rule,* pp. 149–150.

9. Sherwin-White, *Roman Society and Roman Law,* pp. 32–43.

### Chapter 2: Mobility and Mission

1. Nils A. Dahl, "Letter," *The Interpreter's Dictionary of the Bible,* suppl. vol. (Abingdon, 1976), pp. 538–541; Stanley K. Stowers, *Letter Writing in Greco-Roman Antiquity* (Library of Early Christianity; Westminster Press, in preparation).

2. H. Stuart Jones, "Claudius and the Jewish Question at Alexandria," *Journal of Roman Studies* 16 (1926), pp. 27–28.

3. Ramsay MacMullen, *Paganism in the Roman Empire* (Yale University Press, 1981), pp. 109–110; Helmut Engelmann, *The Delian Aretalogy of Sarapis,* tr. by Ewald Osers (E. J. Brill, 1975).

4. MacMullen, *Paganism,* pp. 3–4.

5. Ibid., pp. 90–94; John Ferguson, *The Religions of the Roman Empire* (Cornell University Press, 1970), pp. 211–243.

6. Walter Burkert, "Craft Versus Sect: The Problem of Orphics and Pythagoreans," *Jewish and Christian Self-Definition,* ed. by B. F. Meyer and E. P. Sanders, vol. 3 (Fortress Press, 1982), pp. 1–22.

7. Abraham J. Malherbe, "Self-Definition Among Epicureans and Cynics," *Jewish and Christian Self-Definition,* vol. 3, pp. 46–59; Bernard Frischer, *The Sculpted Word: Epicureanism and Philosophical Recruitment in Ancient Greece* (University of California Press, 1982), esp. pp. 67–86.

8. Ramsay MacMullen, *Enemies of the Roman Order* (Harvard University Press, 1966), pp. 46–94.

9. A. T. Kraabel, "The Diaspora Synagogue: Archaeological and Epigraphic Evidence Since Sukenik," *Aufstieg und Niedergang der römischen Welt* (cited elsewhere in this chapter as *ANRW*), ed. by H. Temporini and W. Haase, vol. 2.19.1 (Walter de Gruyter, 1979), pp. 477–510; "Social Systems of Six Diaspora Synagogues," *Ancient Synagogues: The State of Research,* ed. by Joseph Gutmann (Scholars Press, 1981), pp. 79–91.

10. S. W. Baron, *A Social and Religious History of the Jews,* 2nd ed., vol. 1 (Columbia University Press, 1952), p. 171.

11. Smallwood, *Jews Under Roman Rule,* pp. 416–417.

12. T. M. Taylor, "The Beginnings of Jewish Proselyte Baptism," *New Testament Studies* 2 (1955–56), pp. 193–198; Smallwood, *Jews Under Roman Rule,* p. 430.

13. Victor Tcherikover, *Hellenistic Civilization and the Jews,* pp. 302–303; Schmuel Safrai and M. Stern, eds., *The Jewish People in the First Century,* vol 1 (Fortress Press, 1974), pp. 488, 500.

14. Sukkah 51b, quoted and discussed by Tcherikover, *Hellenistic Civilization and the Jews,* pp. 337–338.

15. Victor Tcherikover, *The Jews in Egypt in the Hellenistic-Roman Age in the Light of the Papyri* (1963), pp. 146–159 (in Hebrew), pp. xiv–xxvi (in English).

16. Folker Siegert, "Gottesfürchtige und Sympathisanten," *Journal for the Study of Judaism* 4 (1973), 144–145.

17. Tcherikover, *Hellenistic Civilization and the Jews,* p. 352.

18. Jones, "Claudius" (note 2 above), pp. 17–35; Smallwood, *Jews Under Roman Rule,* pp. 246–250; R. Goldenberg, "The Jewish Sabbath in the Roman World up to the Time of Constantine the Great," *ANRW,* vol. 2.19.1, pp. 418–421.

19. W. H. C. Frend, *Martyrdom and Persecution in the Early Church* (New York University Press, 1967), pp. 100–105, 145.

20. Robin Scroggs, "The Earliest Hellenistic Christianity," *Religions in Antiquity,* ed. by Jacob Neusner (E. J. Brill, 1970), pp. 176–206.

21. E. A. Judge, *The Social Pattern of Christian Groups in the First Century* (Tyndale Press, 1960), p. 57.

22. Henneke Gülzow, "Soziale Gegebenheiten der altkirchlichen Mission," in *Die Alte Kirche,* ed. by Heinzgünter Fröhnes and Uwe W. Knorr (Chr. Kaiser Verlag, 1974), p. 196; Wayne A. Meeks, *The First Urban Christians* (Yale University Press, 1983), pp. 25–30.

23. Elisabeth Schüssler Fiorenza, *In Memory of Her* (Crossroad, 1983), pp. 208–218.

24. D. Lührmann, "Neutestamentliche Haustafeln und antike Oekonomie," *New Testament Studies* 27 (1980), pp. 83–97; David L. Balch, *Let Wives Be Submissive: The Domestic Code in 1 Peter* (Scholars Press, 1981); Fiorenza, *In Memory of Her.*

25. D. W. Riddle, "Early Christian Hospitality, a Factor in the Gospel Transmission," *Journal of Biblical Literature* 57 (1938), pp. 141–154; A. J. Malherbe, "The Inhospitality of Diotrephes," in *God's Christ and His People: Studies in Honour of Nils Alstrup Dahl,* ed. by Jacob Jervell and Wayne A. Meeks (Oslo: Universitetsforlaget, 1977), pp. 222–232; reprinted in *Social Aspects of Early Christianity,* 2nd rev. ed. (Fortress Press, 1983), pp. 92–112.

26. Robert M. Grant, *Early Christianity and Society: Seven Studies* (Harper & Row, 1977), ch. 6.

27. Wayne A. Meeks, "In One Body: The Unity of Humankind in Colossians and Ephesians," *God's Christ and His People,* pp. 209–221.

28. Meeks, *First Urban Christians,* p. 147.

29. Balch, *Wives.*

**Chapter 3: The Ancient Economy**

1. A. R. Hands, *Charities and Social Aid in Greece and Rome* (Cornell University Press, 1968).

2. L. William Countryman, *The Rich Christian in the Church of the Early Empire: Contradictions and Accommodations* (Edwin Mellen Press, 1980), ch. 3.

3. John H. D'Arms, *Commerce and Social Standing in Ancient Rome* (Harvard University Press, 1981).

4. Richard Duncan-Jones, *The Economy of the Roman Empire: Quantitative Studies* (Cambridge University Press, 1974), ch. 1, "The Finances of a Senator," pp. 17–32.

5. G. E. M. de Ste. Croix, *The Class Struggle in the Ancient Greek World* (Cornell University Press, 1981), pp. 428–432.

6. P. Veyne, "Vie de Trimalcion," *Annales (Economies, Sociétés, Civilisations)* 16 (1961), pp. 213–247.

7. *Corpus Inscriptionum Latinarum,* vol. 8, no. 11824; Ramsay MacMullen, *Roman Social Relations* (Yale University Press, 1974), p. 74.

8. J. B. Frey, *Corpus Inscriptionum Judaicarum,* vol. 1 (Rome, 1936), no. 945.

9. H. Kreissig, "Free Labour in the Hellenistic Age," in *Non-Slave Labour in the Greco-Roman World,* ed. by Peter Garnsey (Cambridge Philological Society, 1980), pp. 30–33.

10. Ste. Croix, *Class Struggle,* esp. pp. 172–173; Moses Finley, *The Ancient Economy* (University of California Press, 1973), pp. 62–94.

11. Finley, *Ancient Economy,* pp. 53–55, 142–143.

12. Ste. Croix, *Class Struggle,* pp. 164, 170.

13. Laura Breglia, "Circolazione monetale ed aspetti di vita economica a Pompei," *Pompeiana* (Biblioteca della Parola del Passato, no. 4, 1950), pp. 47–48.

14. Frederick W. Danker, *Benefactor: Epigraphic Study of a Graeco-Roman and New Testament Semantic Field* (Clayton Publishing House, 1982).

15. Finley, *Ancient Economy,* pp. 129–149.

16. Michael H. Crawford, "Money and Exchange in the Roman World," *Journal of Roman Studies* 60 (1970), pp. 40–48.

17. Pliny, *Natural History* 18.88–90; *Corpus Inscriptionum Latinarum,* vol. 4, nos. 1679, 5380.

## Chapter 4: Society in Palestine

1. Michael Avi-Yonah in *The Jewish People in the First Century,* sec. 1, vol. 1, ed. by Safrai and Stern (Fortress Press, 1974), pp. 108–110. More recent figures are given by Applebaum (note 2 below).

2. S. Applebaum in *Aufstieg und Niedergang der römischen Welt,* 2.8, p. 376. Cited elsewhere in this chapter as *ANRW.*

3. Safrai in *Jewish People,* sec. 1, vol. 2, p. 791. This section and the secondary literature cited often depend on rabbinic sources from the second century C.E. and later, which means that the illustrations and conclusions occasionally may not shed light on the period before the two Jewish wars with Rome, when the Pharisaic views were not dominant and had not yet been changed by those traumas.

4. A. T. Kraabel, "The Diaspora Synagogue: Archaeological and Epigraphic Evidence Since Sukenik," *ANRW* 2.19.1 (1979), pp. 477–510, at pp. 491–494.

5. Schürer/Vermes, *History of the Jewish People* (T. & T. Clark, 1979), vol. 2, pp. 425–426.

6. James F. Strange in *ANRW* 2.19.1, pp. 656–657.

7. Safrai in *Jewish People,* sec. 1, vol. 2, p. 927.

8. Eric M. Meyers and James F. Strange, *Archaeology, the Rabbis, and Early Christianity* (Abingdon Press, 1981), p. 145.

9. G. Mussies in *Jewish People,* sec. 1, vol. 2, p. 1044.

10. Joseph A. Fitzmyer, "The Languages of Palestine in the First Century A.D.," *Catholic Biblical Quarterly* 32 (1970), p. 514 has text and translation.

11. Strange in *ANRW* 2.19.1, pp. 660–661. The Theodotus inscription is translated in C. K. Barrett, *The New Testament Background: Selected Documents* (Harper & Row, 1961), no. 50.

12. Fitzmyer, "Languages," p. 523.

13. Nahman Avigad, *Beth She'arim,* vol. 3: *Catacombs 12–23* (Rutgers University Press, 1971), pp. 277–278.

14. Schürer/Vermes, *History of the Jewish People,* vol. 2, sec. 23.

15. A. N. Sherwin-White, *Roman Society and Roman Law in the New Testament* (Oxford University Press, 1963), p. 127.

16. Ibid., p. 139.

17. Applebaum in *ANRW* 2.8, pp. 361, 364.

18. Sean Freyne, *Galilee from Alexander the Great to Hadrian* (Michael Glazier, 1980).

19. Eric M. Meyers in *ANRW* 2.19.1, pp. 697–698.

20. Freyne, *Galilee,* p. 294.

21. See Schürer/Vermes, *History of the Jewish People,* vol. 2, p. 123, on Antiochan citizens at Ptolemais.

22. John Wilkinson, *Jerusalem as Jesus Knew It* (Thames and Hudson,

1978), pp. 138–144; but see Jack Finegan, *The Archaeology of the New Testament* (Princeton University Press, 1969), p. 157.

23. Wilkinson, *Jerusalem,* p. 62.

24. Schürer/Vermes, *History of the Jewish People,* vol. 2, pp. 384–387.

25. Joachim Jeremias, *Jerusalem in the Time of Jesus* (Fortress Press, 1969), ch. 9.

26. Schürer/Vermes, *History of the Jewish People,* vol. 2, p. 257.

27. Jeremias, *Jerusalem,* pp. 113, 234.

28. Jacob Neusner, *From Politics to Piety* (Prentice-Hall, 1973), p. 86.

29. Neusner in *ANRW* 2.19.2 (1979), p. 22.

30. Ibid.

31. Neusner, *From Politics to Piety,* p. 90.

32. J. Klausner in *The World History of the Jewish People,* vol. 7: *The Herodian Period,* ed. by Michael Avi-Yonah and Zui Baras (Rutgers University Press, 1975), p. 186.

33. Gerd Theissen, *Sociology of Early Palestinian Christianity* (Fortress Press, 1977), p. 33.

34. Ibid., p. 40.

35. E. Rivkin, "The Internal City," *Journal for the Scientific Study of Religion* 5 (1965–66), pp. 225–240, at pp. 232–233.

36. James A. Sanders, "Adaptable for Life: The Nature and Function of Canon," in *Magnalia Dei: The Mighty Acts of God,* ed. by F. M. Cross et al. (Doubleday & Co., 1976), pp. 531–560, at p. 535.

37. Louis Finkelstein, *The Pharisees: The Sociological Background of Their Faith* (Jewish Publication Society, 1946) vol. 1, pp. 125–126; Jacob Neusner, *A Life of Rabban Johanan ben Zakkai. Ca. 1–80 CE.* (E. J. Brill, 1962), p. 50.

38. Jeremias, *Jerusalem,* p. 376.

39. Martin Hengel, "Maria Magdalena und die Frauen als Zeugen," in *Abraham Unser Vater.* Festschrift Otto Michel, ed. by O. Betz et al. (E. J. Brill, 1963), pp. 243–256.

40. Fiorenza, *In Memory of Her,* pp. 115–118.

41. M. Jack Suggs, *Wisdom, Christology, and Law in Matthew's Gospel* (Harvard University Press, 1970).

42. Balch, *Wives,* pp. 69–72, and Fiorenza, *In Memory of Her,* pp. 130–135.

43. Hengel "Maria Magdalena," p. 243; James M. Robinson, "Jesus as Sophos and Sophia: Wisdom Tradition and the Gospels," in *Aspects of Wisdom in Judaism and Early Christianity,* ed. by Robert L. Wilken (University of Notre Dame, 1975), pp. 1–16.

44. Theissen, *Sociology,* p. 85; James A. Sanders, "Torah and Paul," in *God's Christ and His People: Studies in Honour of Nils Alstrup Dahl,* ed. by Jacob Jervell and Wayne A. Meeks (Oslo: Universitetsforlaget, 1977), pp. 132–140.

45. Wolfgang Stegemann, "Wanderradikalismus in Urchristentum?" in *Der Gott der Kleinen Leute* (Kaiser, 1979), pp. 101, 106.

46. Fiorenza, *In Memory of Her,* p. 142.

47. David L. Balch, "Early Christian Criticism of Patriarchal Authority: I Peter 2:11–3:12," *Union Seminary Quarterly Review* 39 (1984), pp. 161–174.

**Chapter 5: City Life**

1. A. K. McKay, *Houses, Villas, and Palaces in the Roman World* (Cornell University Press, 1975), pp. 212–217.

2. Bruce W. Frier, *Landlords and Tenants in Imperial Rome* (Princeton University Press, 1980), pp. 3–20.

3. Thucydides 2.45; *Inscriptiones Latinae Selectae,* ed. by H. Dessau, no. 8394; G. Clark, "Roman Women," *Greece and Rome,* 2nd series, 28 (1981), pp. 193–212; J. P. V. D. Balsdon, *Roman Women: Their History and Habits* (John Day Co., 1963); and Sarah B. Pomeroy, *Goddesses, Whores, Wives and Slaves* (Schocken Books, 1975).

4. Moses I. Finley, "Aulus Kapreilius Timotheus, Slave Trader," *Aspects of Antiquity: Discoveries and Controversies* (Viking Press, 1960), p. 166.

5. Peter Garnsey, *Social Status and Legal Privilege in the Roman Empire* (Oxford University Press, 1970), pp. 260–271, 277–280.

6. Gerd Theissen, "Social Integration and Sacramental Activity: An Analysis of 1 Cor. 11:17–34," *The Social Setting of Pauline Christianity,* ed. and tr. by John H. Schütz (Fortress Press, 1982), pp. 145–174.

7. Wayne A. Meeks, *The First Urban Christians* (Yale University Press, 1983), pp. 22–23, 59–61.

8. Ramsay MacMullen, *Roman Social Relations* (Yale University Press, 1974), pp. 69–72, 132–135.

9. Ronald F. Hock, *The Social Context of Paul's Ministry: Tentmaking and Apostleship* (Fortress Press, 1980).

10. Donald Sperber, "On Pubs and Policemen in Roman Palestine," *Zeitschrift der Deutschen Morgenländischen Gesellschaft* 120 (1970), pp. 257–263.

11. Michael Grant, *Gladiators* (Delacorte Press, 1967); J. P. V. D. Balsdon, *Life and Leisure in Ancient Rome* (McGraw-Hill, 1969), pp. 244–329.

12. H. I. Marrou, *A History of Education in Antiquity,* tr. by George Lamb (Sheed & Ward, 1956); Stanley F. Bonner, *Education in Ancient Rome* (Methuen, 1977).

13. David L. Balch, *Let Wives Be Submissive: The Domestic Code in 1 Peter* (Scholars Press, 1981), pp. 36, 55, 74, 76.

14. David C. Verner, *The Household of God: The Social World of the Pastoral Epistles* (Scholars Press, 1983) pp. 60–63.

15. Balch, *Wives,* chs. 5–6.

16. Elisabeth Schüssler Fiorenza, *In Memory of Her* (Crossroad, 1983), pp. 145–151.

17. Balch, *Wives,* pp. 54, 97.

18. Ibid., pp. 68–69.

19. MacMullen, *Roman Social Relations,* pp. 72–87; F. M. DeRobertis, *Storia delle corporazioni e del regime associativo nel mondo romano* (Adriatica, 1971).

20. A. D. Nock, *Conversion* (Oxford University Press, 1933), p. 203.

21. Ibid., pp. 228–229.

22. C. Golini, *Protesta e integrazione nella Roma antica* (Adriatica, 1971), chs. 1 and 2.

23. Achille Vogliano and Franz Cumont, "The Bacchic Inscription in the Metropolitan Museum," *American Journal of Archaeology* 37 (1933), pp. 215–270; M. P. Nilsson, *The Dionysiac Mysteries of the Hellenistic and Roman Age* (Skansak Centraltryckeriet, 1957), esp. ch. 5.

24. J. H. W. G. Liebeschuetz, *Continuity and Change in Roman Religion* (Oxford University Press, 1977), p. 60.

25. Nock, *Conversion,* p. 217.

26. Sharon Kelly Heyob, *The Cult of Isis Among Women in the Graeco-Roman World* (E. J. Brill, 1975); cf. ch. 6, note 18.

27. Charles Edson, "Cults of Thessalonica," *Harvard Theological Review* 41 (1948), pp. 181–188.

28. Robert Duthoy, *The Taurobolium: Its Evolution and Terminology* (E. J. Brill, 1969), pp. 103–108.

**Chapter 6: Christianity in the Cities of the Roman Empire**

1. A. D. Nock, *Early Gentile Christianity and Its Hellenistic Background* (Harper Torchbooks, 1964), pp. 134–137; W. R. Wiens, "Mystery Concepts in Primitive Christianity and in Its Environment," *Aufstieg und Niedergang der römischen Welt* (cited elsewhere in this chapter as *ANRW*) 2.23.2 (1980), pp. 1248–1284.

2. Elisabeth Schüssler Fiorenza, *In Memory of Her* (Crossroad, 1983), pp. 160–184; Hans-Josef Klauck, *Hausgemeinde und Hauskirche im frühen Christentum* (Stuttgarter Bibelstudien 103: Katholisches Bibelwerk, 1981); David C. Verner, *The Household of God: The Social World of the Pastoral Epistles* (Scholars Press, 1983).

3. *Sylloge Inscriptionum Graecarum,* ed. by Wilhelm Dittenberger, 3d ed., vol. 3 (S. Hirzelium, 1920), no.1109, lines 63–95; *Inscriptiones Latinae Selectae,* ed. by Hermann Dessau, vol. 2.2 (Weidmann, 1906), no. 7212, lines 25–28.

4. E. A. Judge, "The Early Christians as a Scholastic Community," *Journal of Religious History* 1 (1960), pp. 4–15, 125–137.

5. Wayne A. Meeks, *The First Urban Christians* (Yale University Press, 1983), pp. 78–80.

6. Krister Stendahl, *The School of St. Matthew and Its Use of the Old Testament* (Fortress Press, 1968).

7. Abraham J. Malherbe, *Social Aspects of Urban Christianity* (Fortress Press, 1983), pp. 53–55.

8. Malherbe, "Self-Definition" (ch. 2, note 7); Stanley K. Stowers, *The Diatribe and Paul's Letter to the Romans* (Scholars Press, 1981).

9. Walter Lewis Liefeld, *The Wandering Preacher as a Social Figure in the Roman Empire* (University Microfilms, 1967).

10. Wayne A. Meeks and Robert L. Wilken, *Jews and Christians in Antioch in the First Four Centuries of the Common Era* (Scholars Press, 1978), p. 16.

11. Elma Heinzel, "Zum Kult der Artemis von Ephesos," *Jahreshefte des Oesterreichischen Archaeologischen Instituts in Wien* 50 (1972–73), pp. 243–251; Richard Oster, "The Ephesian Artemis as an Opponent of Early Christianity," *Jahrbuch für Antike und Christentum* 19 (1976), pp. 21–44; Robert M. Grant, *Gods and the One God* (Westminster Press, 1986).

12. John Knox, "Philemon," *The Interpreter's Bible,* vol. 11 (Abingdon Press, 1955), pp. 557–560.

13. Sherman E. Johnson, "Asia Minor and Early Christianity," *Christianity, Judaism and Other Greco-Roman Cults,* ed. by Jacob Neusner (E. J. Brill, 1975), pp. 101–104.

14. Stephen Mitchell, "Population and the Land in Roman Galatia," *ANRW* 2.7.2 (1980), pp. 1073–1075.

15. Winifried Elliger, *Paulus in Griechenland* (Stuttgarter Bibelstudien 92–93: Katholisches Bibelwerk, 1978), p. 50.

16. Ibid., p. 92.

17. Charles Edson, "Cults of Thessalonica," *Harvard Theological Review* 41 (1948), pp. 151–204.

18. *The Oxyrhynchus Papyri,* Part 11, ed. by Bernard P. Grenfell and Arthur S. Hunt (Egypt Exploration Fund, 1915), no. 1380, lines 214–216; cf. David L. Balch, *Let Wives Be Submissive* (Scholars Press, 1981), p. 71.

19. Gerd Theissen, *The Social Setting of Pauline Christianity* (Fortress Press, 1982), pp. 99–110, 145–174.

20. Allen Brown West, *Latin Inscriptions 1896–1926* (*Corinth,* vol. 8.2; Harvard University Press, 1931), no. 111.

21. John H. Kent, *Inscriptions 1926–1960* (*Corinth,* vol. 8.3; American School of Classical Studies at Athens, 1966), p. 100; Meeks, *First Urban Christians,* pp. 58–59.

22. Elliger, *Paulus in Griechenland,* pp. 248–249; James Wiseman, "Corinth and Rome I," *ANRW* 2.7.1 (1979), p. 504, n. 254; Jerome Murphy-O'Connor, *St. Paul's Corinth* (Michael Glazier, 1983), p. 150.

23. W. H. C. Frend, *The Early Church* (J. B. Lippincott Co., 1966), p. 54.

# Suggestions for Further Reading

## Chapter 1: Historical Background

Convenient general histories of the later Roman Republic and the early centuries of the Principate include *The Cambridge Ancient History,* vols. 9–11, ed. by S. A. Cook, F. E. Adcock, and M. P. Charlesworth (Cambridge University Press, 1932–1936); H. H. Scullard, *From the Gracchi to Nero: A History of Rome from 133 B.C. to A.D. 68* (4th ed., Methuen & Co., 1976); and Edward T. Salmon, *A History of the Roman World from 30 B.C. to A.D. 138* (Methuen & Co., 1944).

On the political history of Palestine, see Victor Tcherikover, *Hellenistic Civilization and the Jews* (Atheneum Publishers, 1970); E. Mary Smallwood, *The Jews Under Roman Rule: From Pompey to Diocletian* (E. J. Brill, 1976); and Emil Schürer, *The History of the Jewish People in the Age of Jesus Christ (175 B.C.–A.D. 135),* rev. by G. Vermes, F. Millar, and M. Black (T. & T. Clark, 1979); also Bo Reicke, *The New Testament Era: The World of the Bible from 500 B.C. to A.D. 100,* tr. by David E. Green (Fortress Press, 1968).

On Roman law, see especially A. N. Sherwin-White, *Roman Society and Roman Law in the New Testament* (Oxford University Press, 1963), and in more general terms J. A. Crook, *Law and Life of Rome, 90 B.C.–A.D. 212* (Cornell University Press, 1967).

## Chapter 2: Mobility and Mission

On the mechanics and social aspects of ancient travel, Lionel Casson's *Travel in the Ancient World* (Hakkert, 1974), Raymond Chevallier's *Roman Roads,* tr. by N. H. Field (University of California Press, 1976), and Nigel Sitwell's *The Roman Roads of Europe* (St. Martin's Press, 1981) are well illustrated and readable.

The classic study of methods of evangelizing in pagan cults and philosophical sects is still A. D. Nock, *Conversion: The Old and the New in Religion from Alexander the Great to Augustine of Hippo* (Oxford University Press, 1933); conversion and evangelizing have been recently discussed in Ramsay Mac-

Mullen, *Paganism in the Roman Empire* (Yale University Press, 1981), pp. 94–112, and *Christianizing the Roman Empire* (Yale University Press, 1984).

Three important surveys of Diaspora (as well as Palestinian) Judaism are Schmuel Safrai and M. Stern, eds., *The Jewish People in the First Century* (*Compendia Rerum Iudaicarum ad Novum Testamentum;* Fortress Press, 1974); Victor Tcherikover, *Hellenistic Civilization and the Jews* (Atheneum Publishers, 1970); and E. Mary Smallwood, *The Jews Under Roman Rule: From Pompey to Diocletian* (E. J. Brill, 1976). The extent of syncretism in Diaspora Judaism is discussed by Martin Hengel, *Judaism and Hellenism: Studies in Their Encounter in Palestine During the Early Hellenistic Period* (Fortress Press, 1974, tr. by John Bowden), who stresses its extent and importance, and by A. T. Kraabel, "*Hypsistos* and the Synagogue at Sardis," *Greek, Roman and Byzantine Studies* 10 (1969), pp. 81–93, who minimizes its impact.

The account of the social aspects of early Christianity in the text is heavily dependent on Wayne A. Meeks, *The First Urban Christians: The Social World of the Apostle Paul* (Yale University Press, 1983). Other important discussions are E. A. Judge, *The Social Pattern of Christian Groups in the First Century* (Tyndale Press, 1960); John G. Gager, *Kingdom and Community: The Social World of Early Christianity* (Prentice-Hall, 1975); Abraham J. Malherbe, *Social Aspects of Early Christianity,* 2nd rev. ed. (Fortress Press, 1983); and Elisabeth Schüssler Fiorenza, *In Memory of Her: A Feminist Theological Reconstruction of Christian Origins* (Crossroad, 1983).

**Chapter 3: The Ancient Economy**

Michael I. Rostovtzeff, *Social and Economic History of the Roman Empire,* 2nd ed., rev. by P. M. Fraser (Oxford University Press, 1957), sees the motive power of the ancient economy in an urban middle class of small businessmen and traders. Moses I. Finley, *The Ancient Economy* (University of California Press, 1973), distinguishes between class and status and stresses that the status of social position was the most important factor in ancient society, making the income level of economic class to a large extent irrelevant. Two collections of essays studying specific patterns of commerce within the framework of Finley's work are Peter Garnsey, ed., *Non-Slave Labour in the Greco-Roman World* (Cambridge Philological Society, 1980), and Peter Garnsey, Keith Hopkins, and C. R. Whittacker, eds., *Trade in the Ancient Economy* (University of California Press, 1983). G. E. M. de Ste. Croix, *The Class Struggle in the Ancient Greek World* (Cornell University Press, 1981), gives a wide-ranging Marxist interpretation of the ancient economy up to the fall of Rome. Also of general interest are two works by A. H. M. Jones, *The Greek City from Alexander to Justinian* (Oxford University Press, 1940), esp. ch. 17, "Finance," and *The Roman Economy,* ed. by P. A. Brunt (Basil Blackwell, 1974), esp. chs. 1, 2, 3, 6, and 8. The multivolume *Economic Survey of Ancient Rome,* ed. by Tenney Frank (Johns Hopkins Press, 1933–1940) is still useful as a detailed treatment of data from individual parts of the empire.

**Chapter 4: Society in Palestine**

A survey of the historical geography and demography of Palestine is given by Michael Avi-Yonah in *The Jewish People in the First Century,* sec. 1, vol. 1, ch. 2 of *Compendia Rerum Iudaicarum ad Novum Testamentum,* ed. by Schmuel Safrai and M. Stern (Fortress Press, 1974). See also *The World History of the Jewish People,* vol. 7: *The Herodian Period,* ed. by Michael Avi-Yonah and Zui Baras (Rutgers University Press, 1975), chs. 1–2 (A. Schalit) and 4 (M. Stern). Sean Freyne, *Galilee from Alexander the Great to Hadrian: 323 B.C.E. to 135 C.E.* (Michael Glazier, 1980), argues for the cultural isolation of Galilee. An important primary source is Josephus, quoted in this chapter from the Loeb Classical Library edition and translations by H. St. J. Thackeray, Ralph Marcus, Allen Wikgren, and L. H. Feldman (9 vols., Harvard University Press, 1926–1965).

Freyne's views are corrected by Eric M. Meyers, "The Cultural Setting of Galilee: The Case of Regionalism and Early Judaism," *Aufstieg und Neidergang der römischen Welt* 2.19.1 (1979), pp. 686–702 (hereafter cited as *ANRW*). A. N. Sherwin-White, "The Galilean Narrative and the Graeco-Roman World," *Roman Society and Roman Law in the New Testament* (Oxford University Press, 1963), contains many insights.

Schmuel Safrai gives many details about family and religion in everyday life in *The Jewish People in the First Century,* sec. 1, vol. 2, chs. 14–15 in *Compendia* (Fortress Press, 1976); he discusses the synagogue in ch. 18. Eric M. Meyers and James F. Strange, *Archaeology, the Rabbis, and Early Christianity* (Abingdon Press, 1981), offer new archaeological insights on synagogues in ch. 7.

Joseph A. Fitzmyer, "The Languages of Palestine in the First Century A.D.," *Catholic Biblical Quarterly* 32 (1970) pp. 501–531 is updated by James F. Strange, "Archaeology and the Religion of Judaism in Palestine," *ANRW* 2.19.2 (1979), pp. 659–661. See also C. Rabin and G. Mussies in *Jewish People,* sec. 1, vol. 2, chs. 21 and 22. Emil Schürer, *The History of the Jewish People in the Age of Jesus Christ (175 B.C.–A.D. 135),* rev. by G. Vermes, F. Millar, and M. Black (T. & T. Clark, 1979), vol. 2, pp. 20–28, 74–80 is very cautious about the amount of Greek spoken.

Greek cities are surveyed in the same volume (Schürer/Vermes), pp. 85–183; and by Victor Tcherikover, *Hellenistic Civilization and the Jews* (Atheneum Publishers, 1970), part 1, ch. 2. Freyne, *Galilee,* ch. 4, discusses Galilean cities. The art of the country is surveyed by G. Foerster in *Jewish People,* sec. 1, vol. 2, ch. 20 and brilliantly interpreted by Nahman Avigad, *Beth She'arim,* vol. 3: *Catacombs 12–23* (Rutgers University Press, 1971), ch. 7.

S. Applebaum has two summary articles on peasants and the economy of Palestine, one in *Jewish People,* sec. 1, vol. 2, ch. 12, and another in *ANRW* 2.8 (1977) pp. 355–396. In general, see Ramsay MacMullen, *Roman Social Relations, 50 B.C. to A.D. 284* (Yale University Press, 1974).

Pilgrimage is described by Schmuel Safrai in *Jewish People,* sec. 1, vol. 1, pp. 191–201, and vol. 2, pp. 898–904. Compare Joachim Jeremias, *Jerusalem in the Time of Jesus* (Fortress Press, 1969), ch. 3, and Freyne, *Galilee,* ch. 7.

John Wilkinson, *Jerusalem as Jesus Knew It: Archaeology as Evidence* (Thames and Hudson, 1978), is an exceptional popular summary. Jack Finegan, *The Archeology of the New Testament* (Princeton University Press, 1969), and Michael Avi-Yonah in *World History,* vol. 7, ch. 6, have much information on the city of Jerusalem. M. Stern in *Jewish People,* sec. 1, vol. 1, pp. 340–346, has important comments on the city's status, as does Jeremias, *Jerusalem.*

Jacob Neusner's summary of his research on the Pharisees is in *ANRW* 2.19.2 (1979), pp. 3–42; an earlier summary is *From Politics to Piety: The Emergence of Pharisaic Judaism* (Prentice-Hall, 1973). Compare Schürer/Vermes, *History of the Jewish People,* vol. 2, secs. 24 and 26. There are many data in Jeremias, *Jerusalem,* chs. 8–11, and in Safrai, *Jewish People,* sec. 1, vol. 1, ch. 7. False definitions with some good insights are given by E. Rivkin, "The Internal City: Judaism and Urbanization," *Journal for the Scientific Study of Religion* 5 (1965–66), pp. 225–240.

Crafts and occupations are discussed by J. Klausner in *World History,* vol. 7, ch. 5, and by Jeremias, *Jerusalem.* In general see Robert M. Grant, *Early Christianity and Society* (Harper & Row, 1977), ch. 4.

Important beginnings have been made in defining the sociology of the Jesus movement by Gerd Theissen, *Sociology of Early Palestinian Christianity* (Fortress Press, 1977, tr. by John Bowden), and by Elisabeth Schüssler Fiorenza, *In Memory of Her: A Feminist Theological Reconstruction of Christian Origins* (Crossroad, 1983). An important critique of Theissen is given by Wolfgang Stegemann, "Wanderradikalismus in Urchristentum? Historische und theologische Auseinandersetzung mit einer interessanten These," in *Der Gott der kleinen Leute. Sozialgeschichtliche Bibelauslegungen,* Band 2, *Neues Testament,* ed. by L. Schottroff and W. Stegemann (Kaiser, 1979), pp. 94–120.

**Chapter 5: City Life**

Brief surveys of the design and construction of cities in the New Testament period are available in R. E. M. Wheeler, *Roman Art and Architecture* (Praeger, 1964); J. B. Ward-Perkins, *Cities of Ancient Greece and Italy: Planning in Classical Antiquity* (George Braziller, 1974); and Pierre Grimal, *Roman Cities,* tr. and ed. by Michael Woloch (University of Wisconsin Press, 1983).

The social and political structure of Roman society is discussed in Ramsay MacMullen, *Roman Social Relations, 50 B.C. to A.D. 284* (Yale University Press, 1974); Peter A. Brunt, "The Roman Mob," *Past and Present,* 35 (1966), pp. 1–27; and Donald C. Earl, *The Moral and Political Tradition of Rome* (Cornell University Press, 1967). A brief survey of women in antiquity is Sarah B. Pomeroy, *Goddesses, Whores, Wives and Slaves: Women in Classical Antiquity* (Schocken Books, 1975). Mary R. Lefkowitz and Maureen B. Fant, *Women's Life in Greece and Rome* (Johns Hopkins University Press, 1982), offers an important collection of primary sources in translation.

Good general surveys of Greek and Roman religion are H. J. Rose, *Religion in Greece and Rome* (Harper Torchbooks, 1959); R. M. Ogilvie, *The Romans and Their Gods in the Age of Augustus* (W. W. Norton & Co., 1969); John Ferguson, *The Religions of the Roman Empire* (Cornell University Press, 1970); and Robert M. Grant, *Gods and the One God* (Library of Early Christianity; Westminster Press, 1986). Franz Cumont, *Oriental Religions in Roman Paganism* (Dover Books, 1956) is a classic; its details are brought up to date in the volumes (many in English) of the series *Études préliminaries aux religions orientales dans l'empire romain,* ed. by M. J. Vermaseren (E. J. Brill, 196–).

**Chapter 6: Christianity in the Cities of the Roman Empire**

Convenient general surveys, region by region, are Adolf Harnack, *The Mission and Expansion of Christianity in the First Three Centuries,* tr. and ed. by James Moffatt, vol. 2 (G. P. Putnam's Sons, 1908), and Johannes Weiss, *Earliest Christianity, A History of the Period A.D. 30–150,* ed. by Frederick C. Grant (Harper Torchbooks, 1959). Other works on the contacts, interactions, and reactions between Christians and their environment are Stephen Benko and John J. O'Rourke, eds., *The Catacombs and the Colosseum: The Roman Empire as the Setting of Primitive Christianity* (Judson Press, 1971); R. A. Markus, *Christianity in the Roman World* (Charles Scribner's Sons, 1974); Robin Scroggs, "The Earliest Christian Communities as a Sectarian Movement," *Christianity, Judaism, and Other Greco-Roman Cults,* ed. by Jacob Neusner, vol. 2 (E. J. Brill, 1975), pp. 1–23; Robert M. Grant, *Early Christianity and Society* (Harper & Row, 1977); Bruce Malina, *The New Testament World: Insights from Cultural Anthropology* (John Knox Press, 1981); Robert L. Wilken, *The Christians as the Romans Saw Them* (Yale University Press, 1984). A detailed compendium of information on specific cities, useful as a reference work, is A. H. M. Jones, *The Cities of the Eastern Roman Provinces,* 2nd ed. (Oxford University Press, 1971). Essays in English as well as other languages on many topics relevant to this chapter are found in the volumes of *Aufstieg und Niedergang der römischen Welt,* ed. by Hildegard Temporini and Wolfgang Haase (Walter de Gruyter, 1972– ). Concise archaeological essays on individual cities are contained in *The Princeton Encyclopedia of Classical Sites,* ed. by Richard Stillwell (Princeton University Press, 1976).

On Antioch: Raymond Brown and John P. Meier, *Antioch and Rome: New Testament Cradles of Catholic Christianity* (Paulist Press, 1983); Glanville Downey, *A History of Antioch in Syria: From Seleucus to the Arab Conquest* (Princeton University Press, 1961); Moses Hadas, *The Third and Fourth Books of the Maccabees* (Harper & Row, 1953); Wayne A. Meeks and Robert L. Wilken, *Jews and Christians in Antioch in the First Four Centuries of the Common Era* (Scholars Press, 1978).

On Asia Minor: David Magie, *Roman Rule in Asia Minor* (Princeton University Press, 1950); Merrill M. Parvis, "Ephesus in the Early Christian Era," *Biblical Archaeologist* 8.3 (1945), pp. 61–73; Floyd V. Filson, "Ephesus and the New Testament," ibid., pp. 73–80; Otto F. A. Meinardus, *St. Paul in*

*Ephesus and the Cities of Galatia and Cyprus* (Caratzas Publishing Co., 1979); Sherman E. Johnson, "Laodicea and Its Neighbors," *Biblical Archaeologist* 13.1 (1950), pp. 1–18; Edwin Yamauchi, *The Archaeology of New Testament Cities in Western Asia Minor* (Baker Book House, 1980).

On Macedonia: F. F. Bruce, "St. Paul in Macedonia," *Bulletin of the John Rylands Library* 61 (1979), pp. 337–354.

On Corinth: Oscar Broneer, "The Apostle Paul and the Isthmian Games," *Biblical Archaeologist* 25.1 (1962), pp. 1–31; Carl H. Kraeling, "The Jewish Community at Corinth," *Journal of Biblical Literature* 51 (1932), pp. 130–160; Jerome Murphy-O'Connor, *St. Paul's Corinth: Texts and Archaeology* (Good News Studies 6: Michael Glazier, 1983); Gerd Theissen, *The Social Setting of Pauline Christianity: Essays on Corinth,* ed. and tr. by John H. Schütz (Fortress Press, 1982); James Wiseman, "Corinth and Rome I: 228 B.C.–A.D. 267," *ANRW* 2.7.1 (1979), pp. 438–458.

On Rome: G. LaPiana, "The Roman Church at the End of the Second Century," *Harvard Theological Review* 18 (1925), pp. 201–277; Harry J. Leon, *The Jews of Ancient Rome* (Jewish Publication Society, 1960); Daniel W. O'Connor, *Peter in Rome, The Literary, Liturgical and Archeological Evidence* (Columbia University Press, 1969); Wolfgang Wiefel, "The Jewish Community in Ancient Rome and the Origins of Roman Christianity," *The Romans Debate,* ed. by Karl Paul Donfried (Augsburg Publishing House, 1977), pp. 100–119.

On Alexandria: Peter M. Fraser, *Ptolemaic Alexandria* (3 vols., Oxford University Press, 1972); John Marlowe, *The Golden Age of Alexandria* (Victor Gollancz, 1971).

# Index of Selected Subjects

# Index of New Testament Passages